Jetlagged Comic
Jetway Reunion

Kelly Kincaid

Kelly Kin [signature]

ISBN: 978-0-692-93873-7

Published by IngramSpark

Jetlagged Comic

PO Box 13362

Seattle, WA 98198

www.jetlaggedcomic.com

Foreword

Once a flight attendant, always a flight attendant. It's like the Marines. That might sound crazy to some people. It's true though. Only another flight attendant can truly understand what the job is like. It doesn't matter which airline we work for, we all have the same experiences. At times, it might seem difficult or bizarre, it's also totally amazing. There's no other job like it.

"Don't ever quit," is something flight attendants tell each other all the time. "Take a leave. Work part-time. Never quit." We all know former colleagues who quit and then regretted it.

After my best friend quit, her husband, a pilot, noticed how much she missed going to work, and suggested she become a teacher when the kids got a little older, since she's so good with kids.

"I don't want to teach!" she said over the phone to me one day. "I only want to serve Coke."

To hear your best friend cry about wanting to serve Coke is heartbreaking. It's also funny. Only a flight attendant can understand this. You see it's not just a job, it's a lifestyle, and that lifestyle involves a lot of cans of soda.

Many people think it's easy serving Coke and picking up trash for a living, but nothing could be further from the truth. I guarantee you 99.9% of the population couldn't handle this job. Either on the plane…or off. Most flight attendants either last only a few weeks on the job – or an entire lifetime.

It takes a special person – a person like Kelly Kincaid.

Kelly and I share a profession. And we share a passion. We're flight attendants who enjoy sharing stories about our work … and our lives … and the insane ways the two intersect.

When I wrote my book, *Cruising Attitude: Tales of Crashpads, Crew Drama, and Crazy Passengers at 30,000 Feet*, I was determined to make it different from the many other books about travel. I wanted it to be more than just stories about flying and the madness of modern airline flight. That's why half of it takes place on the ground. Most people don't realize just how much the job affects your family life, love life, every single little thing in your life. You can't escape it.

While it takes me a few pages to describe certain aspects of our lives, Kelly Kincaid does the same thing in a single cartoon. They're brilliant. So unbelievably spot-on. Take for instance my favorite one, the one I share every Thanksgiving and Christmas. In this Jetlagged cartoon there's a Turkey on the table and a family sitting down to eat a festive meal. Off to the side, next to a window, behind a curtain, is an off duty flight attendant holding a plate of food. Somebody sitting at the table asks where she is. "Behind the curtain again," someone else says.

A regular person might think, huh? Why is she standing behind the window curtain eating a turkey leg. But anyone who's worked as a flight attendant knows what it's like to eat a majority of their meals standing up. Only a flight attendant has to hide when they want to eat. Only a flight attendant understands what it's like to scarf down a meal in a half a second just to avoid being interrupted by passengers who want something. That or they're looking for a place to stretch. Which reminds me, the galley is not the place for pilates. I can't tell you the number of many times I've eaten a sandwich with a stranger's butt mere inches from my face. There's a Jetlagged cartoon illustrating that too.

By Heather Poole
Author of
Cruising Attitude: Tales of Crashpads, Crew Drama, and Crazy Passengers at 35,000 Feet

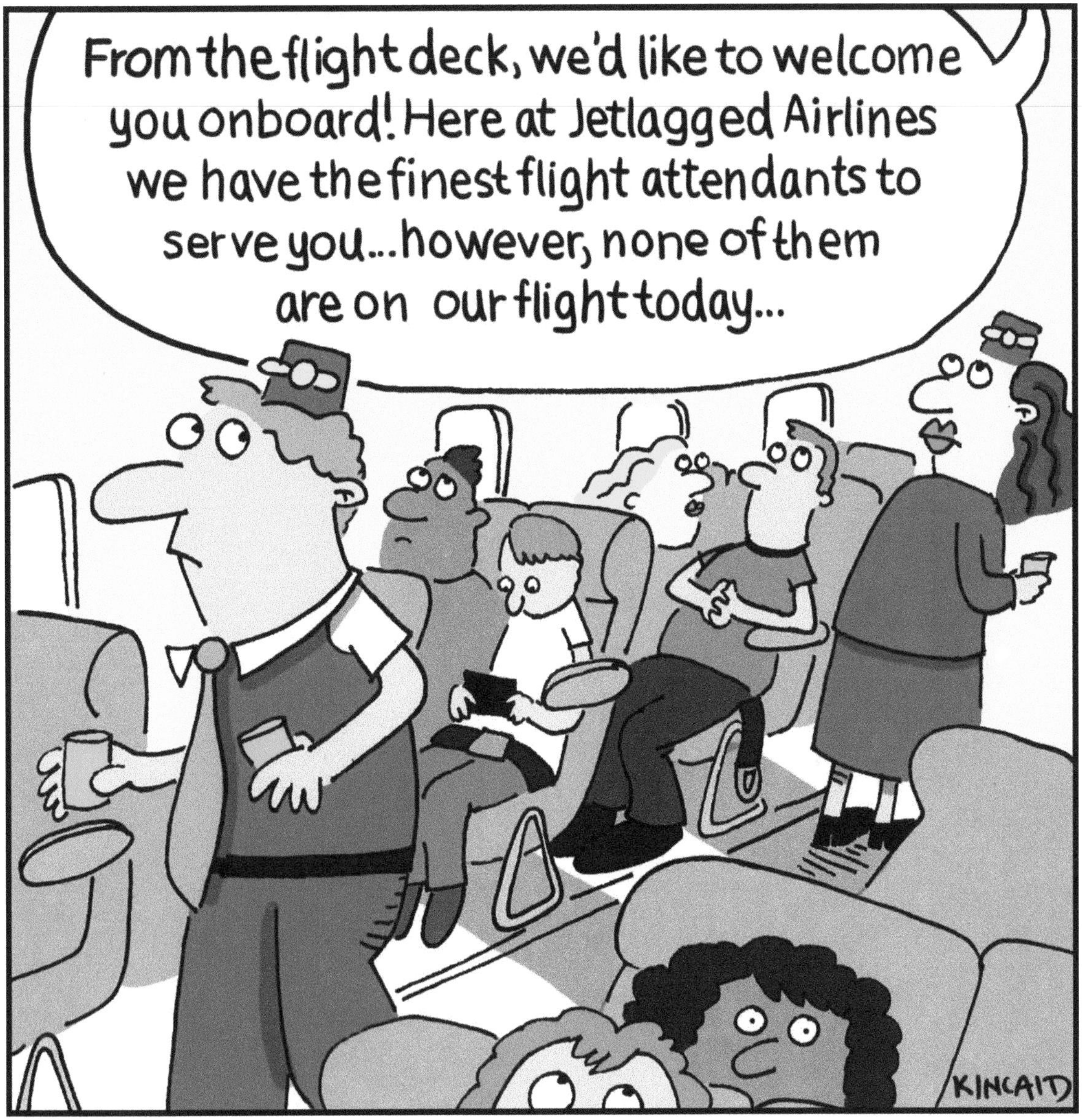
From the flight deck, we'd like to welcome you onboard! Here at Jetlagged Airlines we have the finest flight attendants to serve you...however, none of them are on our flight today...
KINCAID

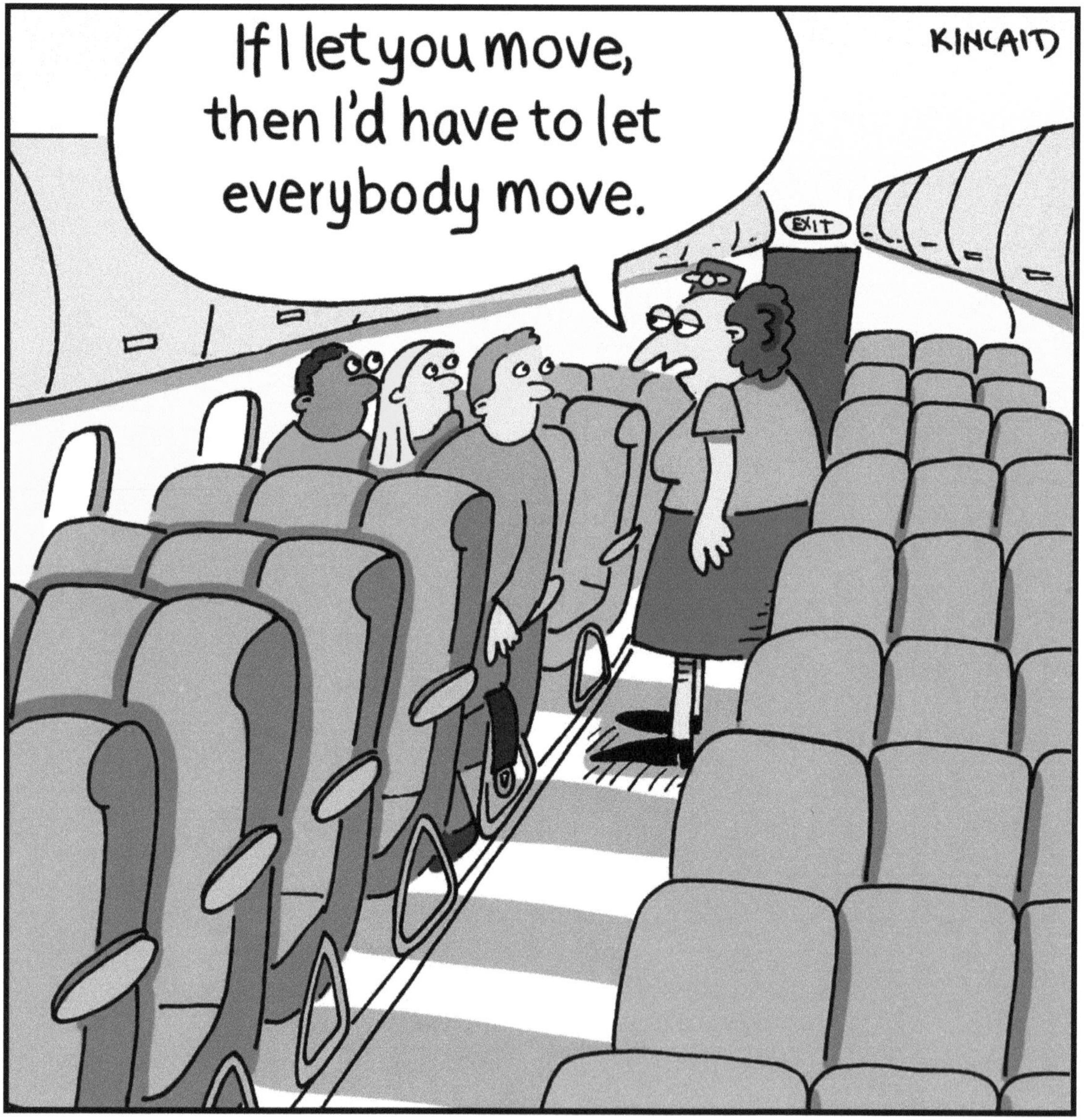
If I let you move, then I'd have to let everybody move.
KINCAID
EXIT

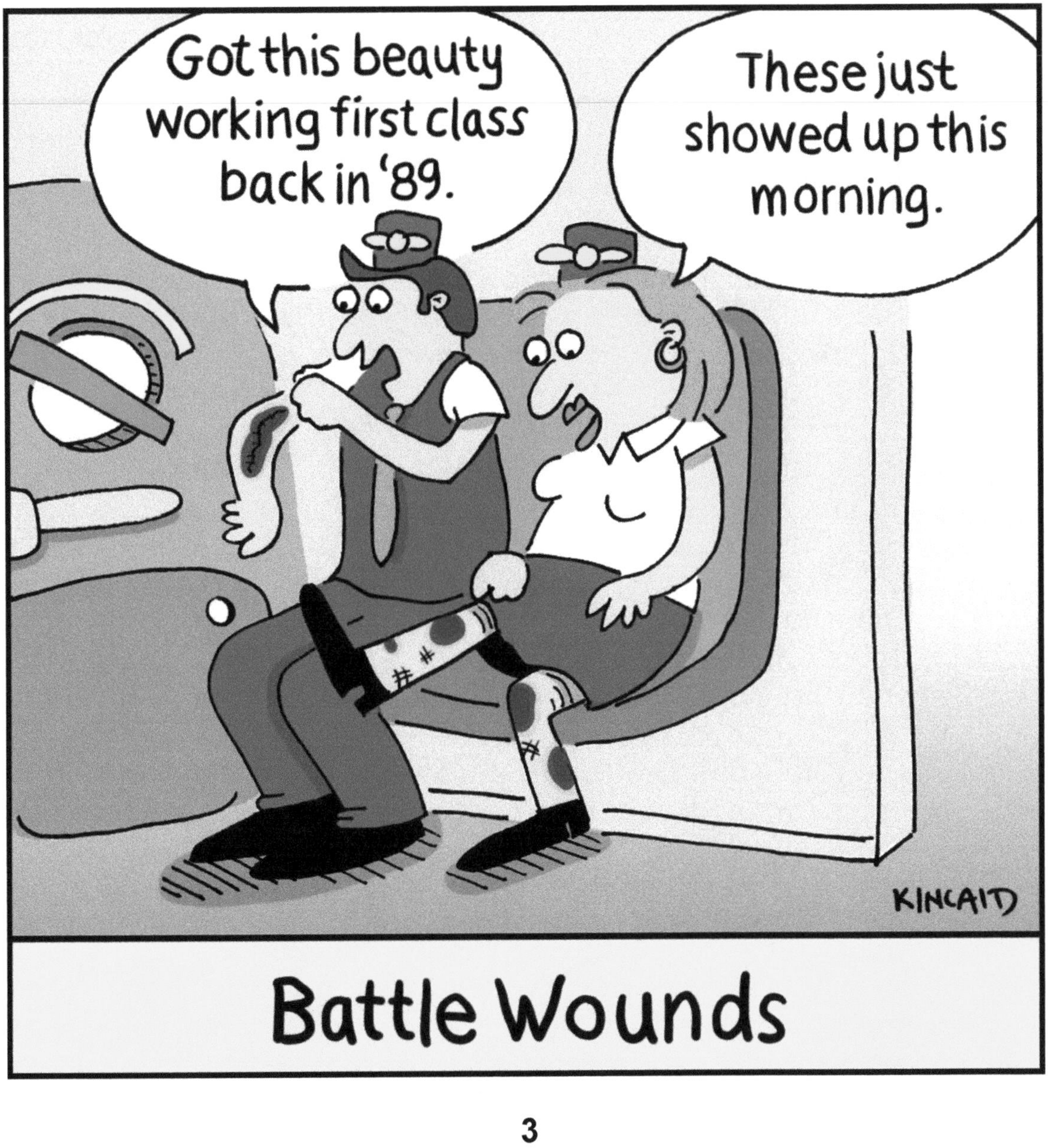
Got this beauty working first class back in '89.
These just showed up this morning.
KINCAID

Battle Wounds

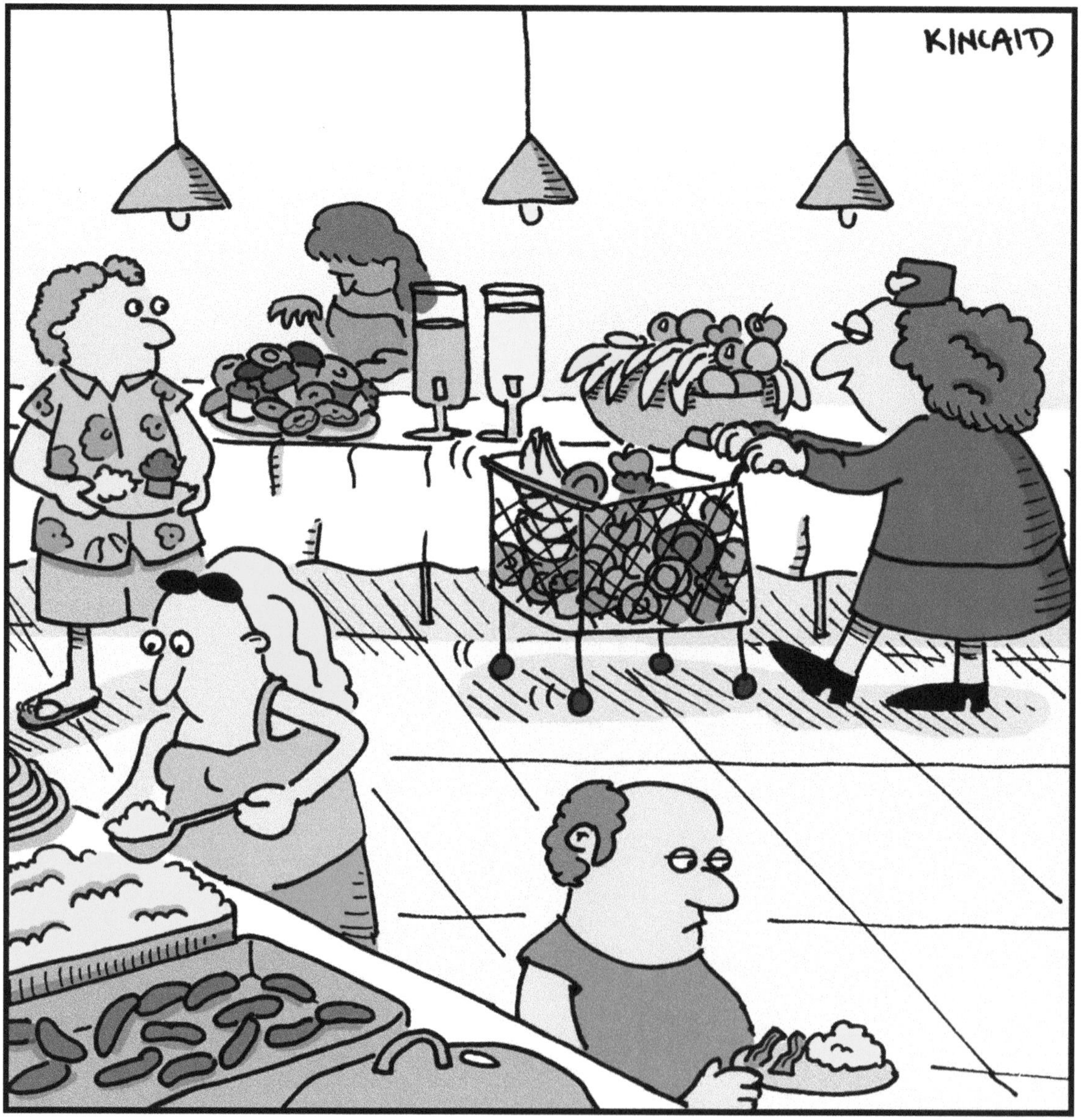
KINCAID

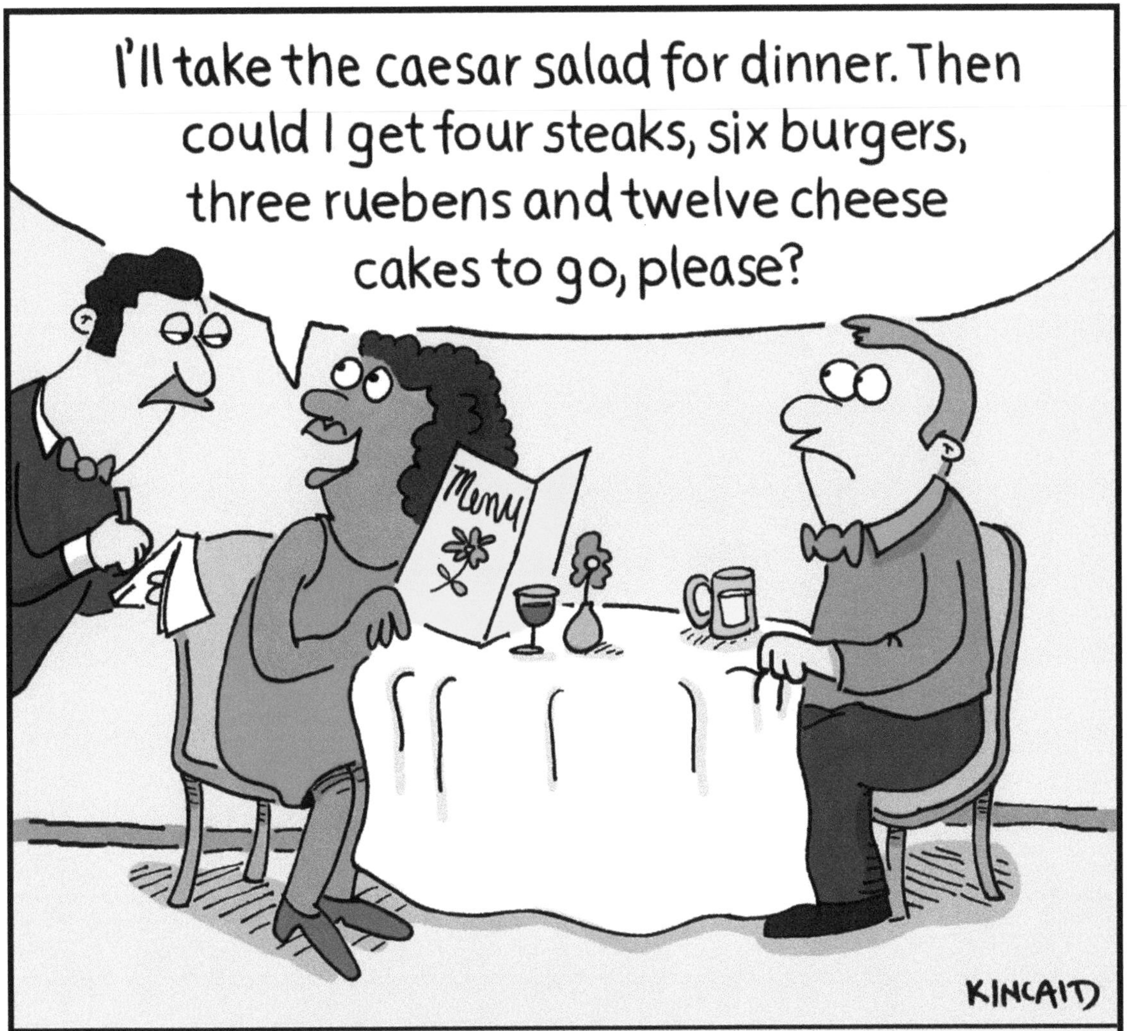
I'll take the caesar salad for dinner. Then could I get four steaks, six burgers, three ruebens and twelve cheese cakes to go, please?
Menu
KINCAID

FIRST DATES WITH FLIGHT ATTENDANTS

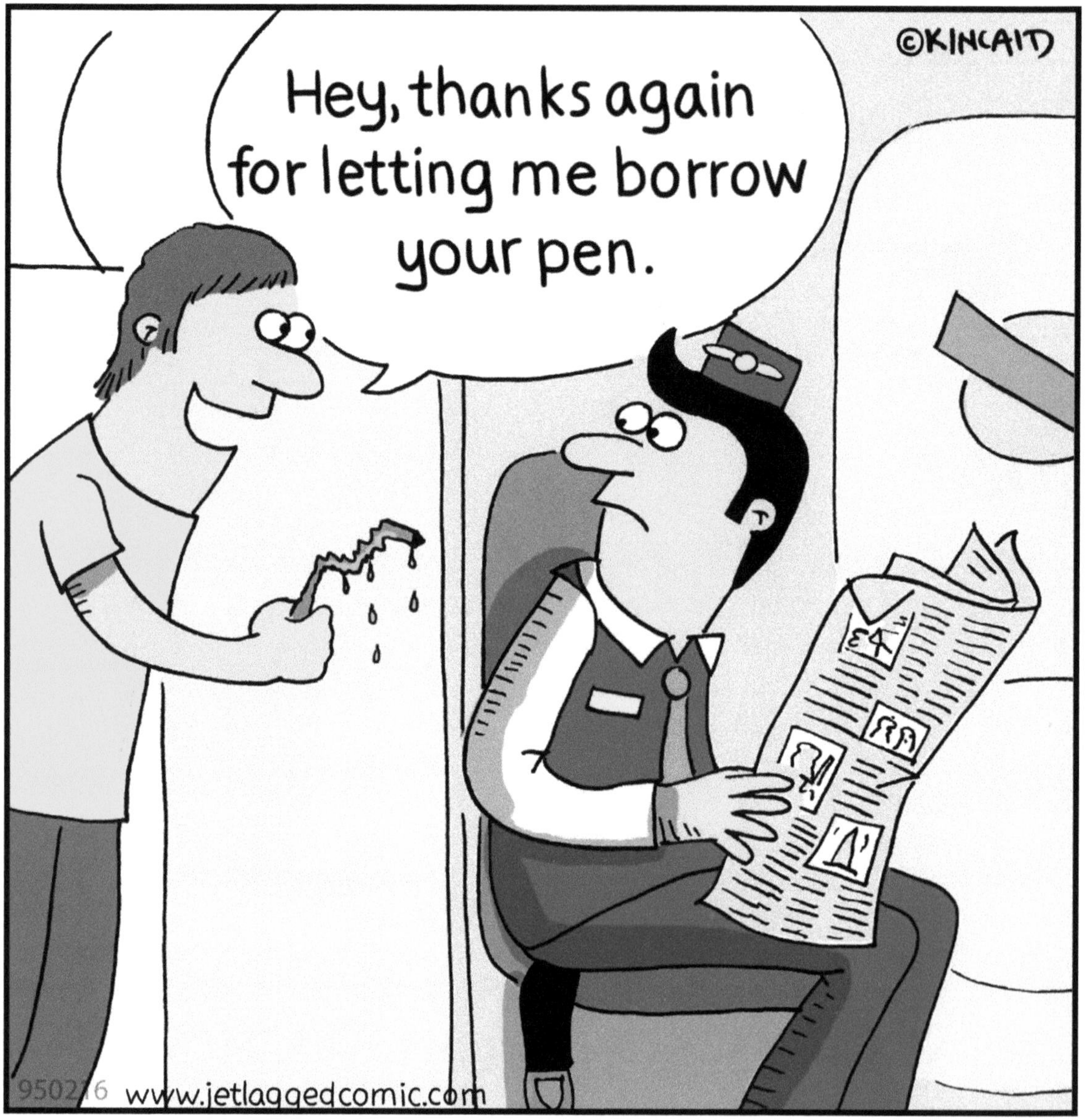
Hey, thanks again for letting me borrow your pen.
©KINCAID
950216 www.jetlaggedcomic.com

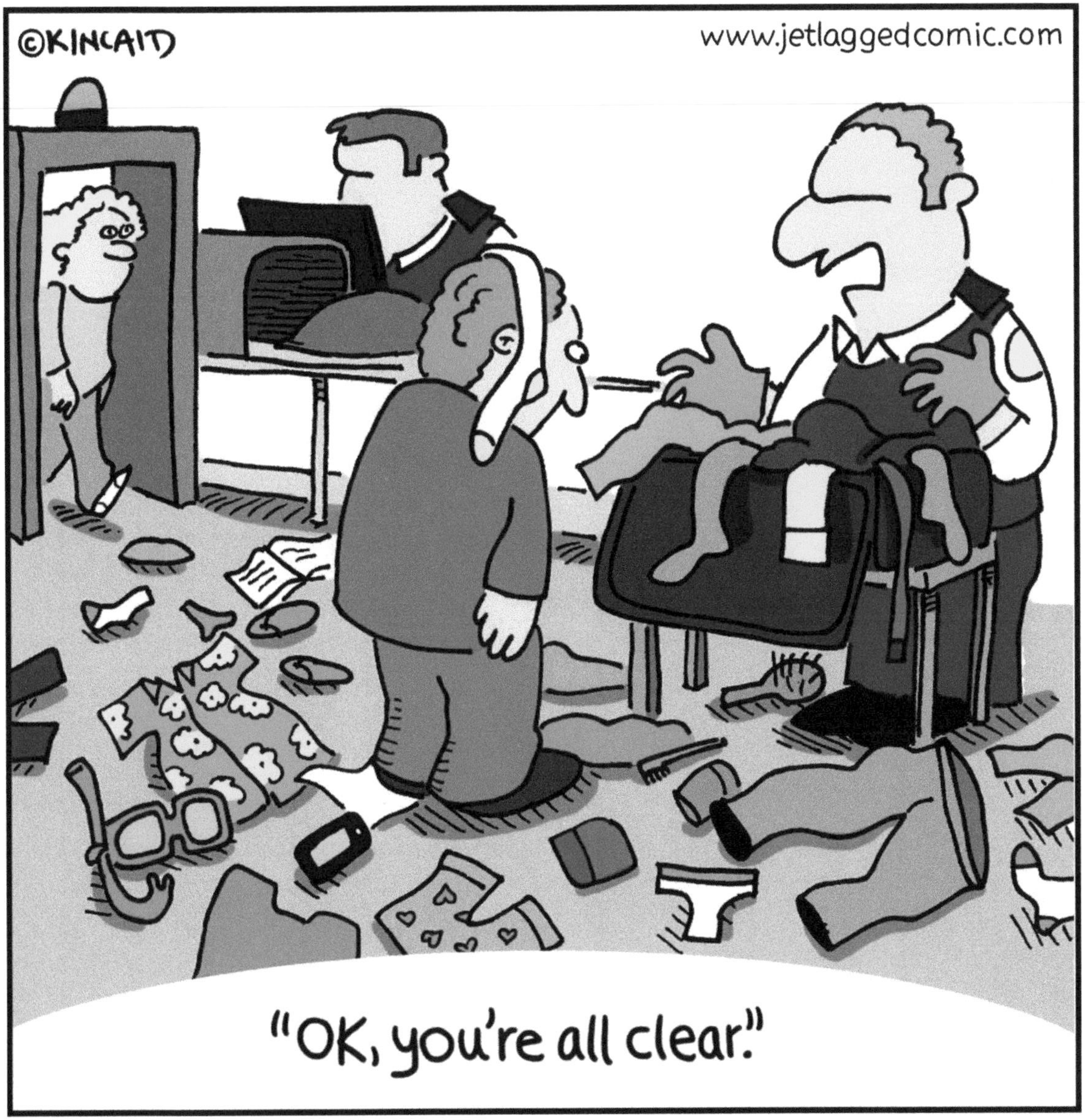
©KINCAID
www.jetlaggedcomic.com
"OK, you're all clear."

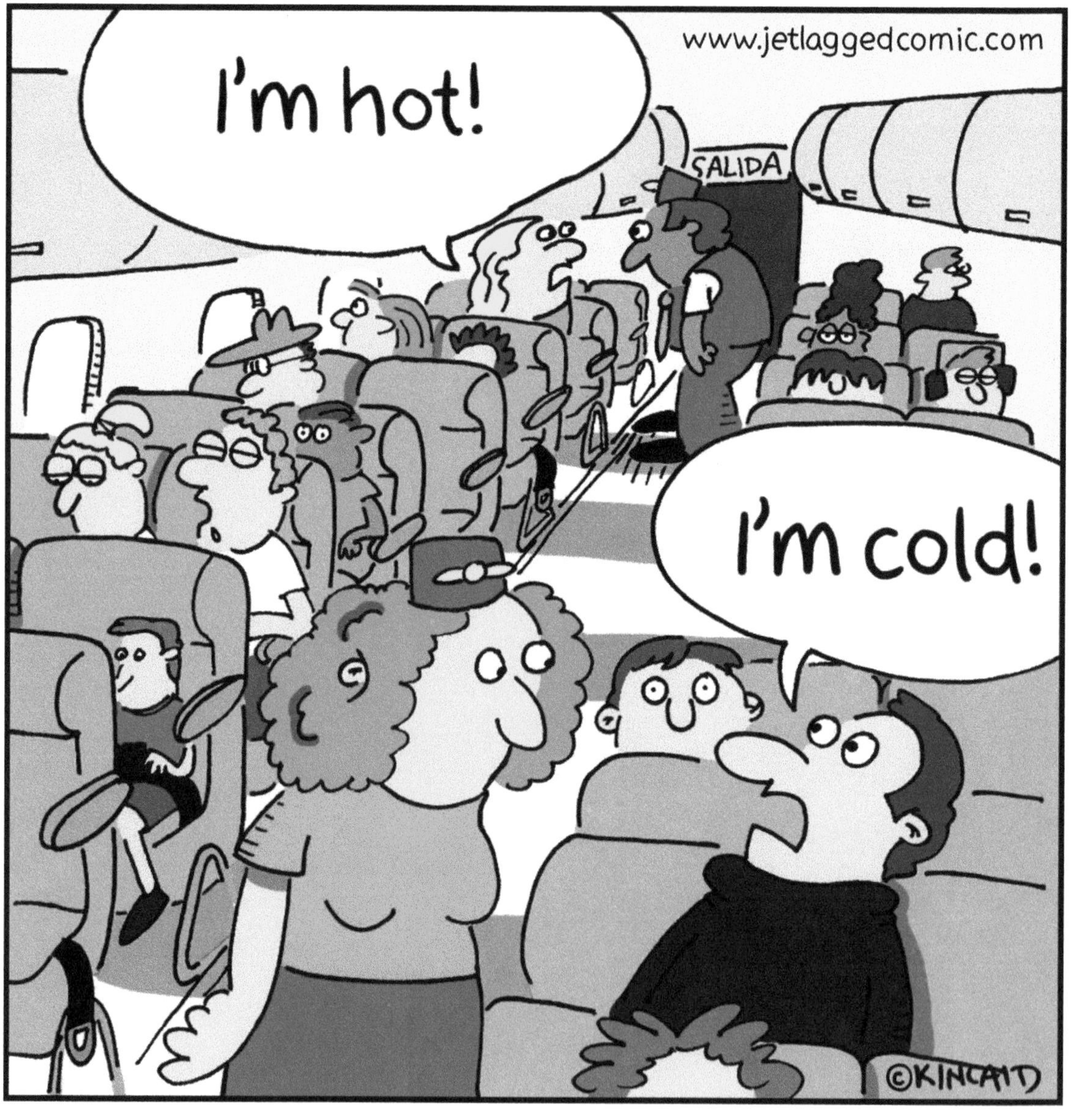
www.jetlaggedcomic.com
I'm hot!
SALIDA
I'm cold!
©KINCAID

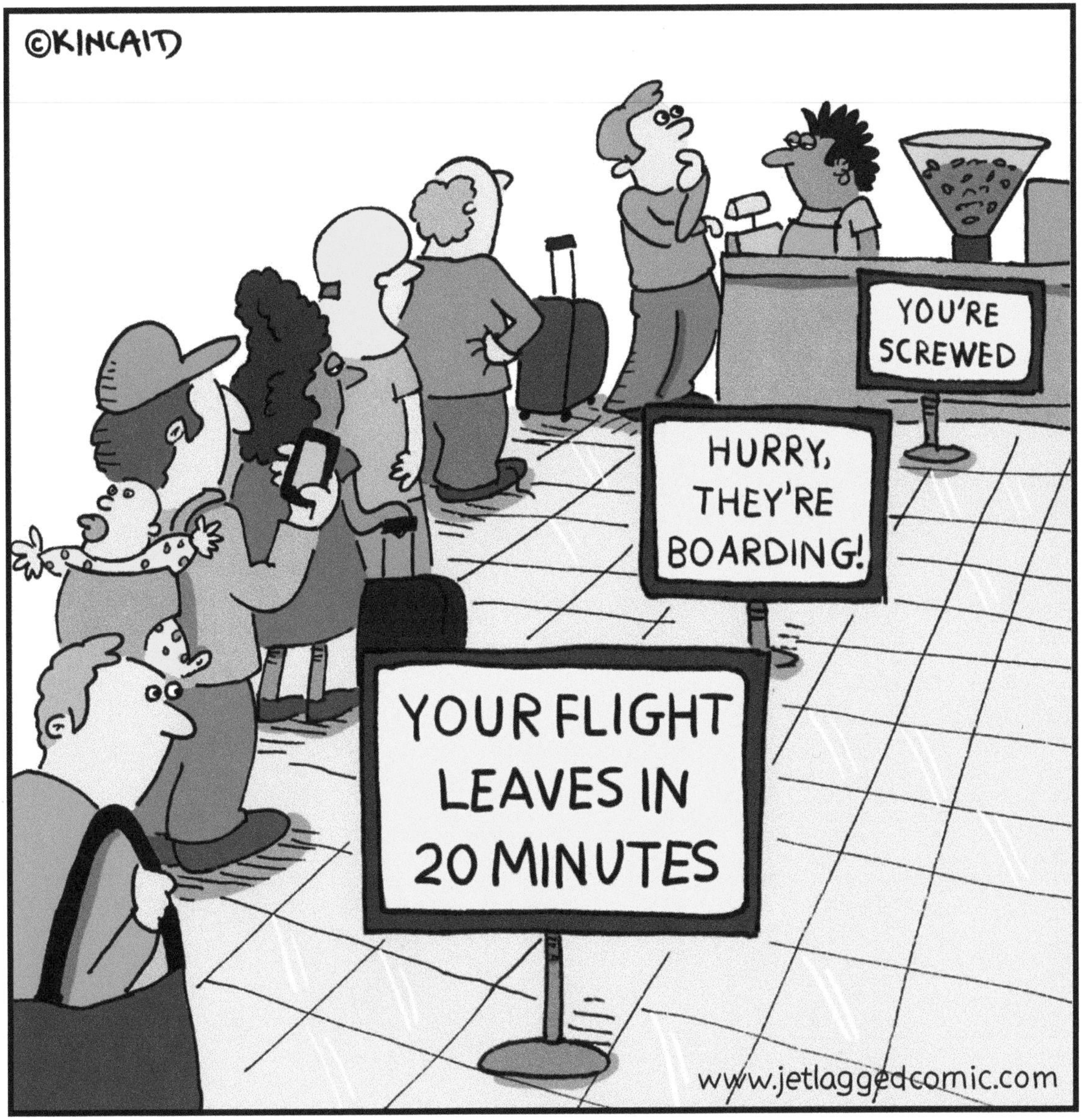
©KINCAID
YOU'RE SCREWED
HURRY, THEY'RE BOARDING!
YOUR FLIGHT LEAVES IN 20 MINUTES
www.jetlaggedcomic.com

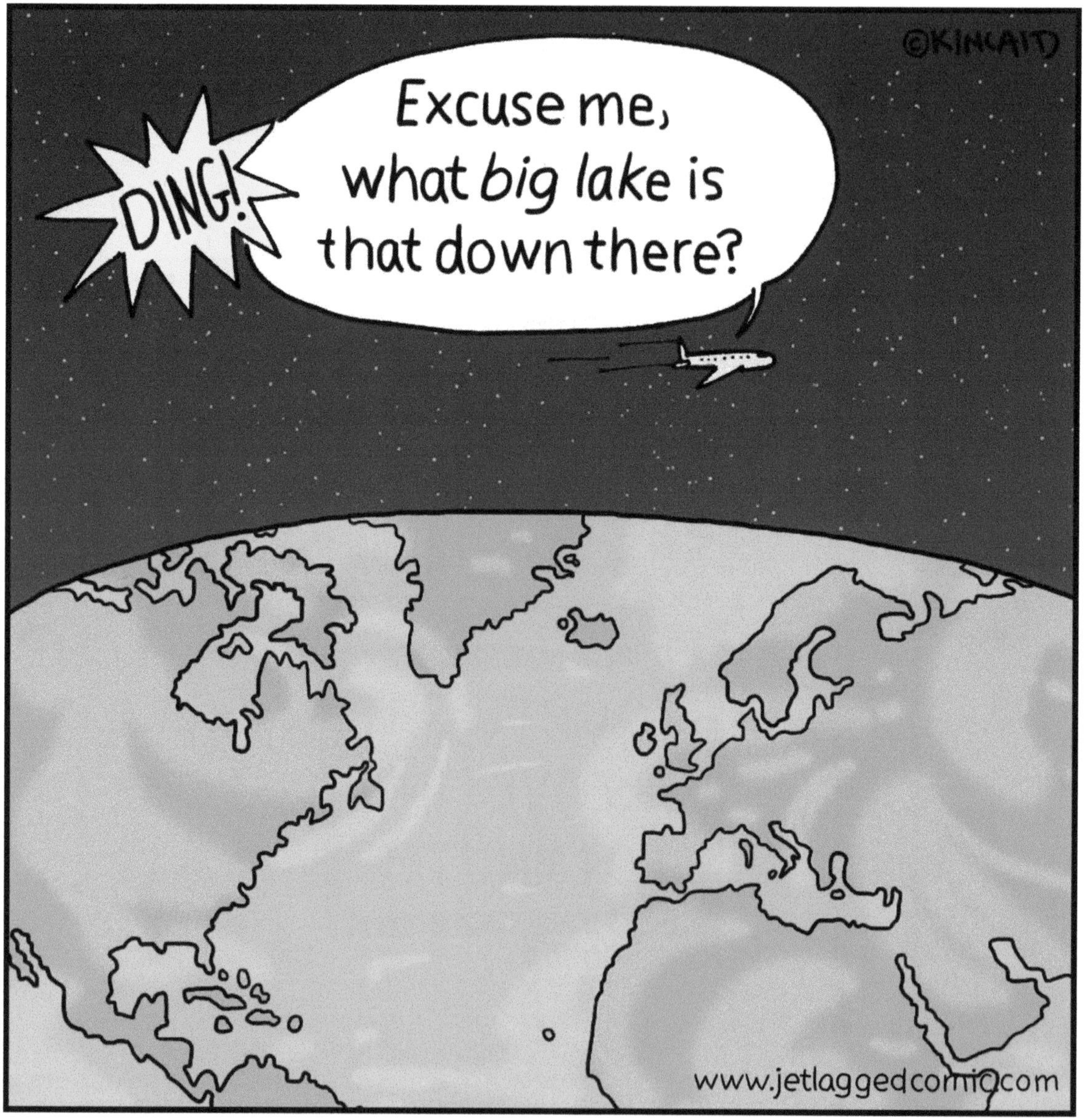
©KINCAID
DING!
Excuse me, what *big lake* is that down there?
www.jetlaggedcomic.com

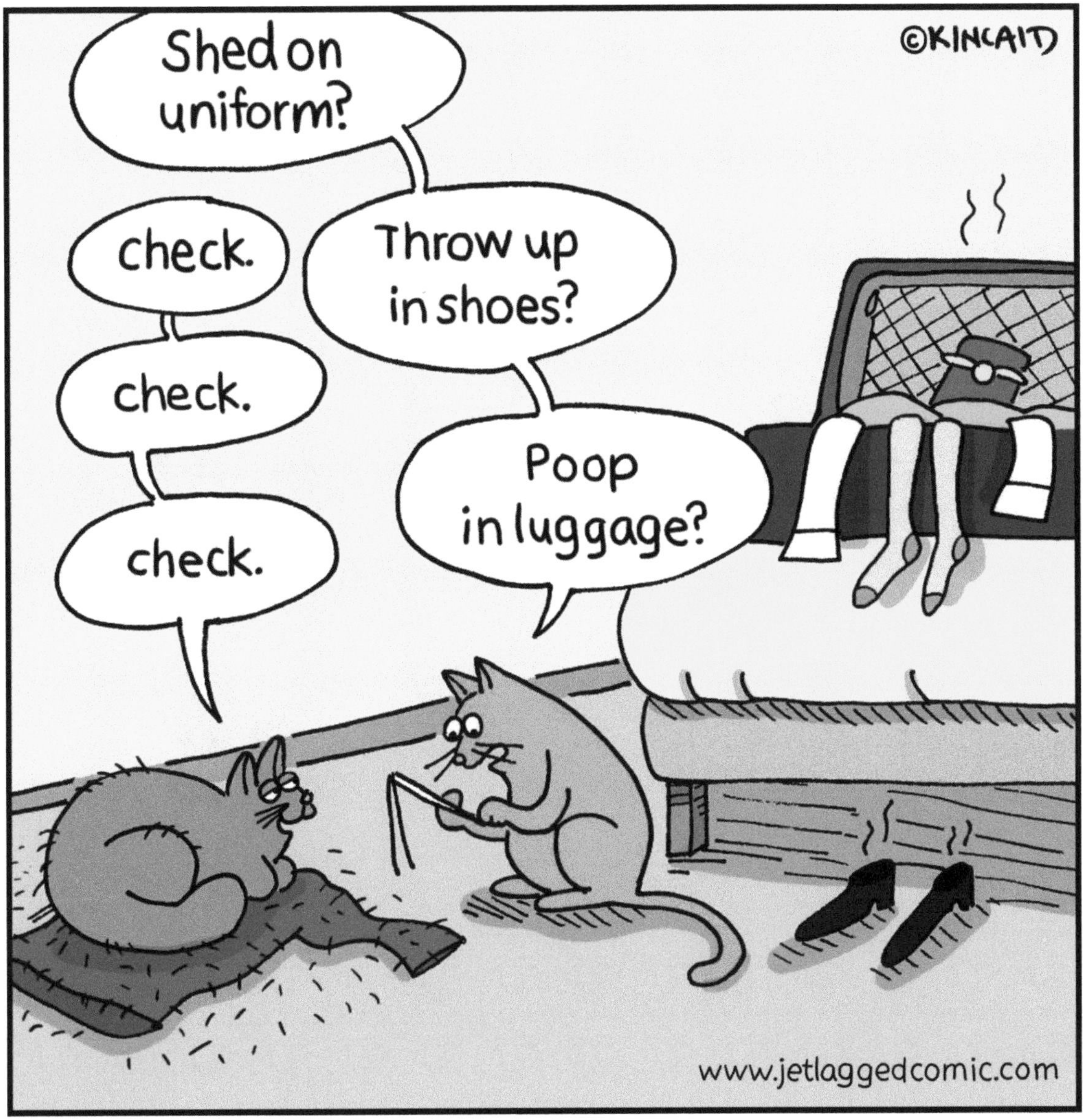
©KINCAID
Shed on uniform?
check.
Throw up in shoes?
check.
Poop in luggage?
check.
www.jetlaggedcomic.com

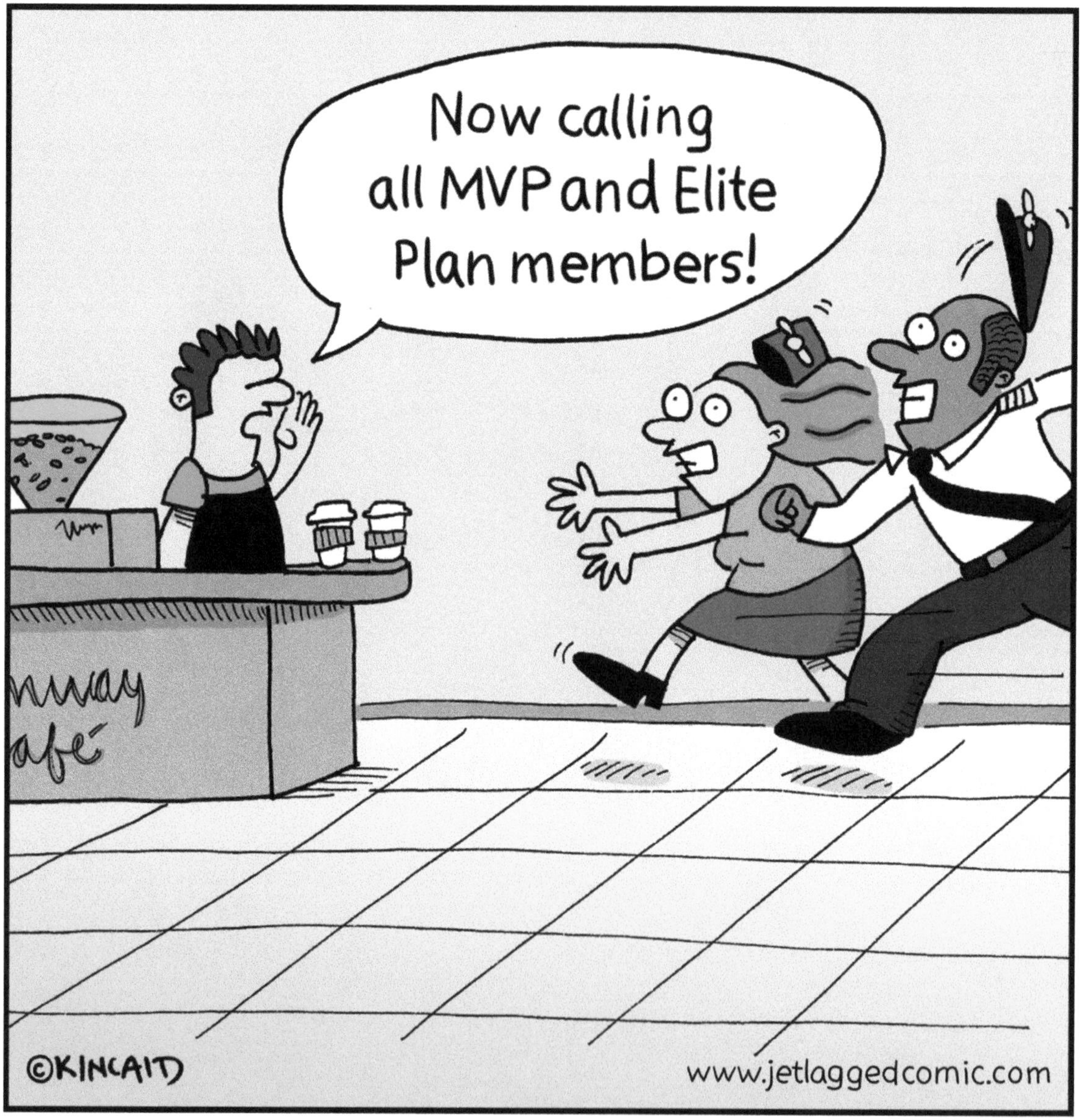
Now calling all MVP and Elite Plan members!
©KINCAID
www.jetlaggedcomic.com

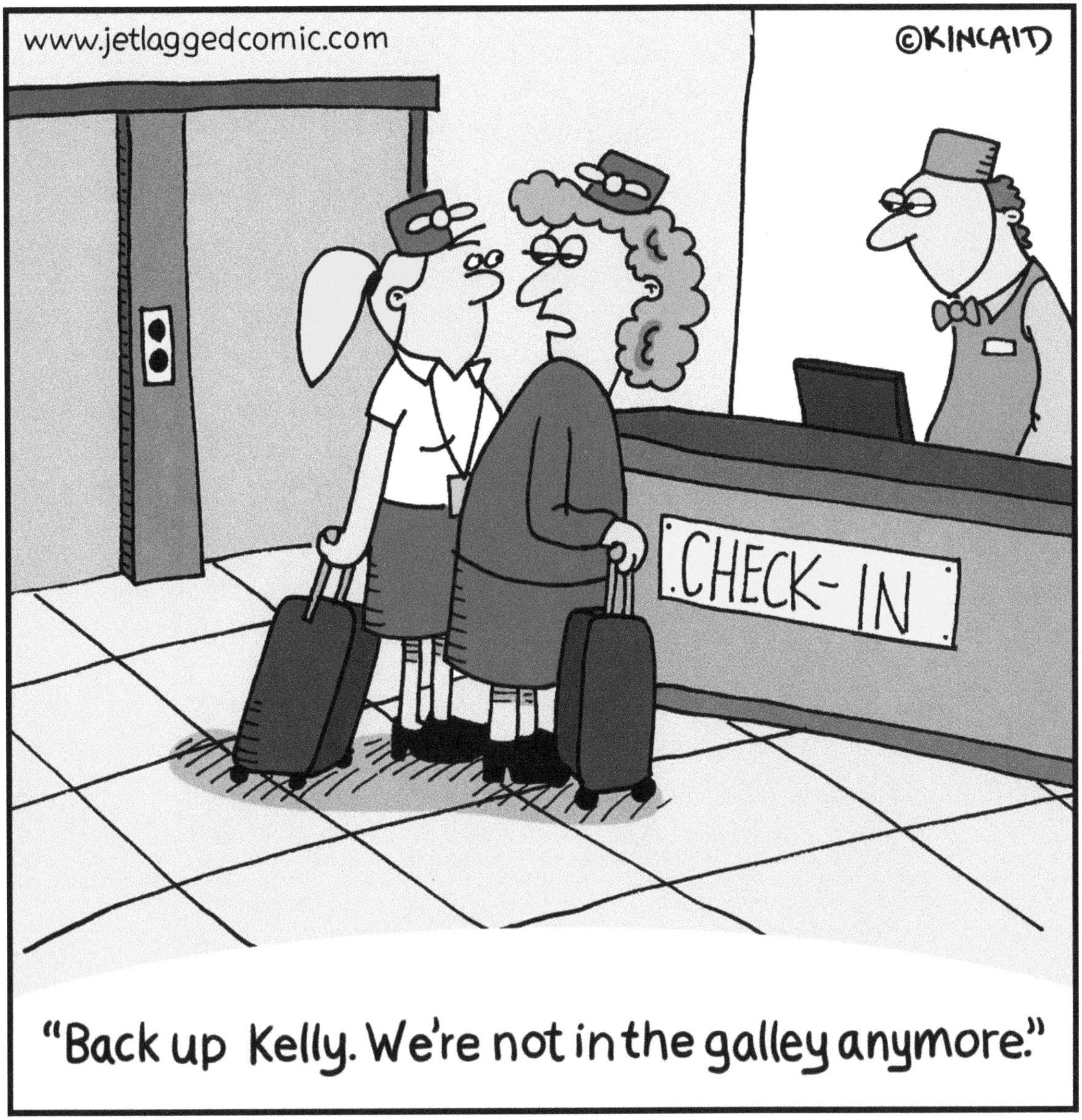
www.jetlaggedcomic.com
©KINCAID
CHECK-IN

"Back up Kelly. We're not in the galley anymore."

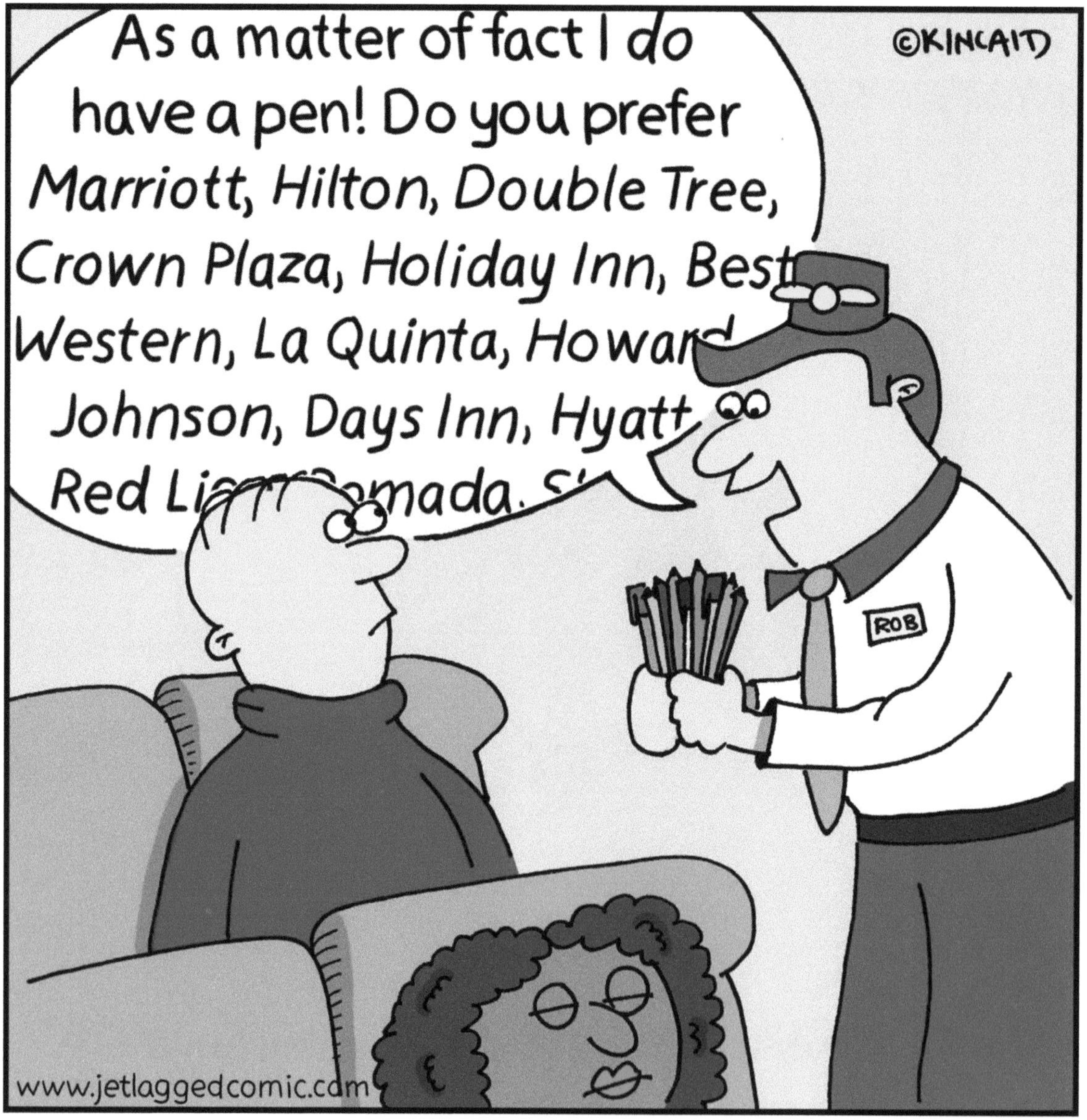
As a matter of fact I do have a pen! Do you prefer Marriott, Hilton, Double Tree, Crown Plaza, Holiday Inn, Best Western, La Quinta, Howar
Johnson, Days Inn, Hyatt, Red Li
©KINCAID
ROB
www.jetlaggedcomic.com

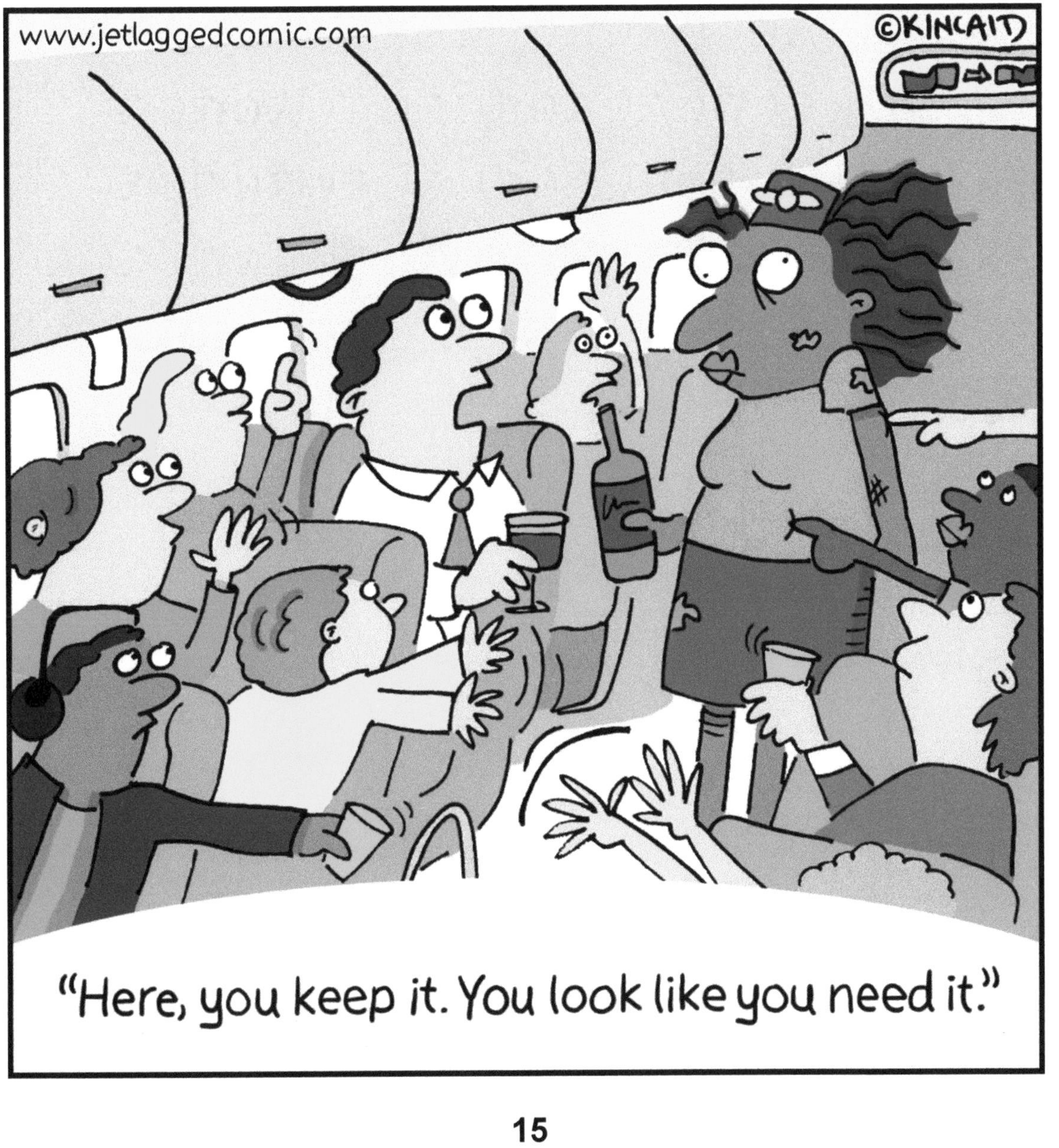
www.jetlaggedcomic.com
©KINCAID

"Here, you keep it. You look like you need it."

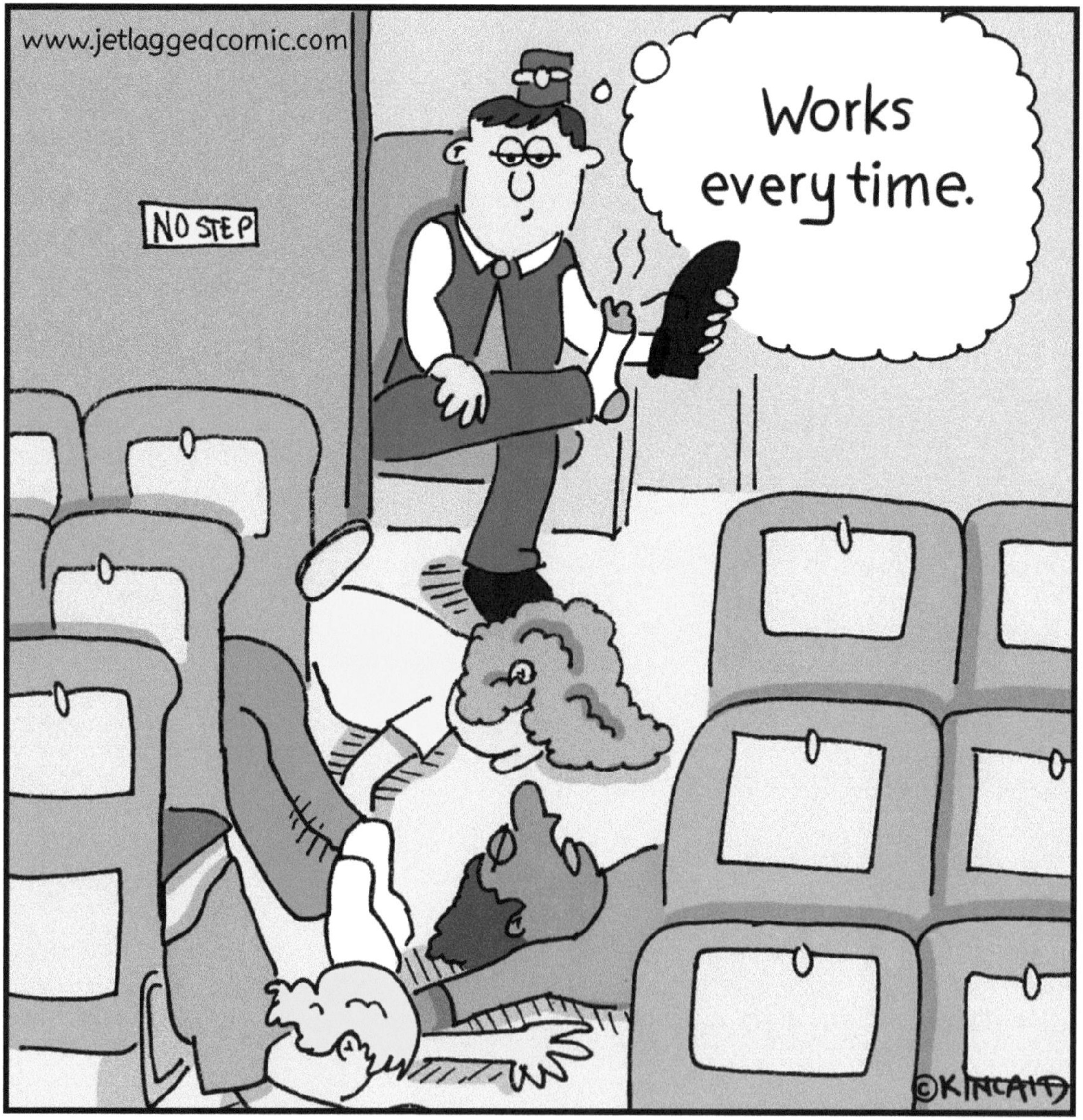
www.jetlaggedcomic.com
NO STEP
Works every time.
©KINCAID

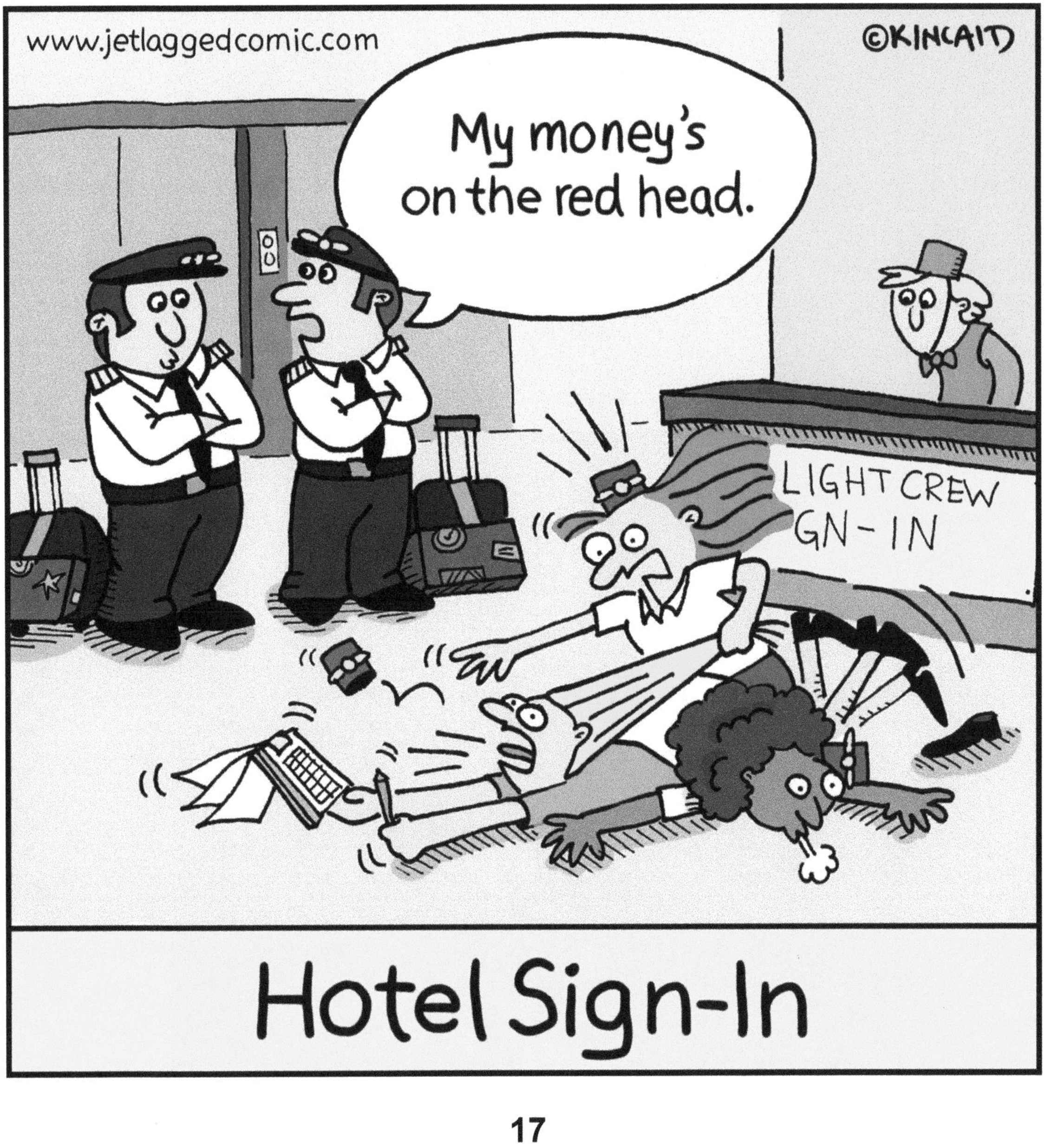
www.jetlaggedcomic.com
©KINCAID
My money's on the red head.
LIGHT CREW
GN-IN

Hotel Sign-In

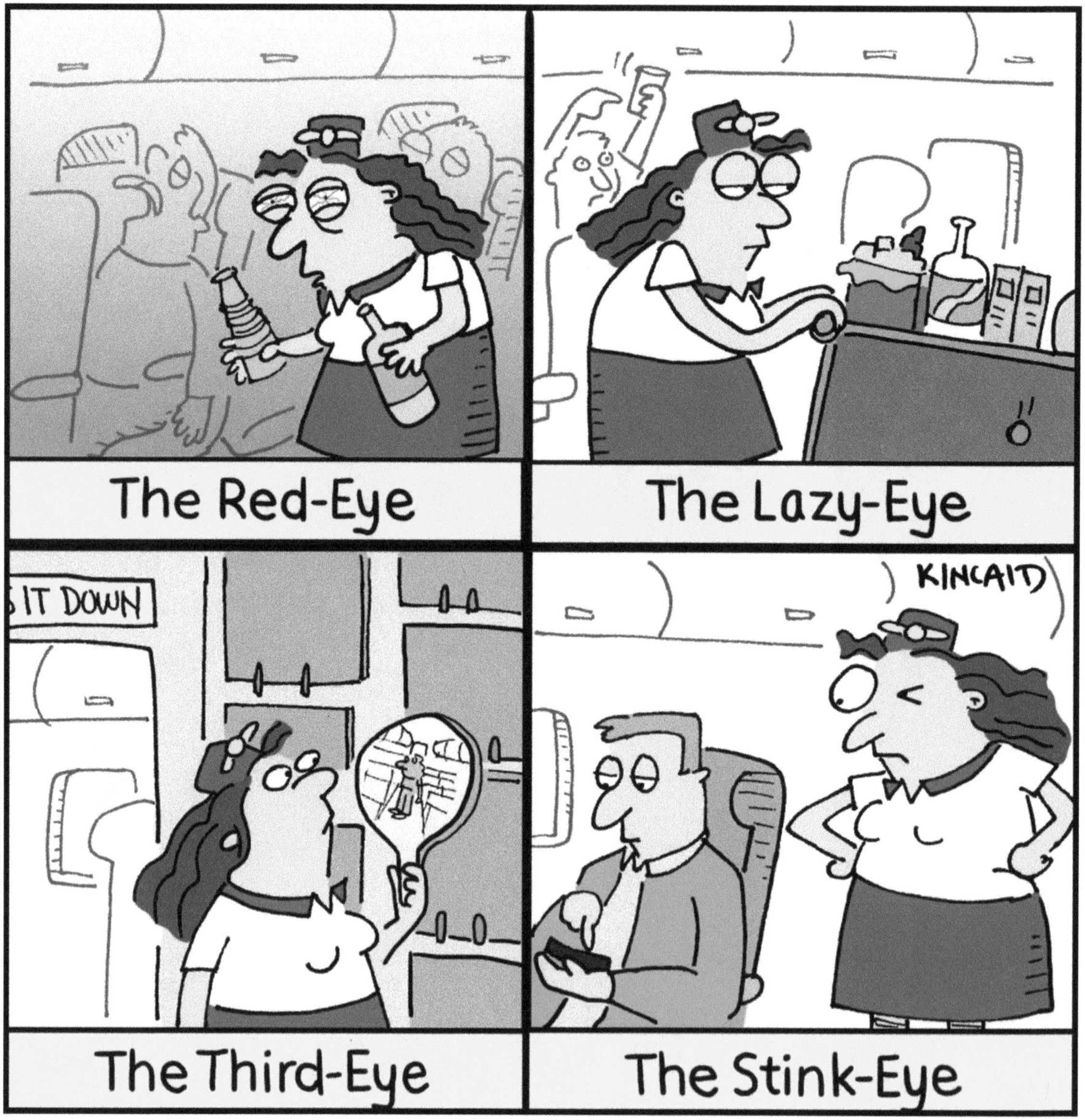
The Red-Eye
The Lazy-Eye
IT DOWN
The Third-Eye
KINCAID
The Stink-Eye

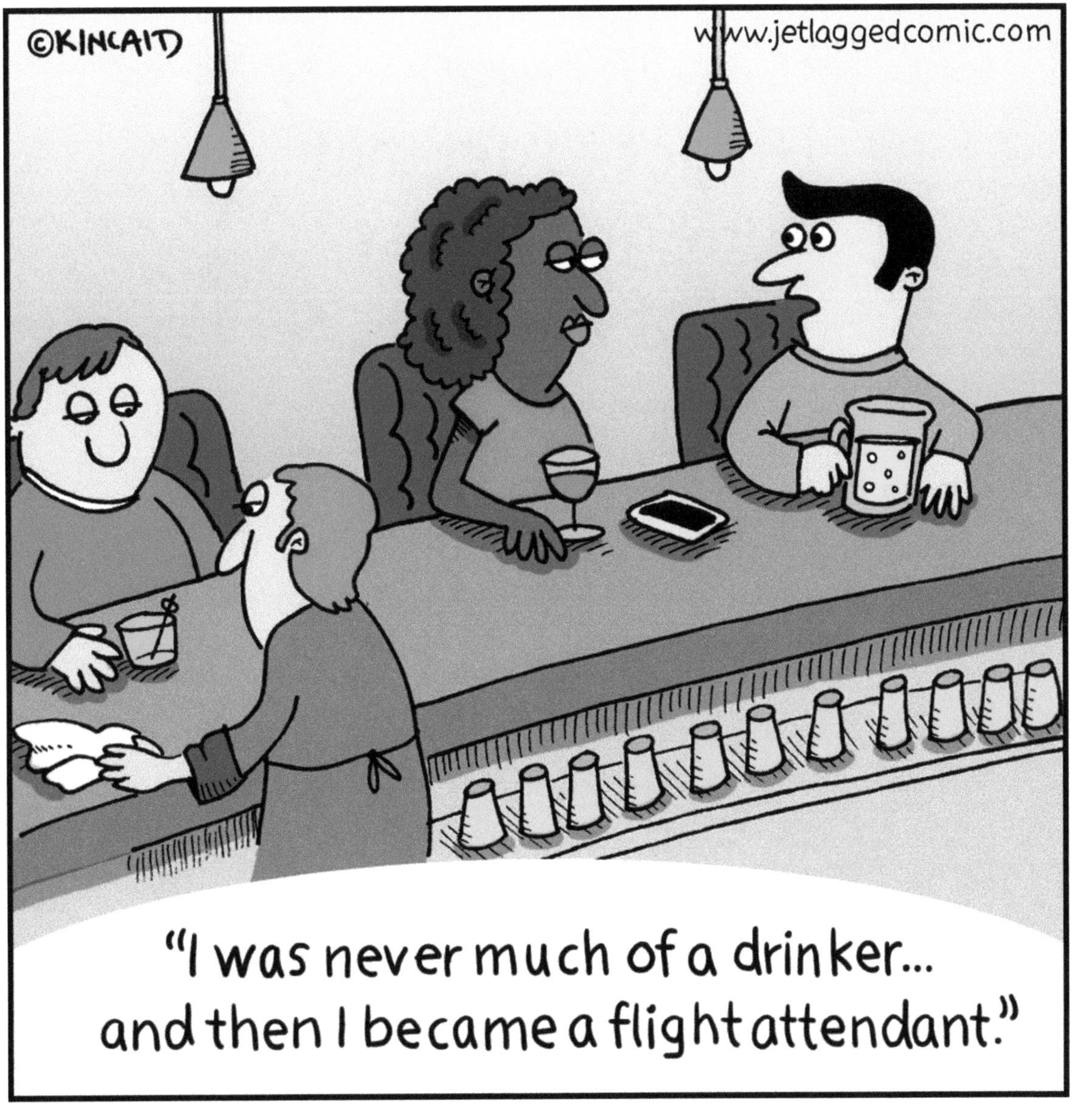
©KINCAID
www.jetlaggedcomic.com
"I was never much of a drinker...
and then I became a flight attendant."

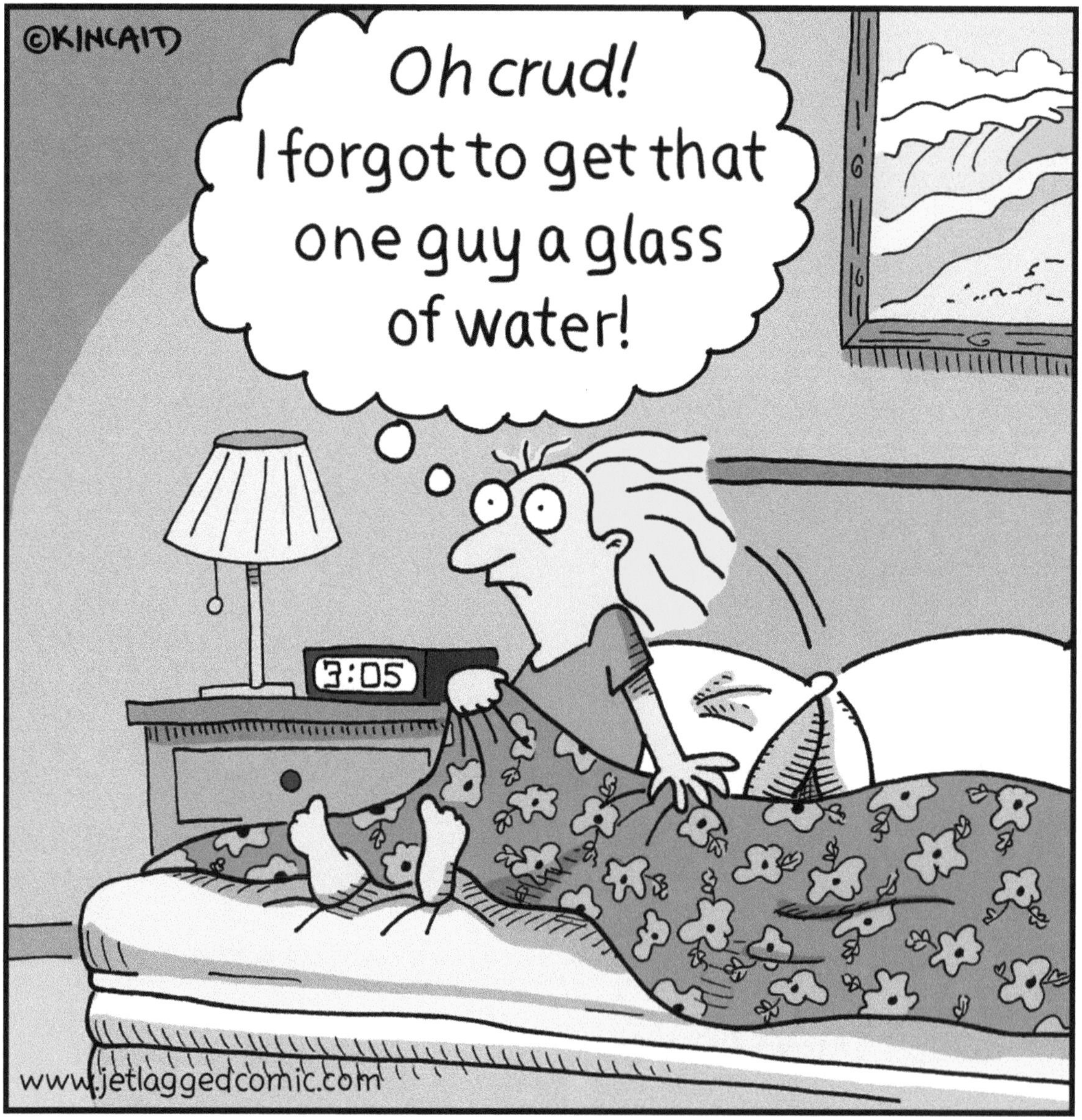
©KINCAID
Oh crud! I forgot to get that one guy a glass of water!
3:05
www.jetlaggedcomic.com

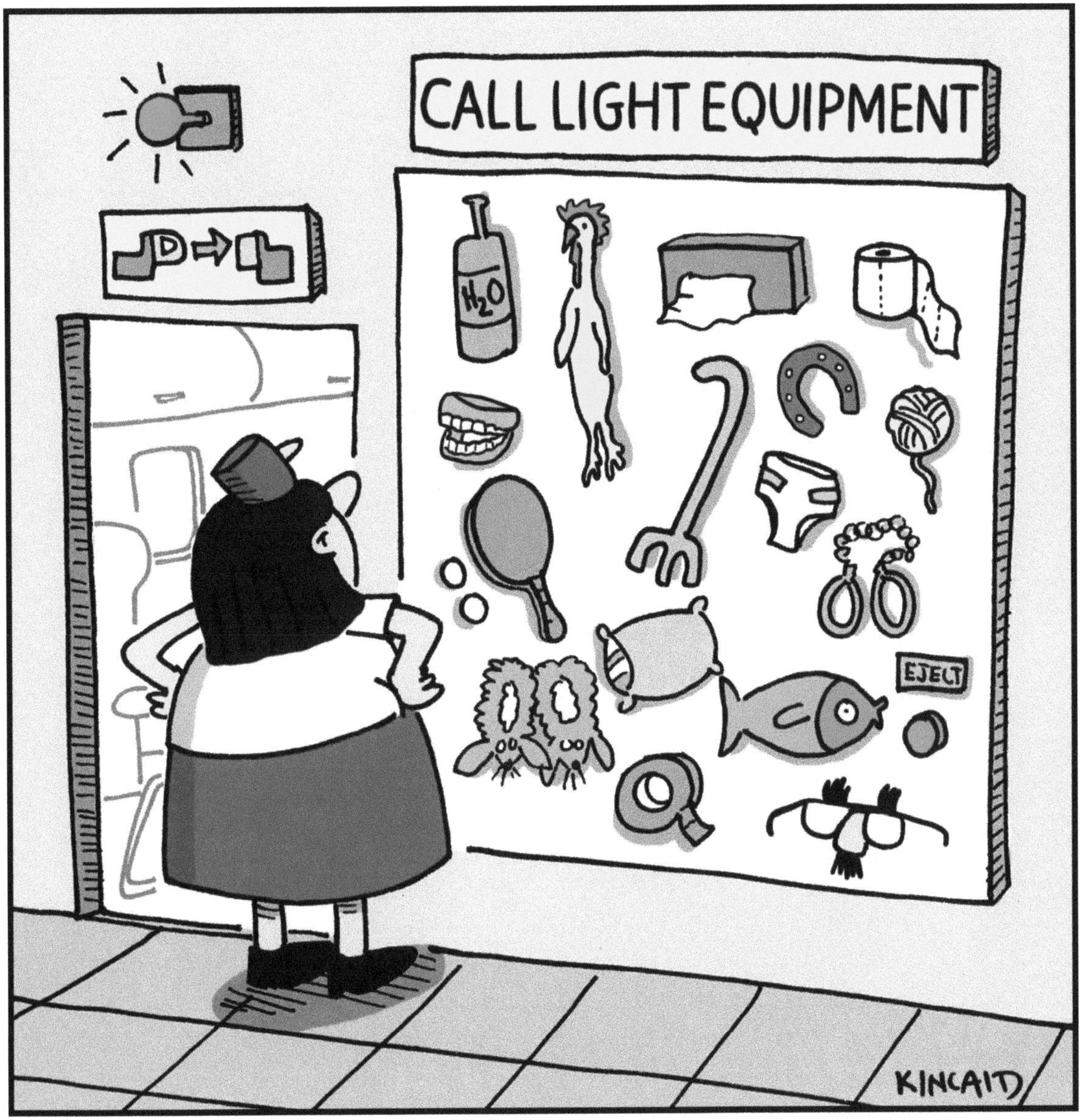
CALL LIGHT EQUIPMENT
H_2O
EJECT
KINCAID

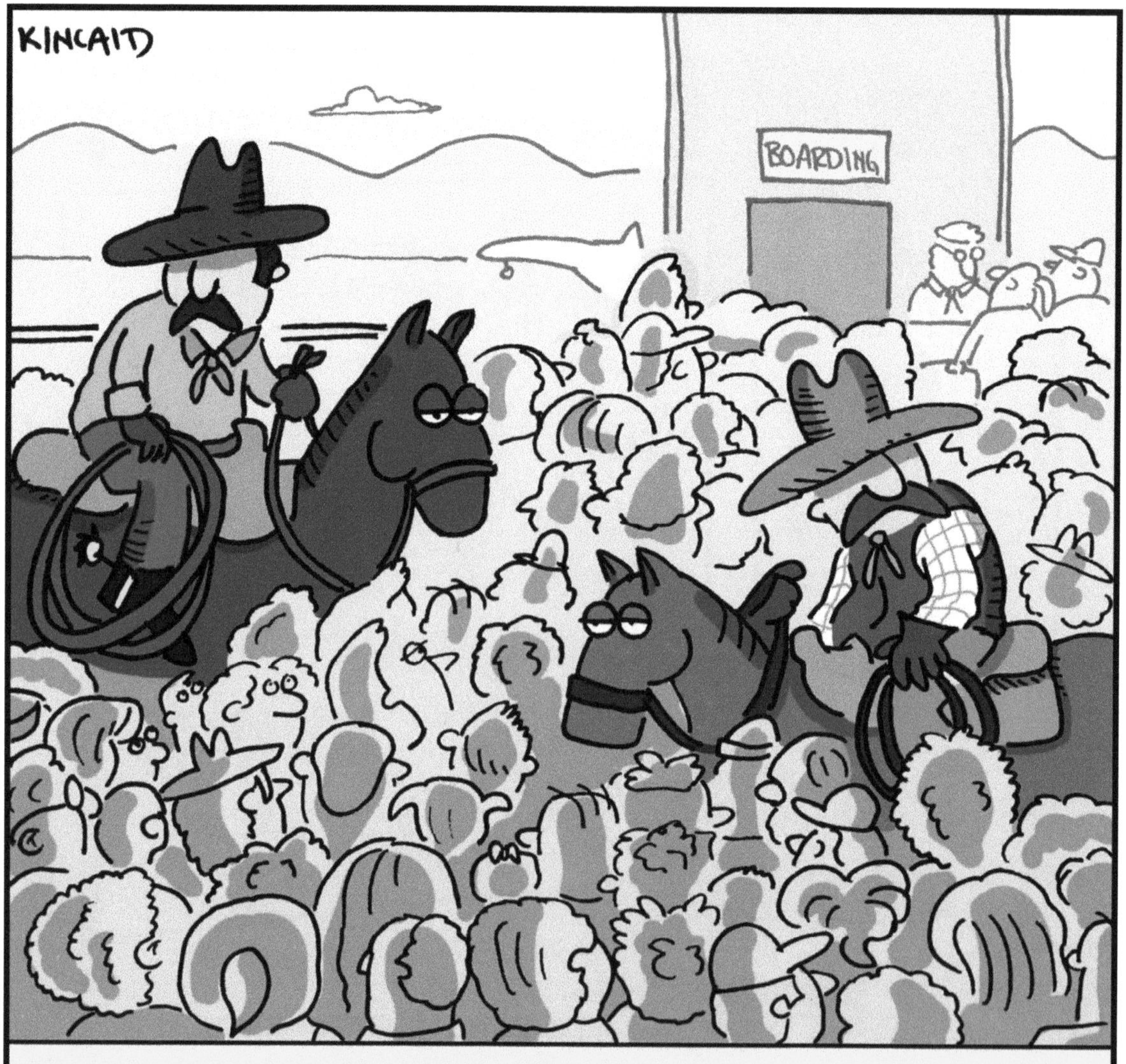
KINCAID
BOARDING

General Boarding

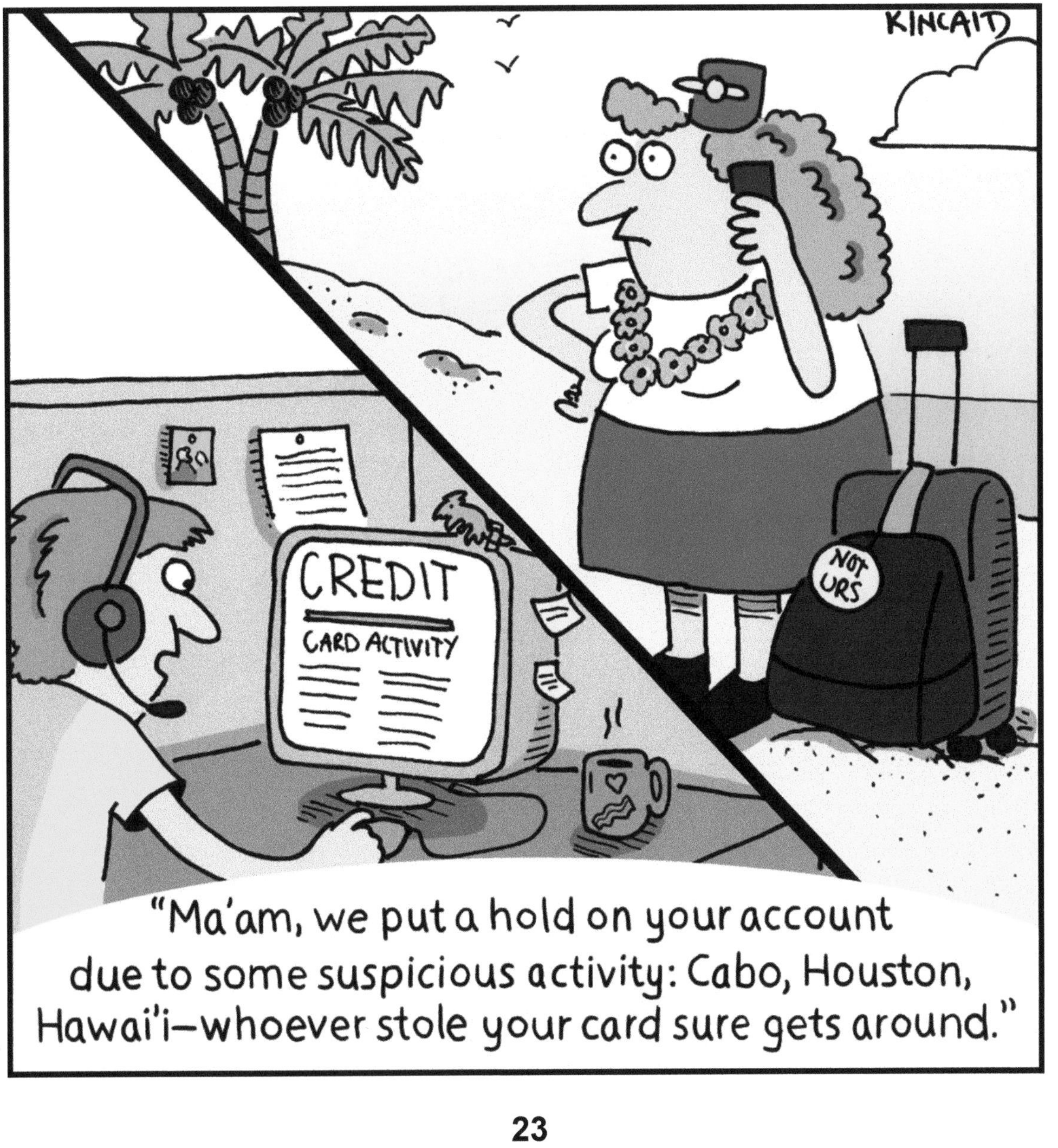
KINCAID
CREDIT
CARD ACTIVITY
NOT URS

"Ma'am, we put a hold on your account due to some suspicious activity: Cabo, Houston, Hawai'i—whoever stole your card sure gets around."

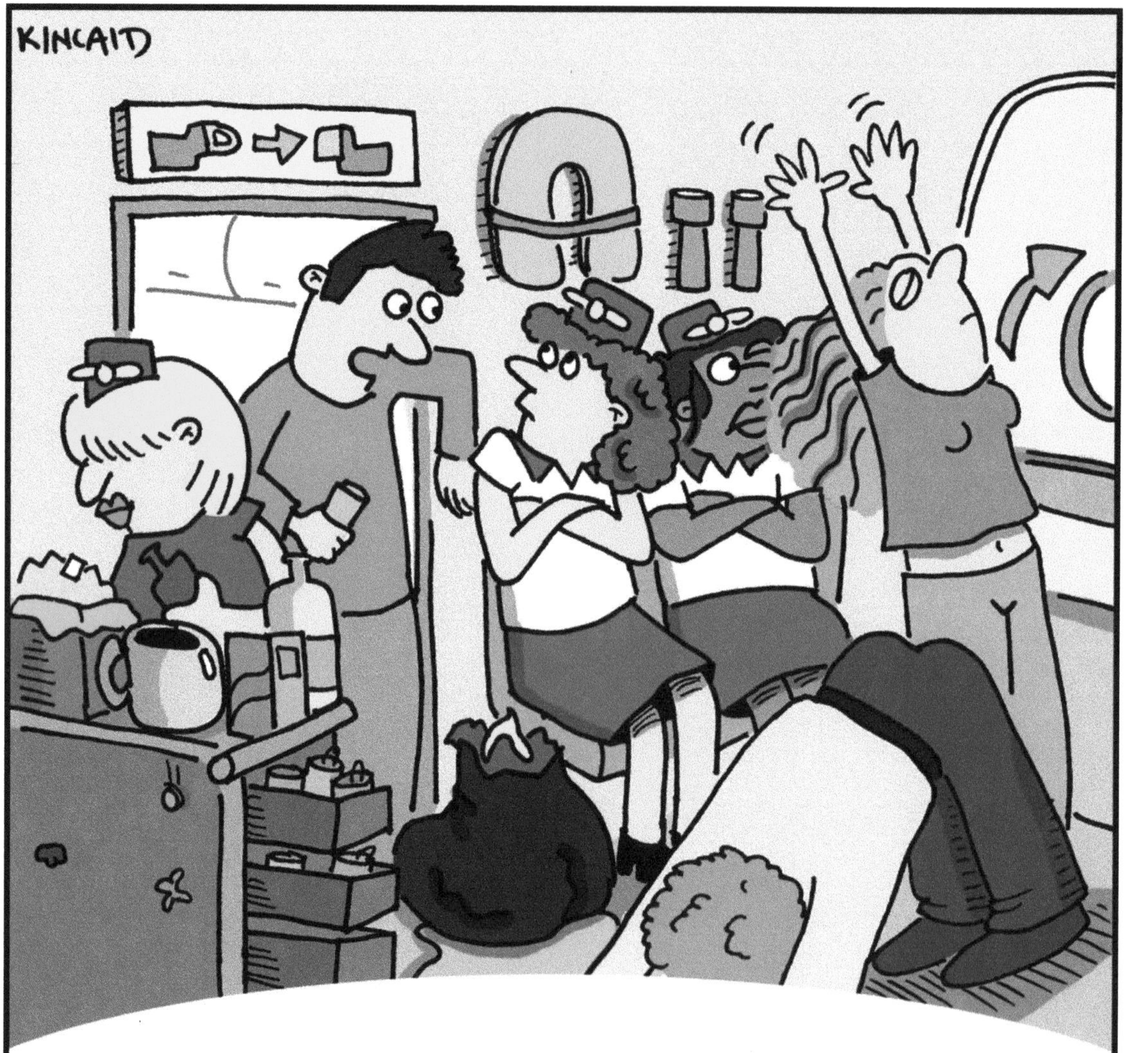
KINCAID

"Are there any open seats? I'm crammed."

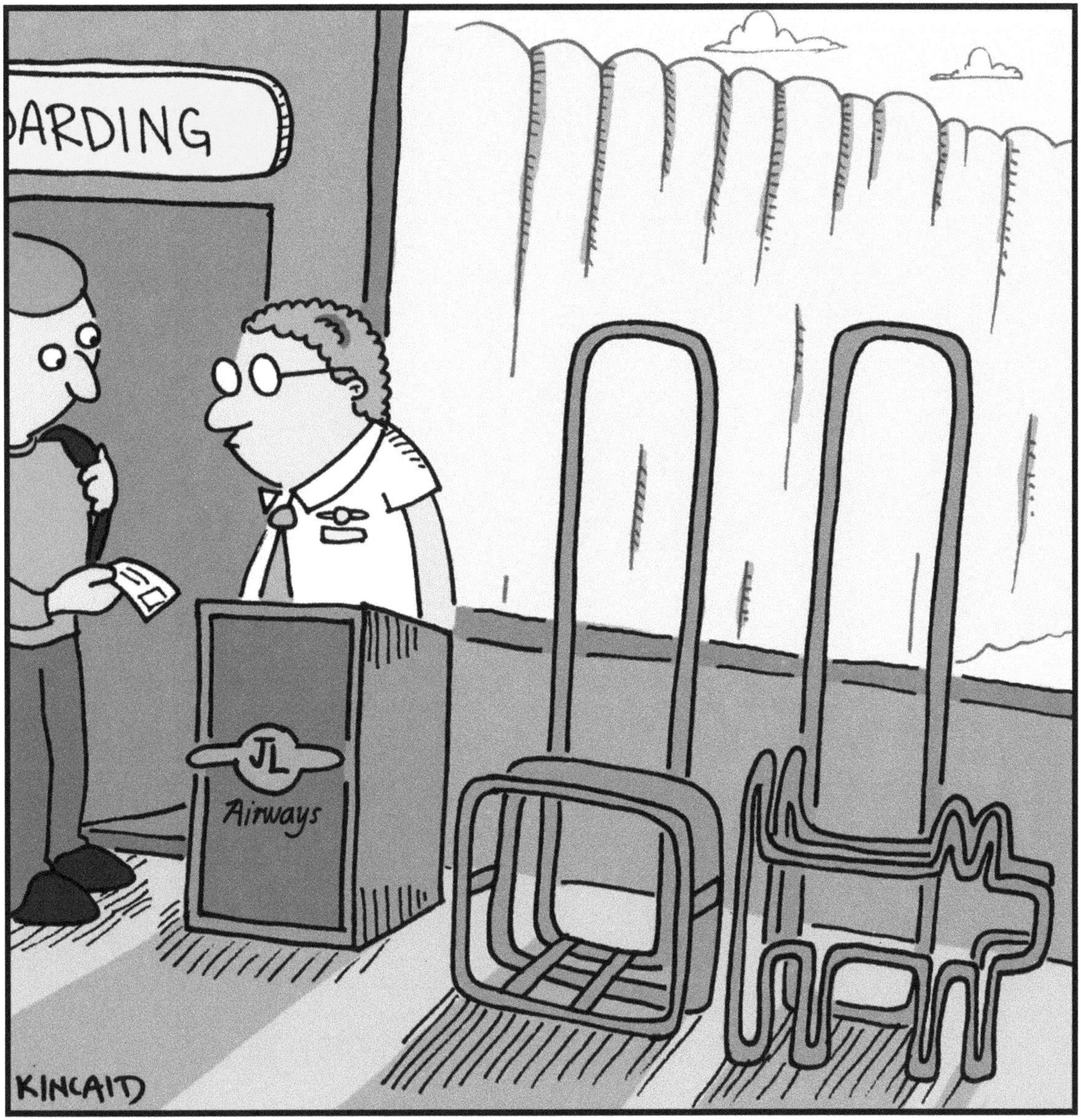
OARDING
JL
Airways
KINCAID

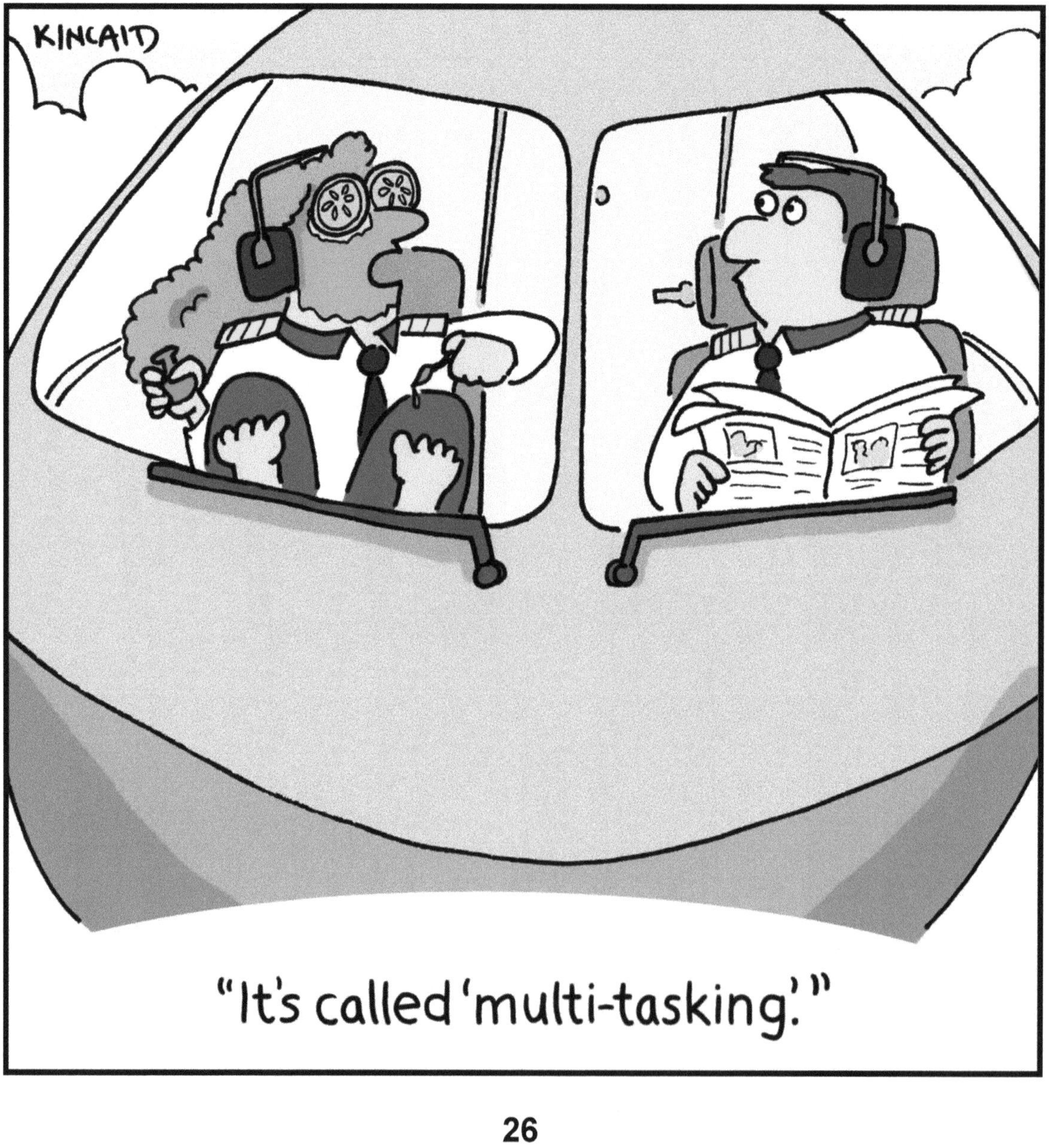
KINCAID

"It's called 'multi-tasking.'"

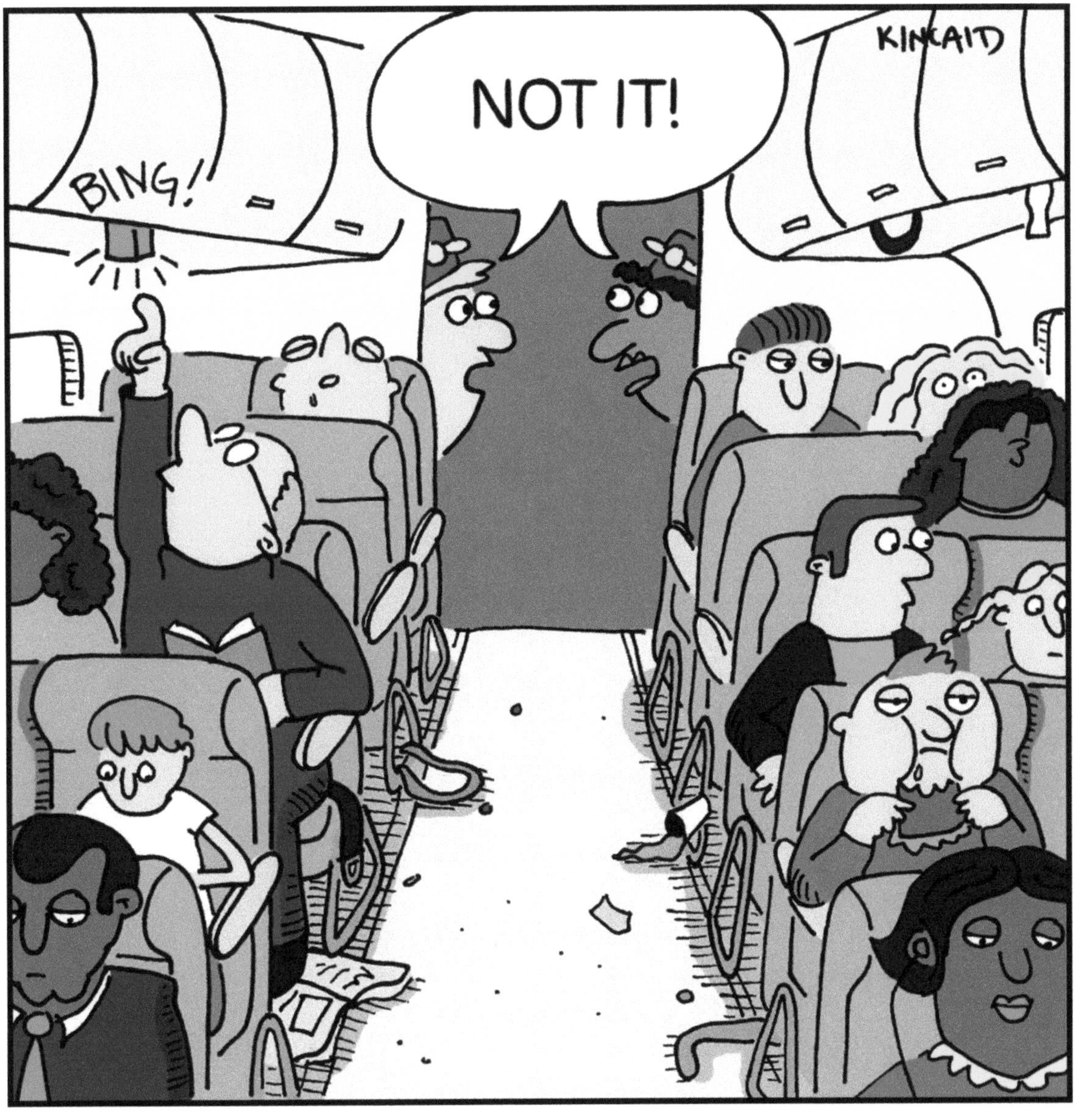
NOT IT!
BING!
KINCAID

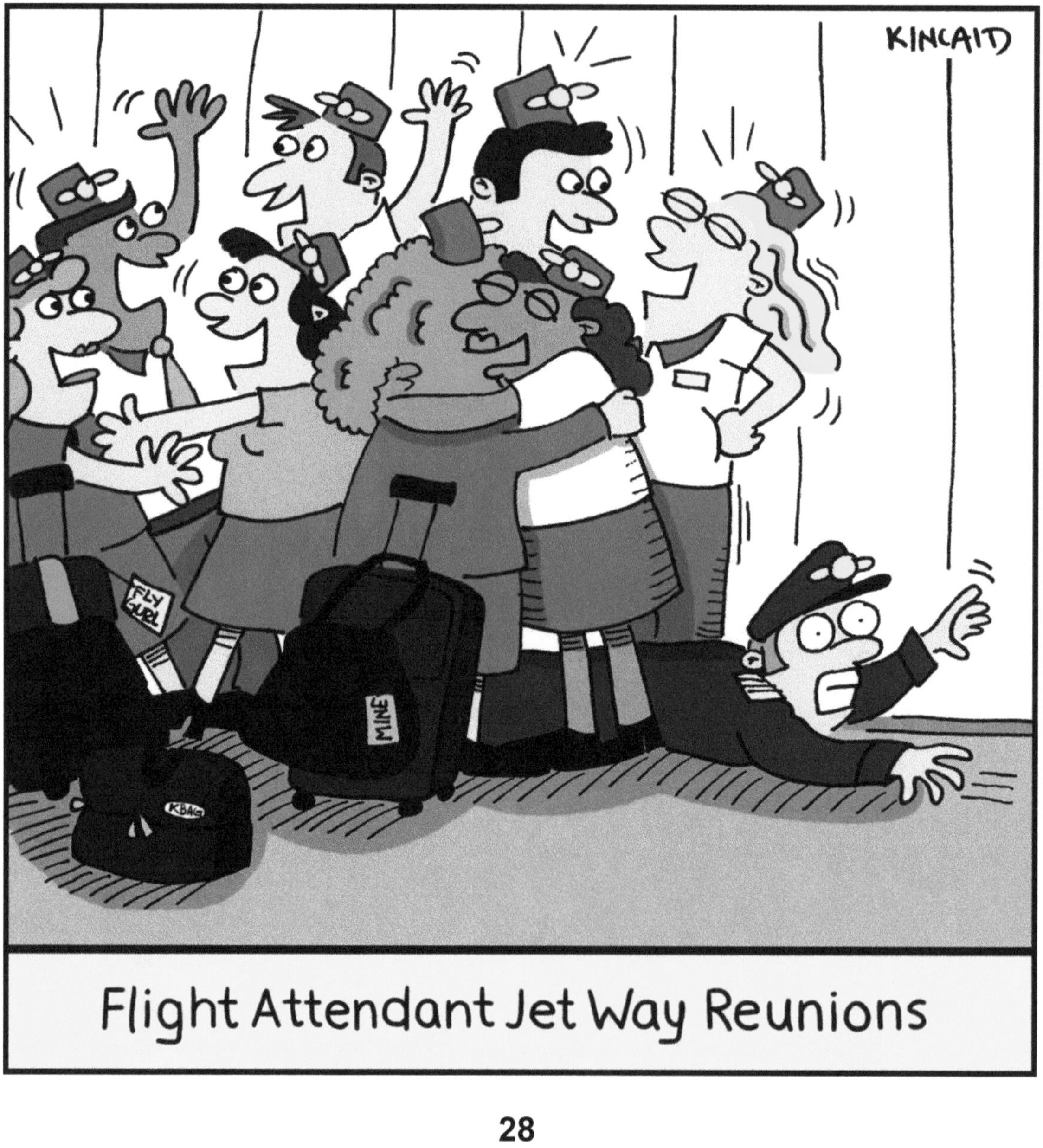
KINCAID
FLY GURL
MINE
KBAG

Flight Attendant Jet Way Reunions

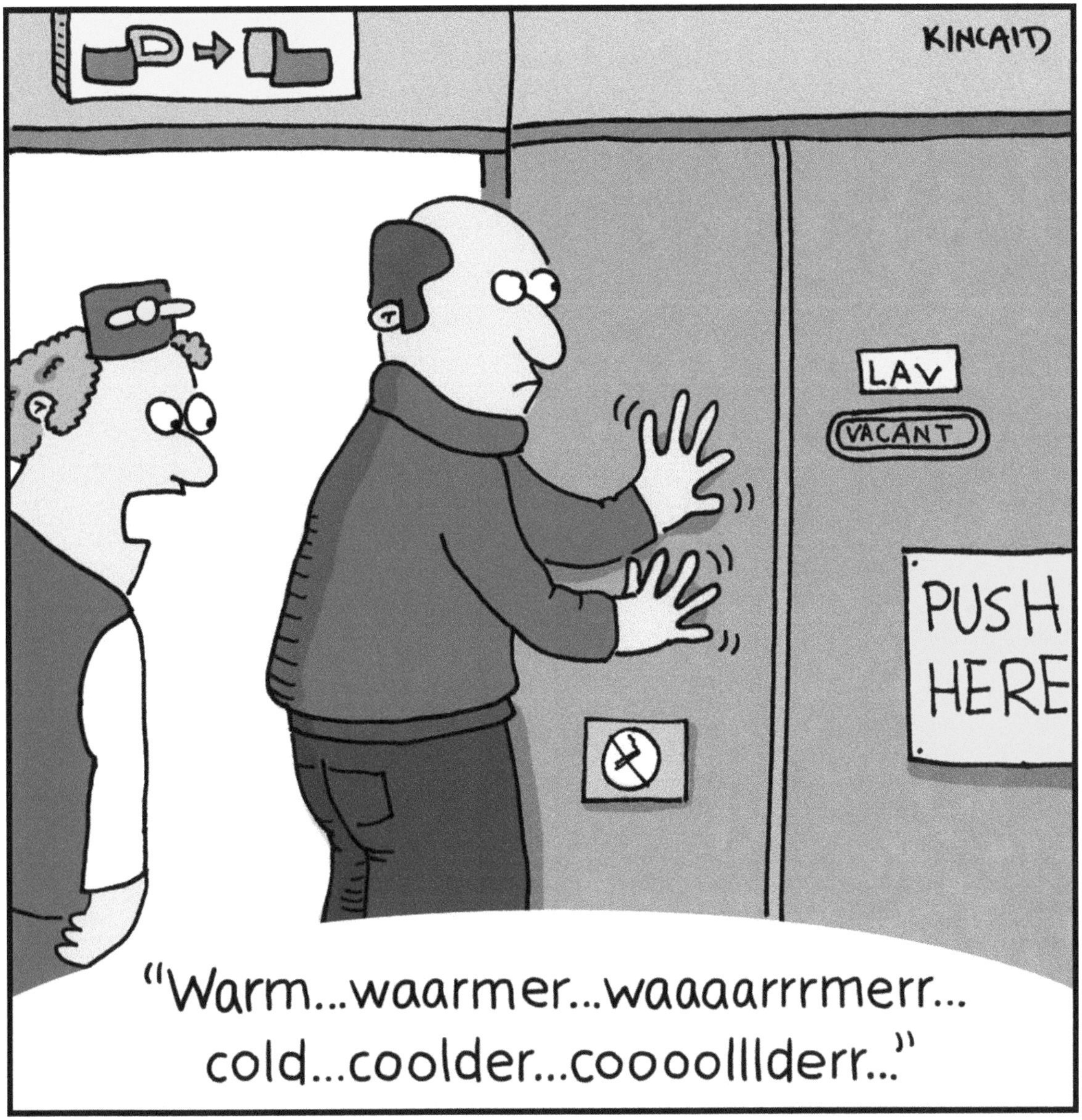
KINCAID
LAV
VACANT
PUSH HERE
"Warm...waarmer...waaaarrrmerr...
cold...coolder...coooollllderr..."

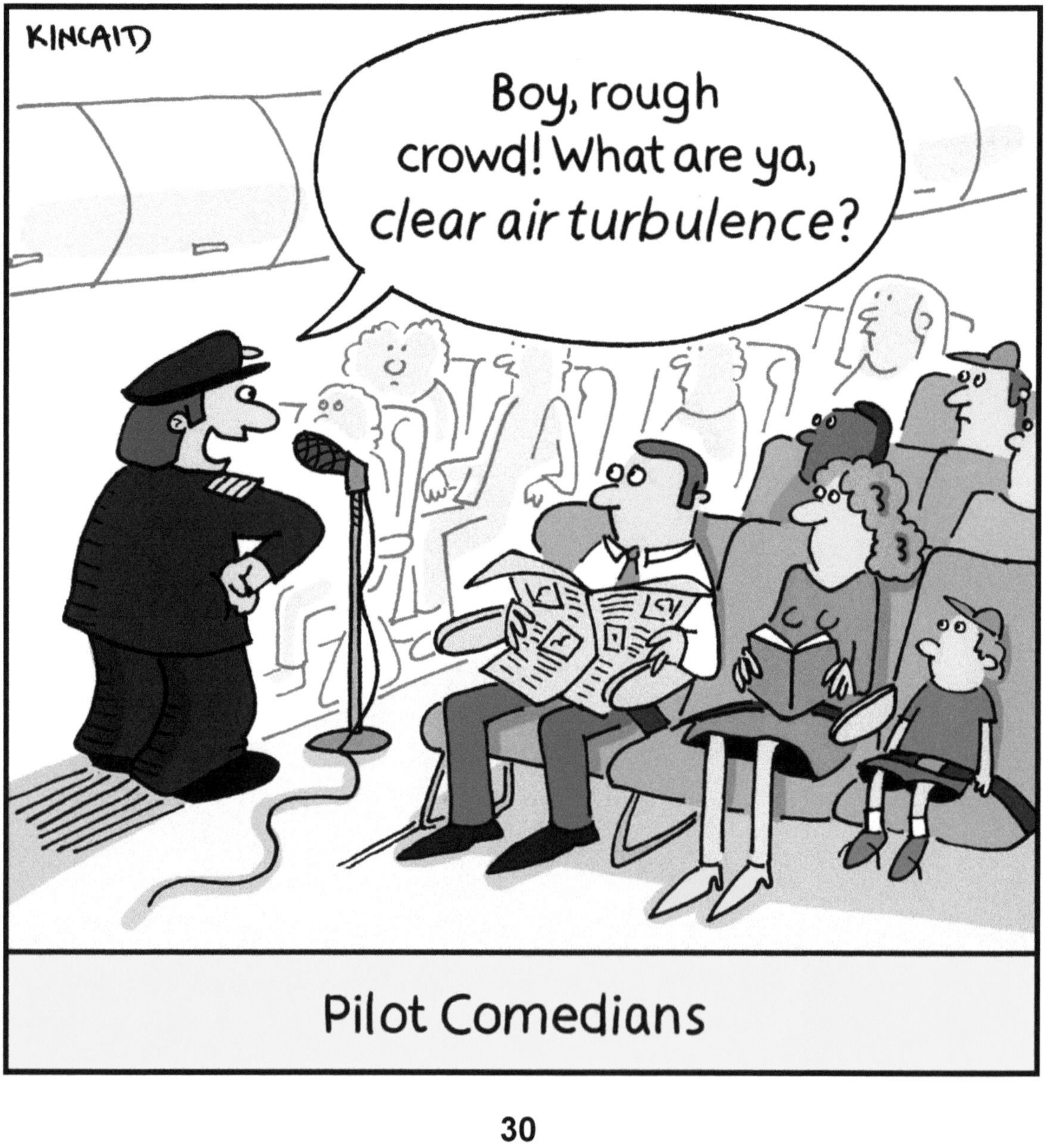
KINCAID
Boy, rough crowd! What are ya, *clear air turbulence?*

Pilot Comedians

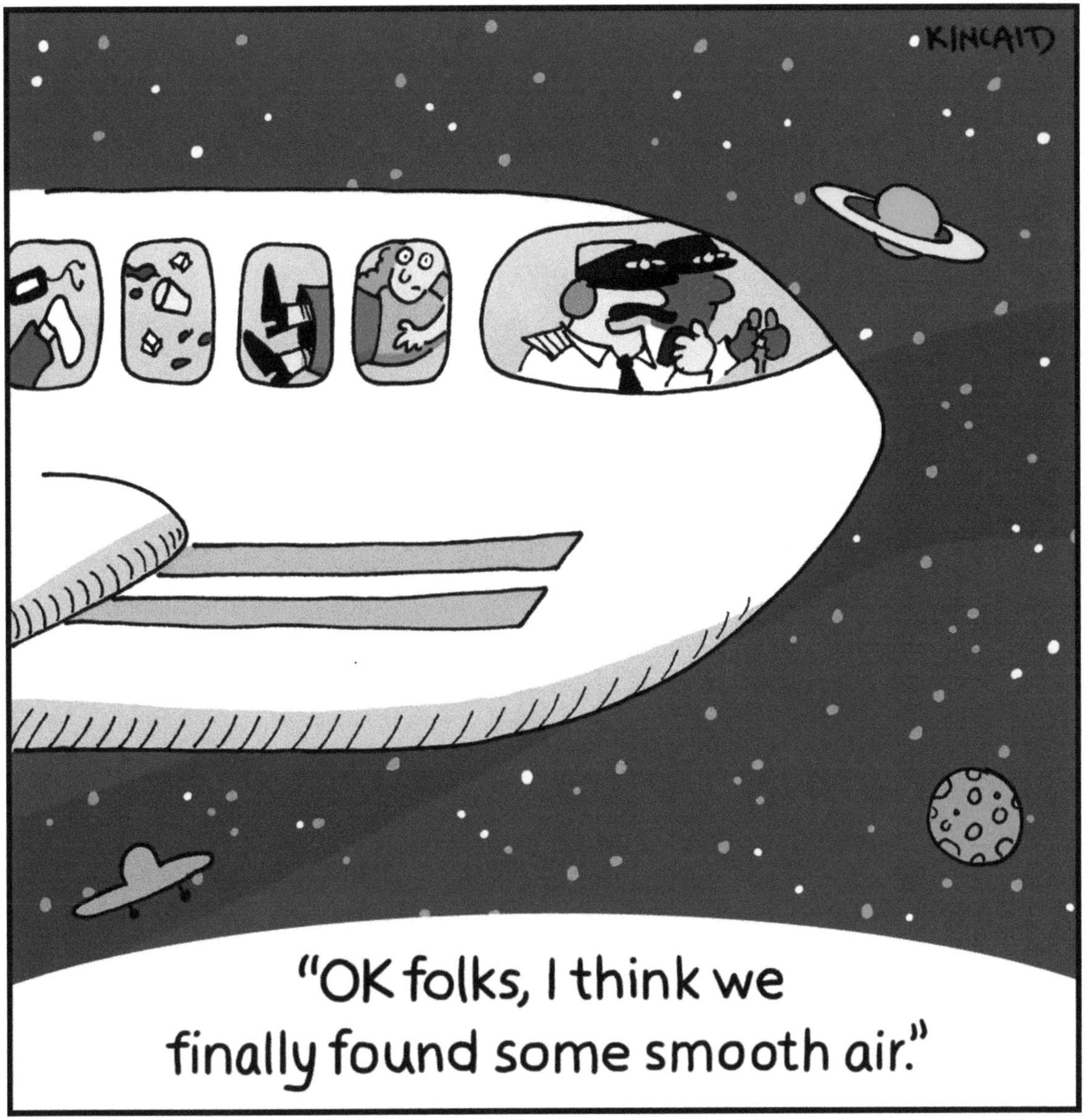
KINCAID

"OK folks, I think we finally found some smooth air."

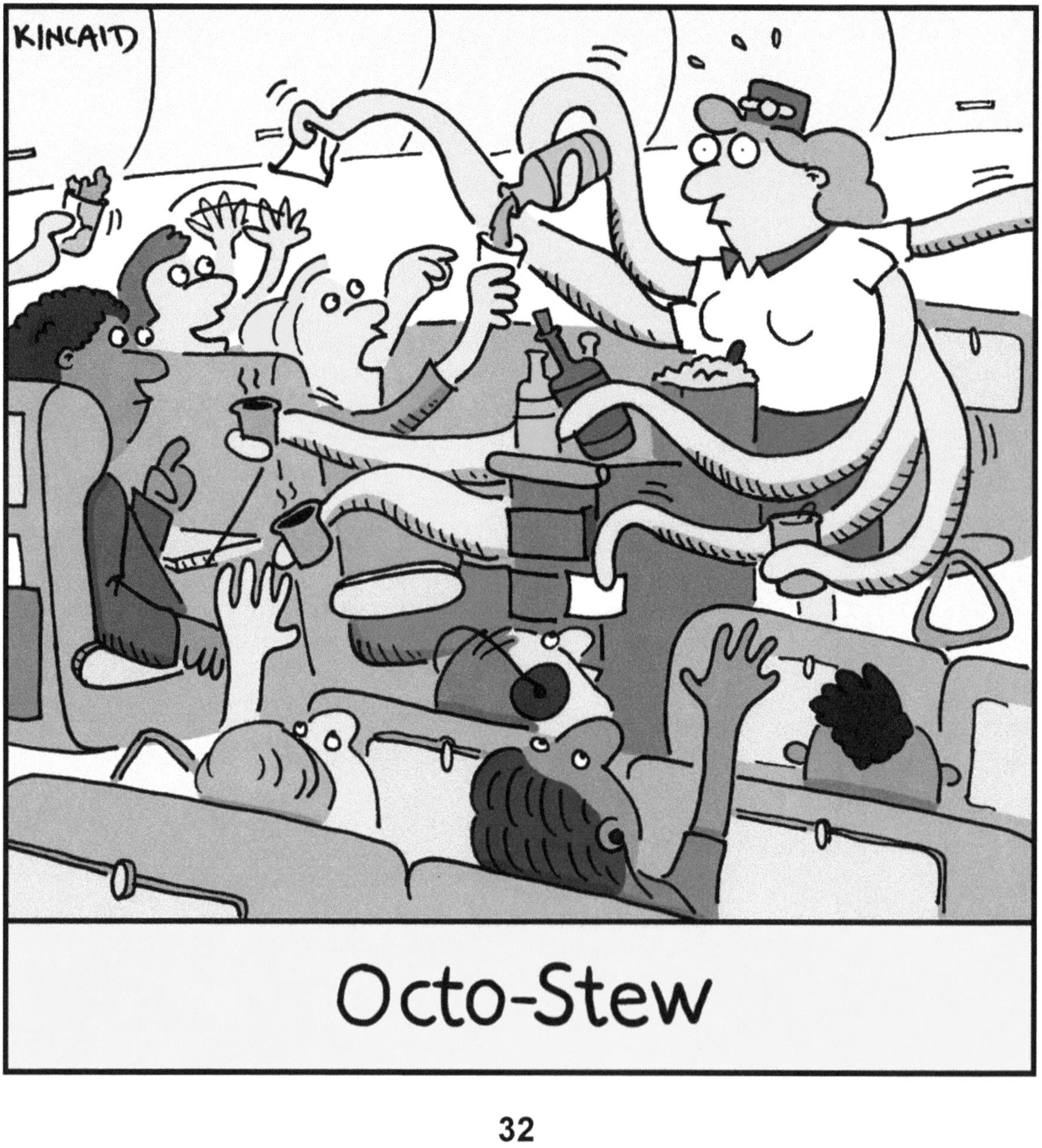
KINCAID

Octo-Stew

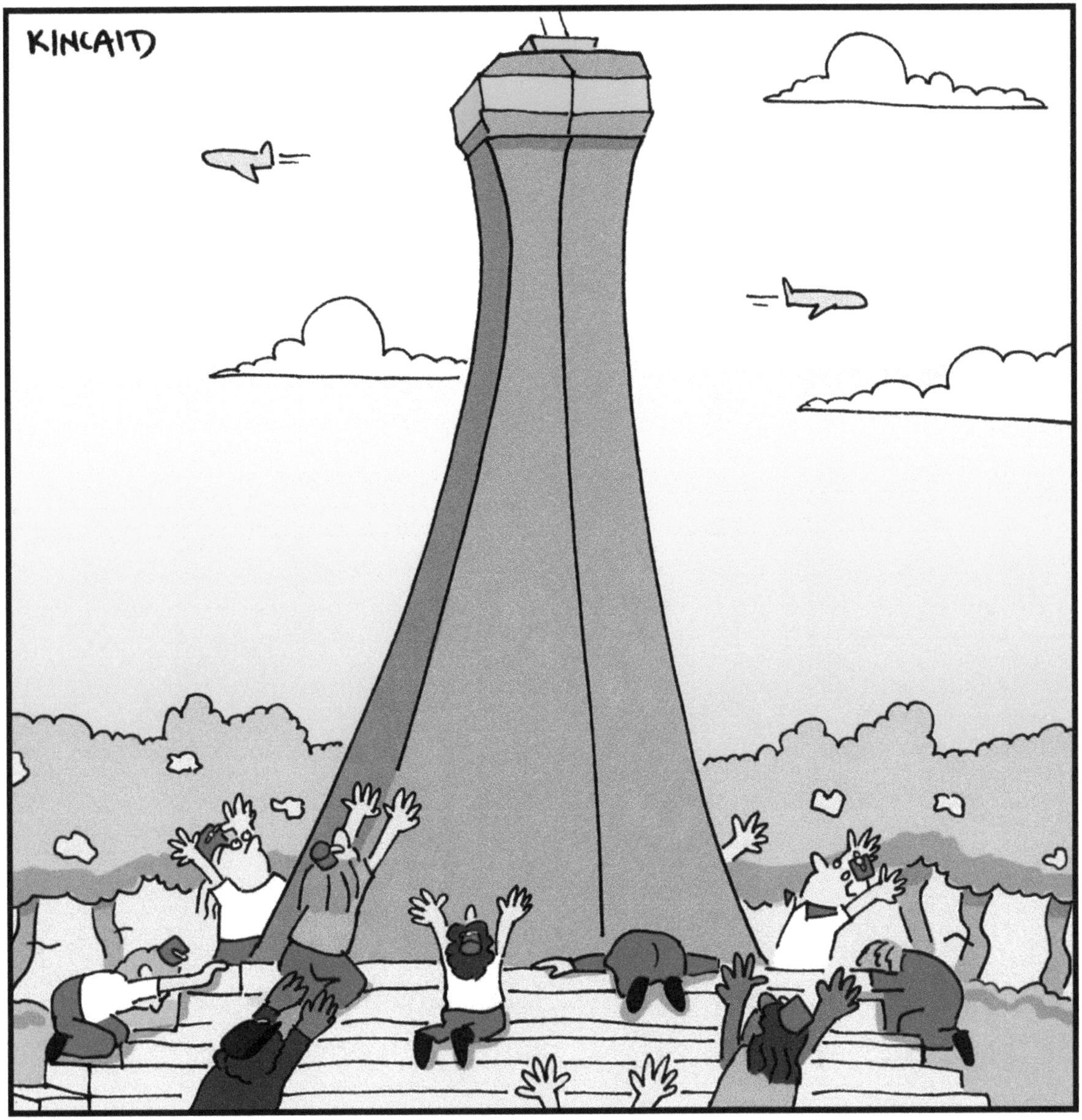
KINCAID

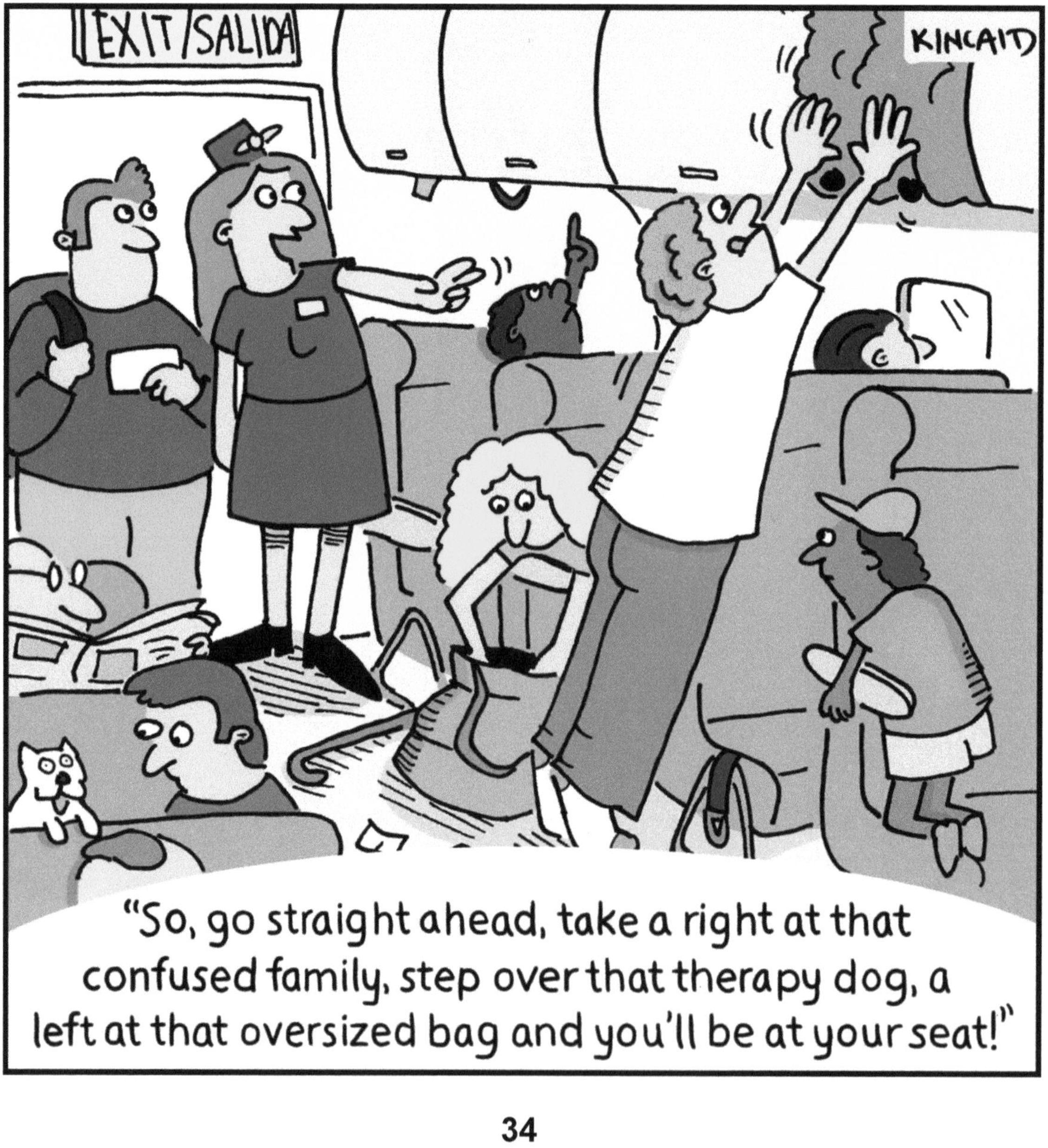
EXIT/SALIDA
KINCAID

"So, go straight ahead, take a right at that confused family, step over that therapy dog, a left at that oversized bag and you'll be at your seat!"

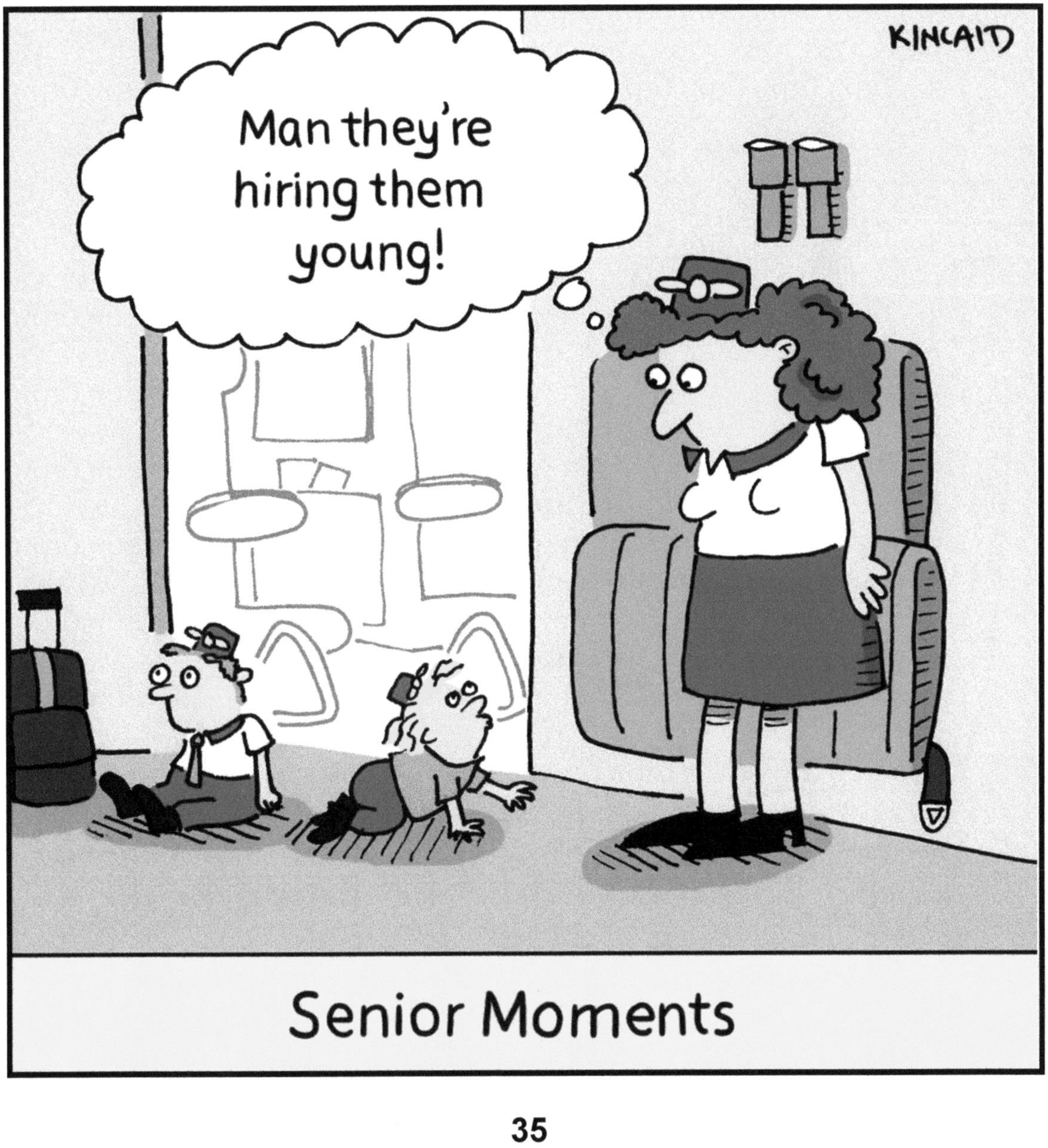
KINCAID
Man they're hiring them young!

Senior Moments

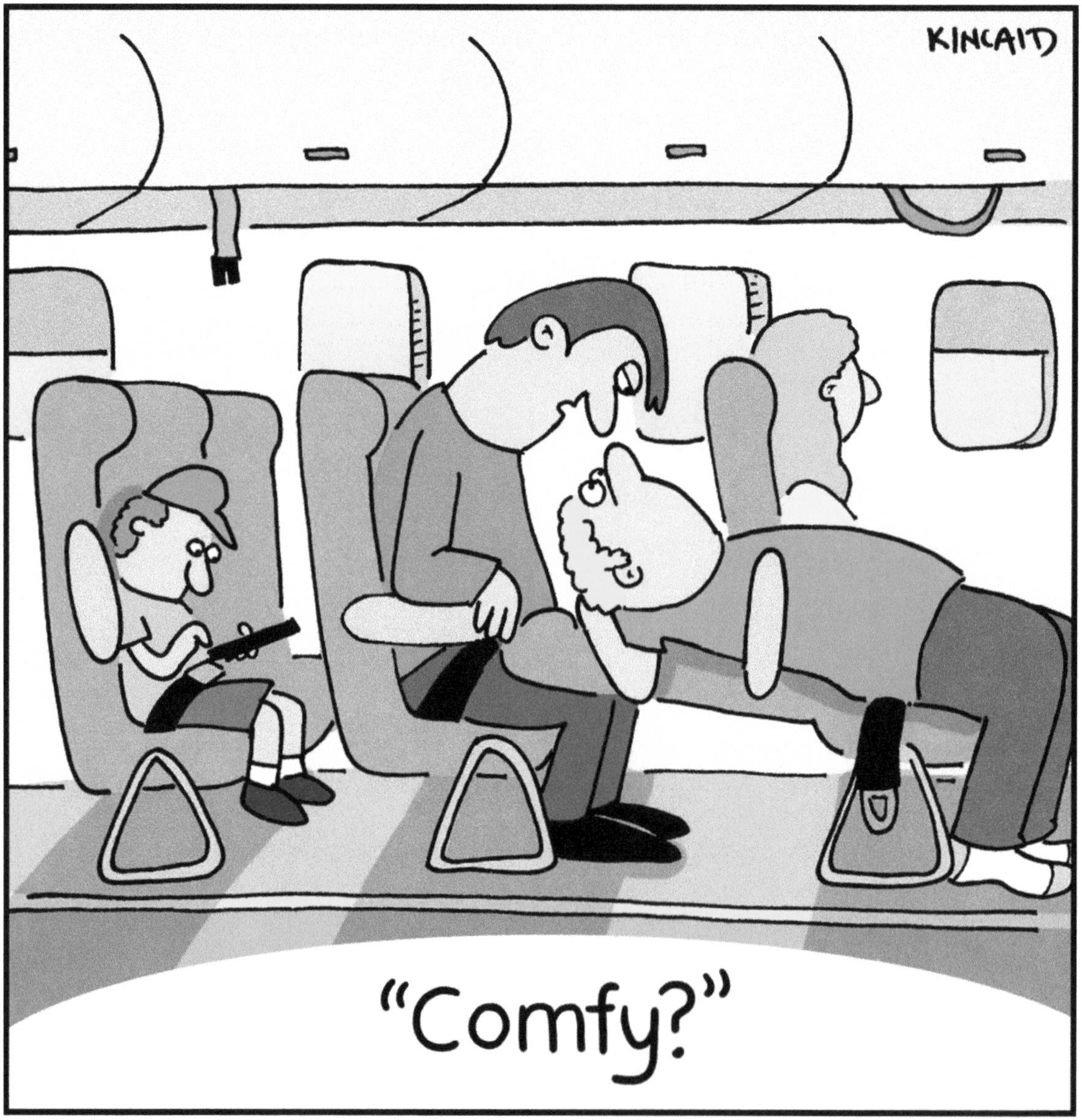
KINCAID

"Comfy?"

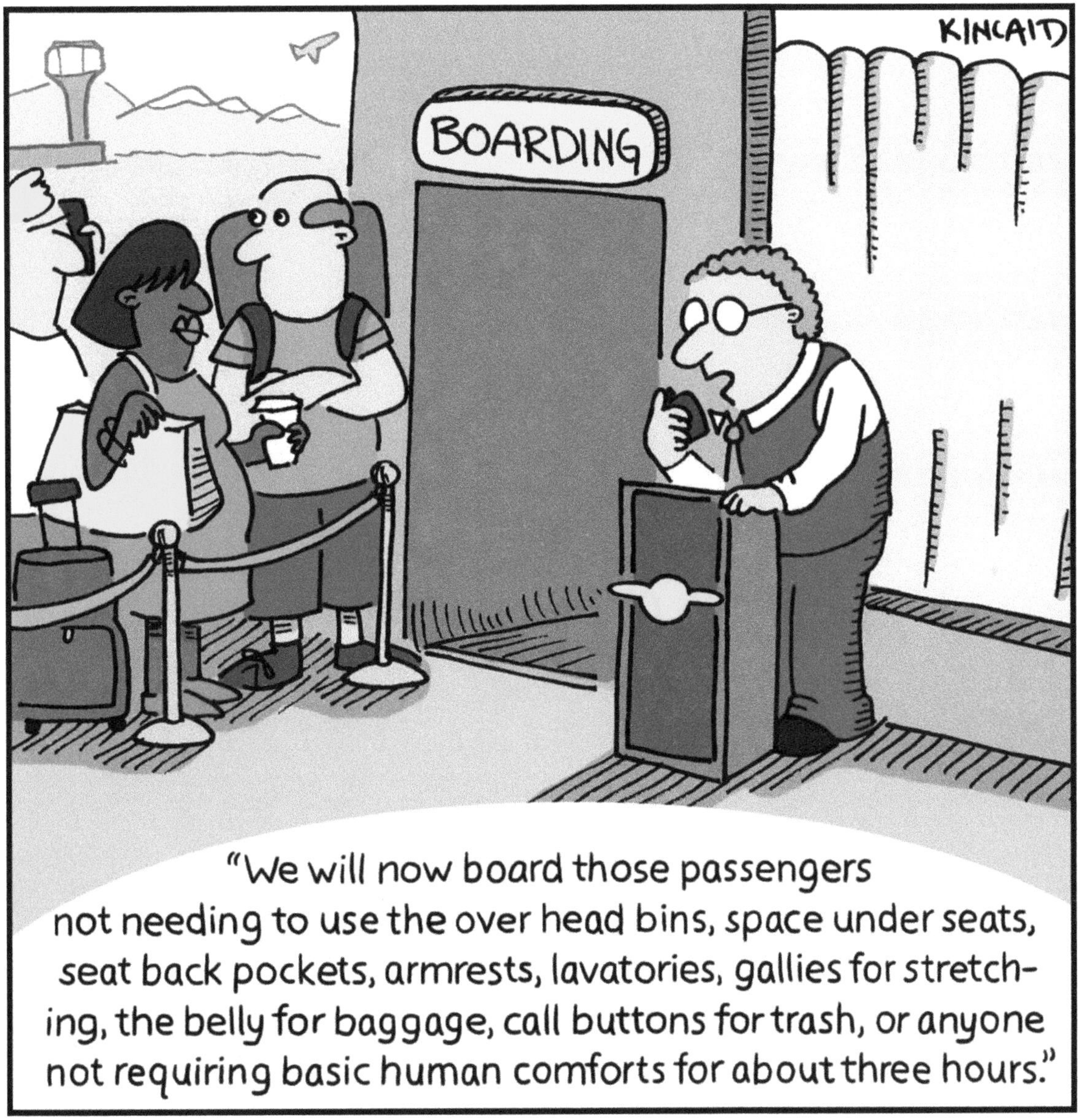
KINCAID
BOARDING

"We will now board those passengers not needing to use the over head bins, space under seats, seat back pockets, armrests, lavatories, gallies for stretching, the belly for baggage, call buttons for trash, or anyone not requiring basic human comforts for about three hours."

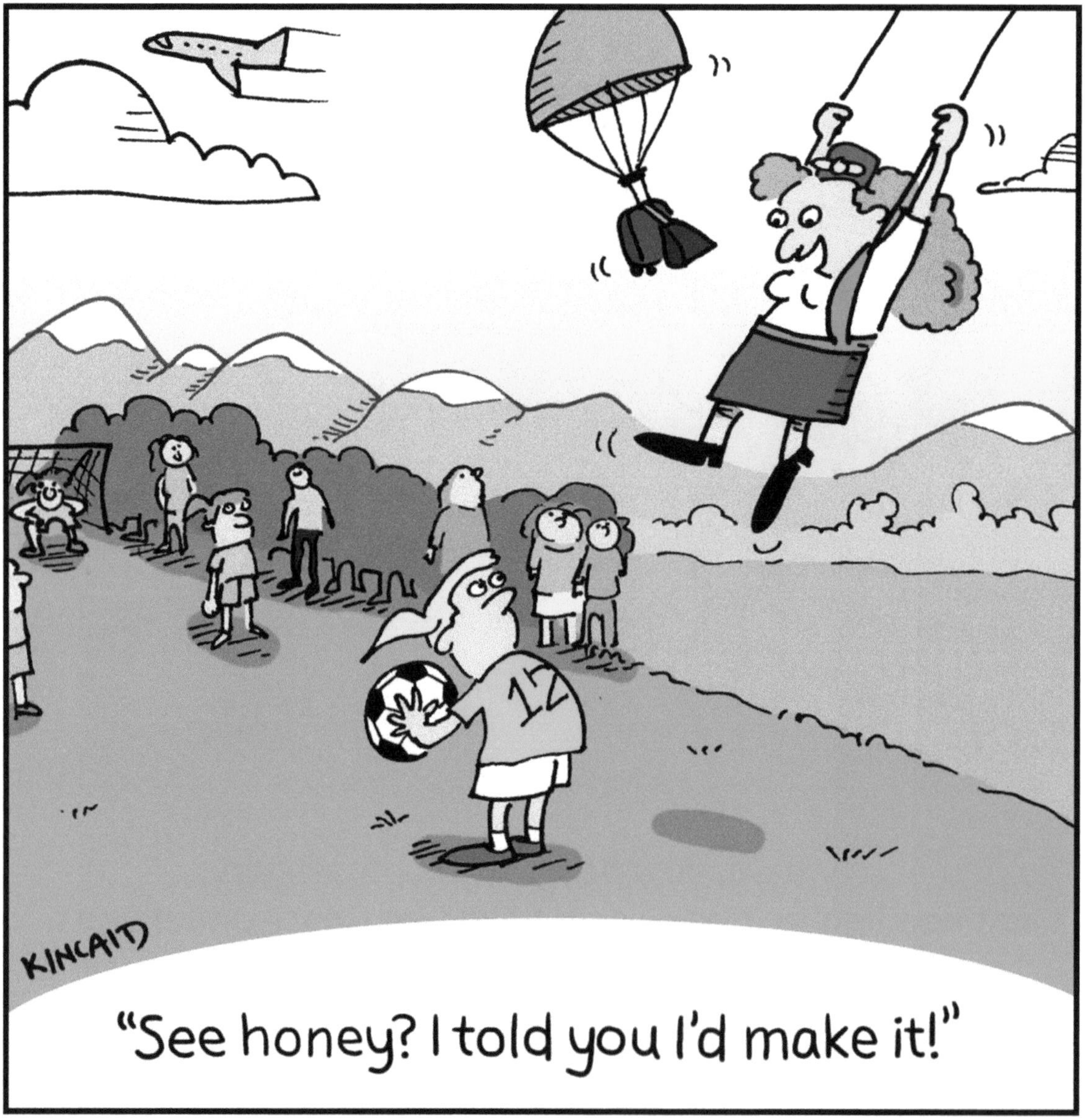
12
KINCAID

"See honey? I told you I'd make it!"

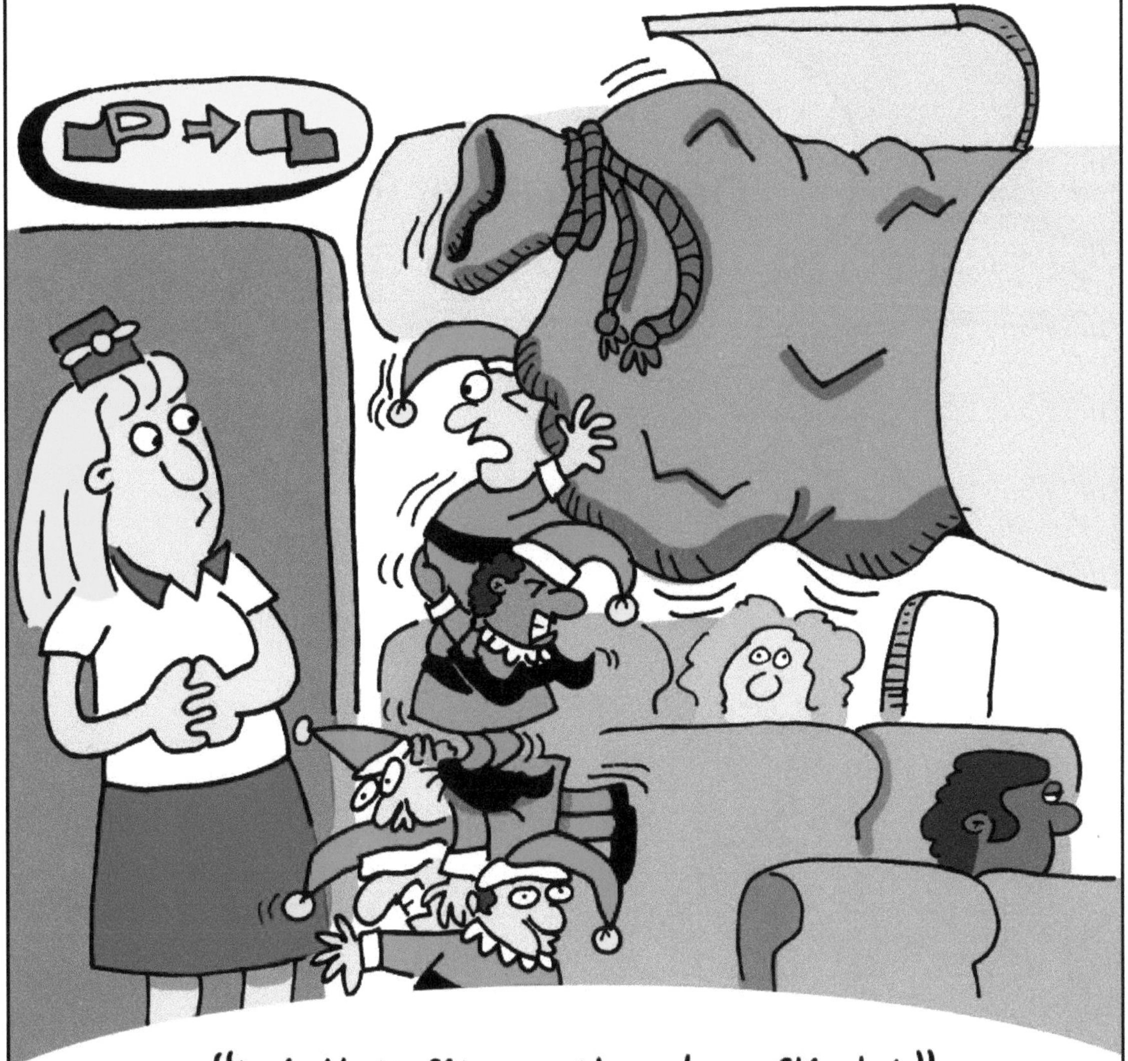

"Well, it fit on the *last* flight."

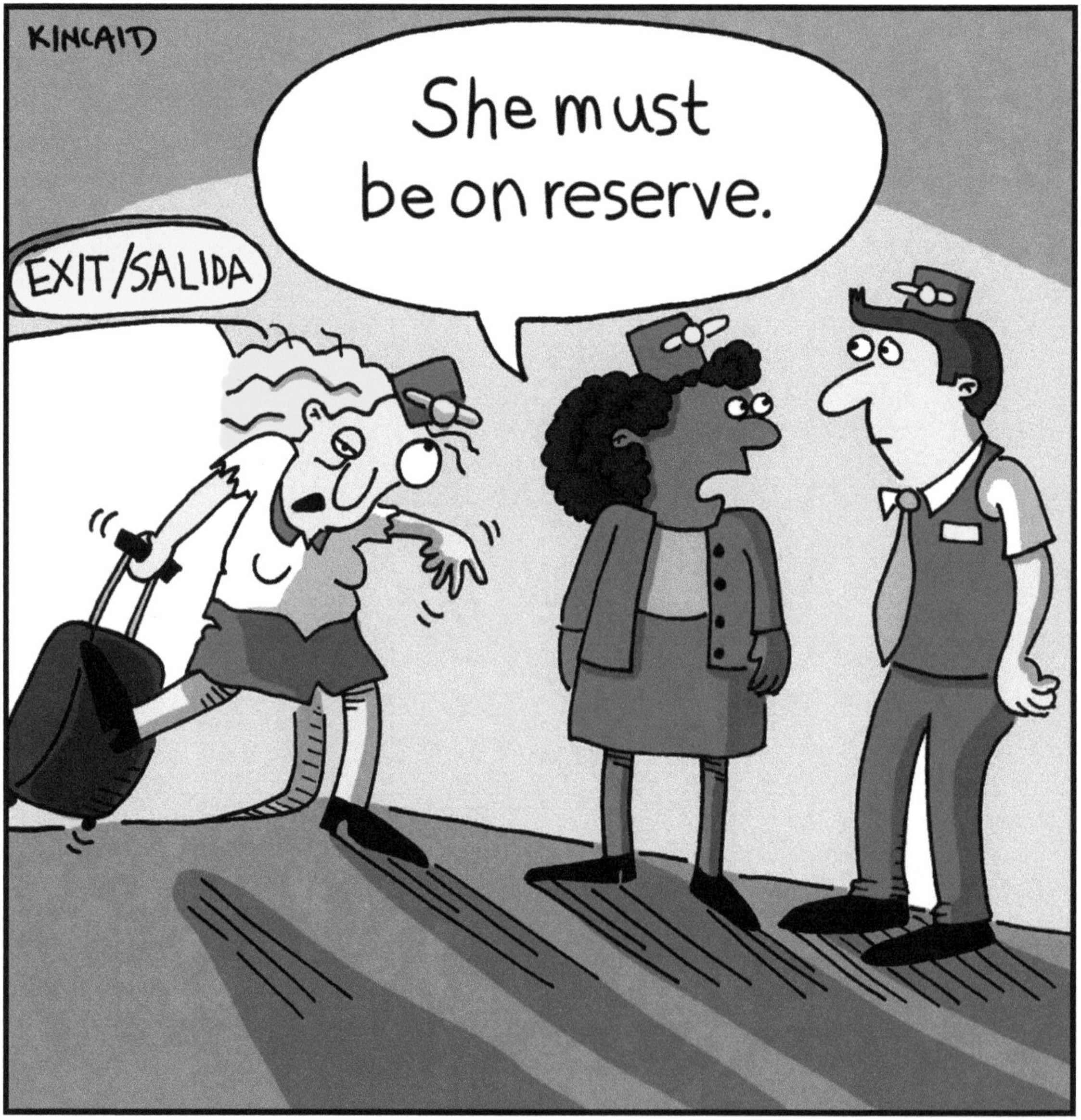
KINCAID
She must be on reserve.
EXIT/SALIDA

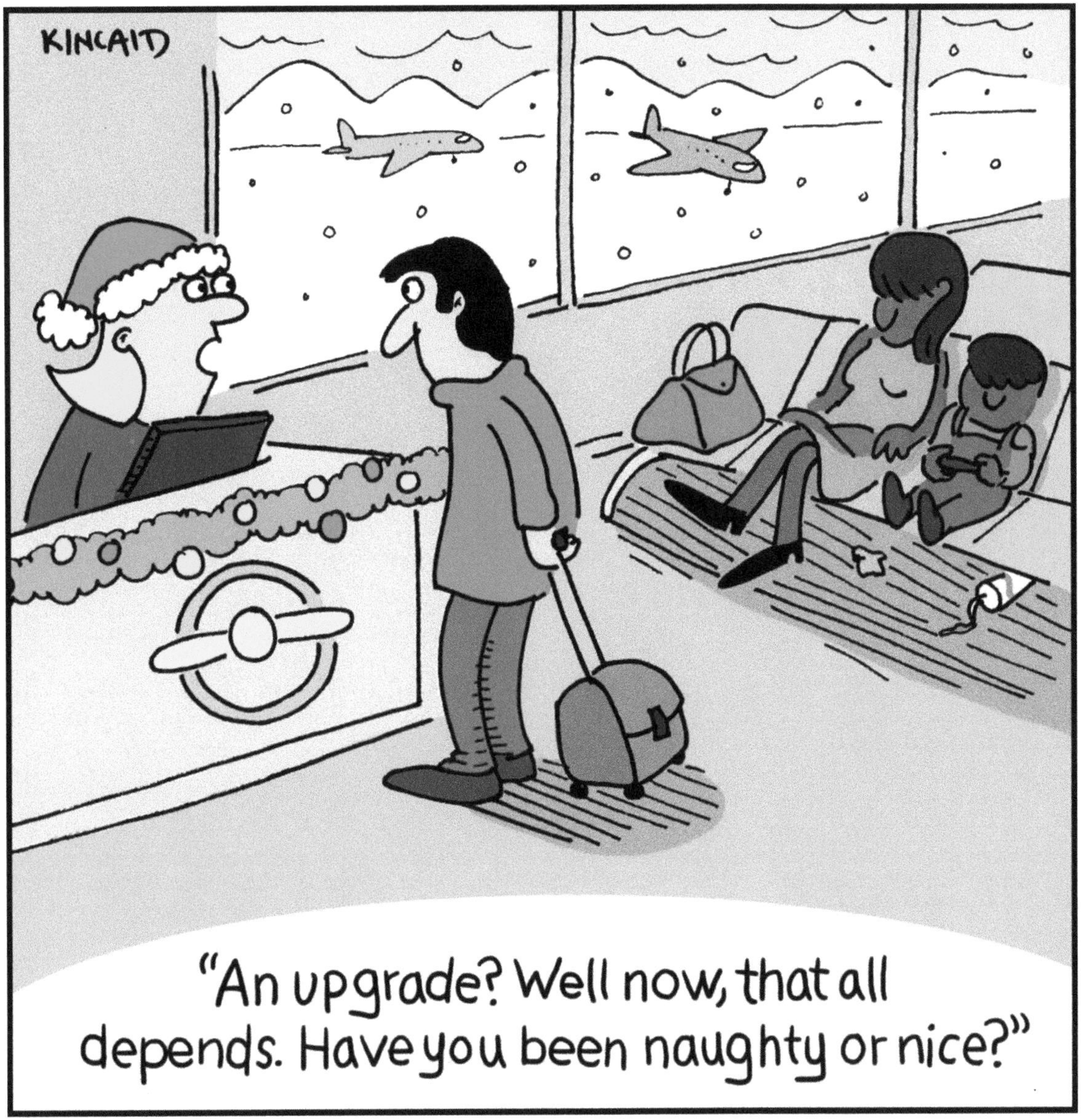
KINCAID

"An upgrade? Well now, that all depends. Have you been naughty or nice?"

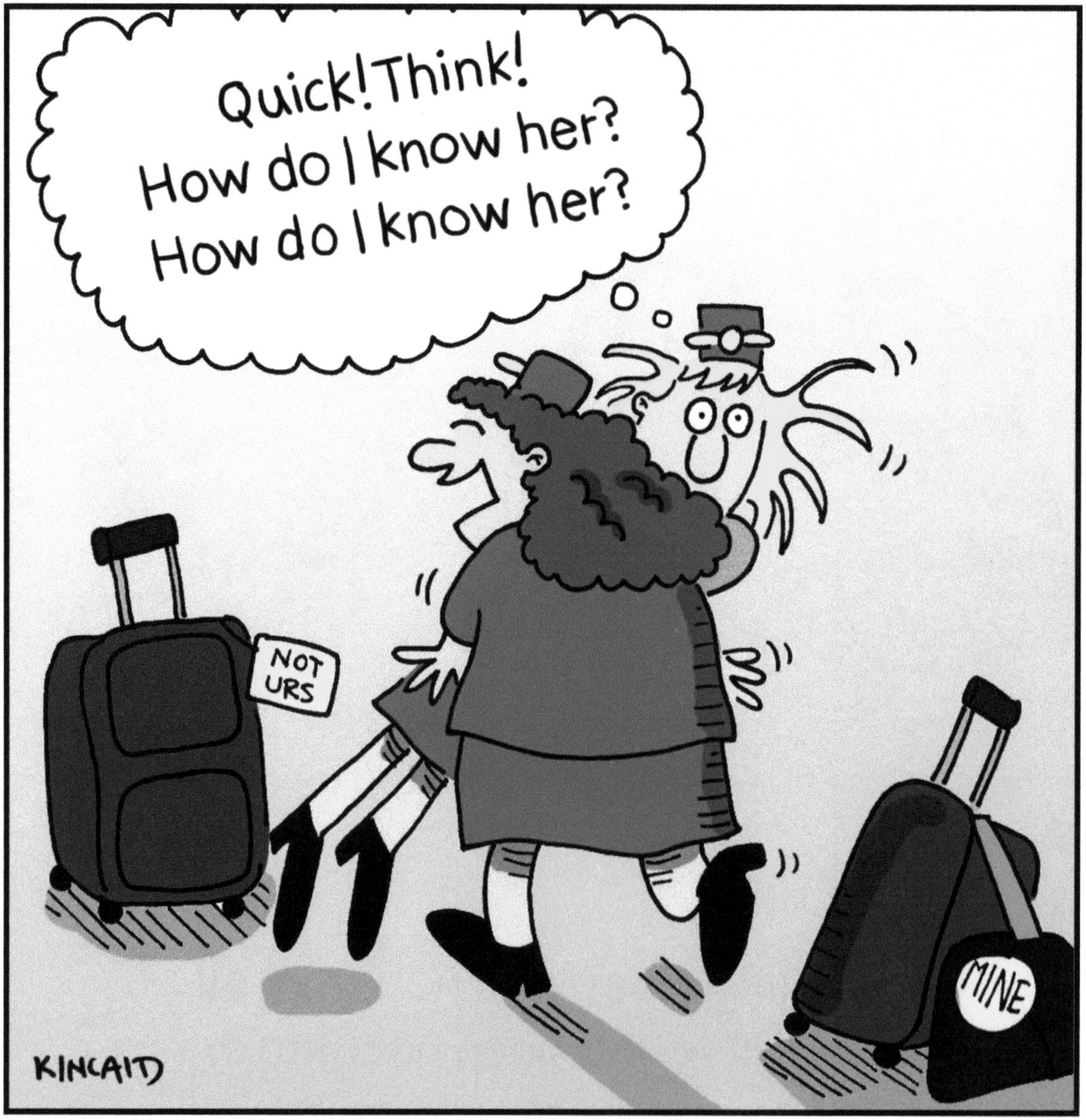
Quick! Think!
How do I know her?
How do I know her?
NOT URS
MINE
KINCAID

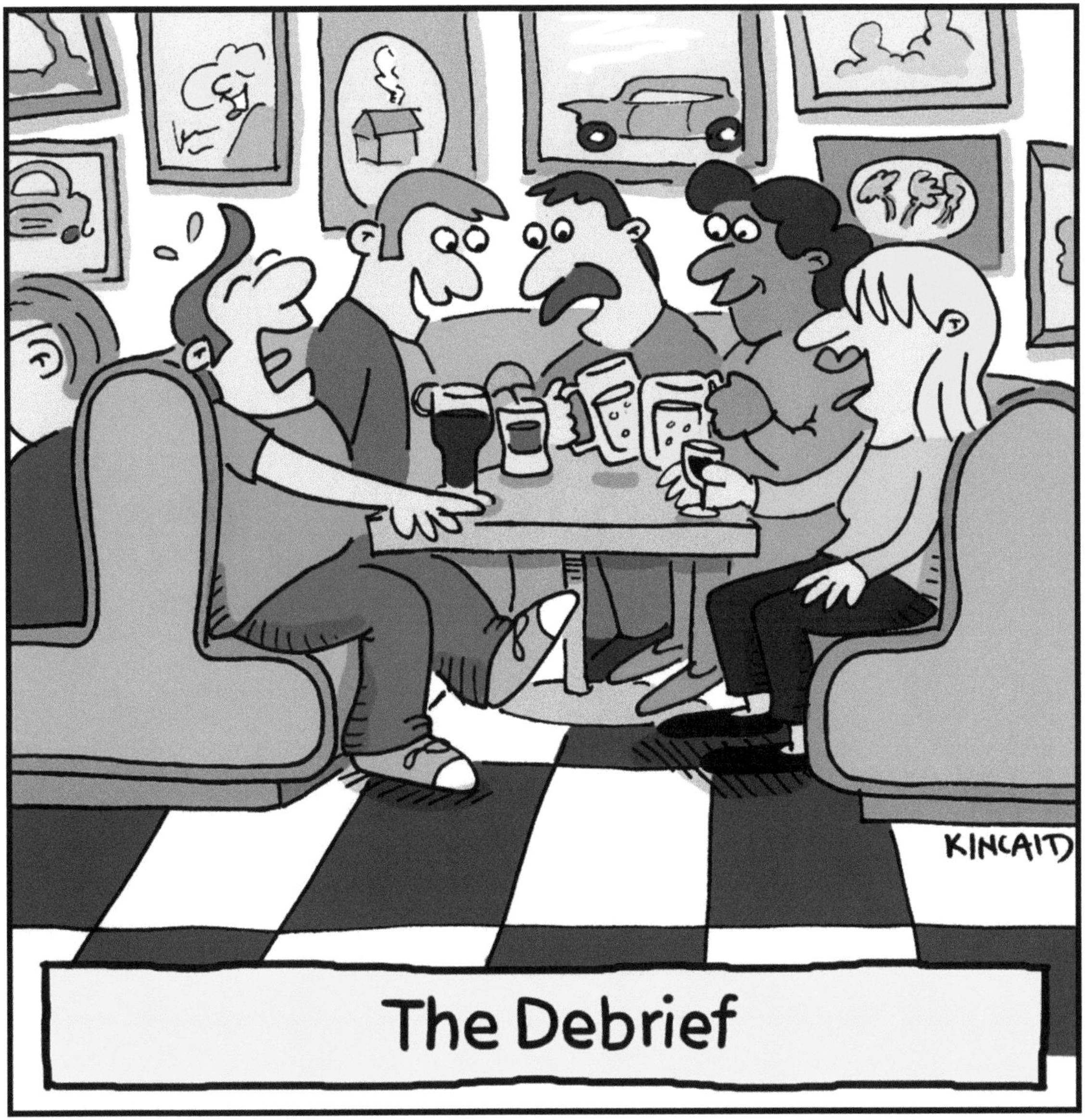
KINCAID
The Debrief

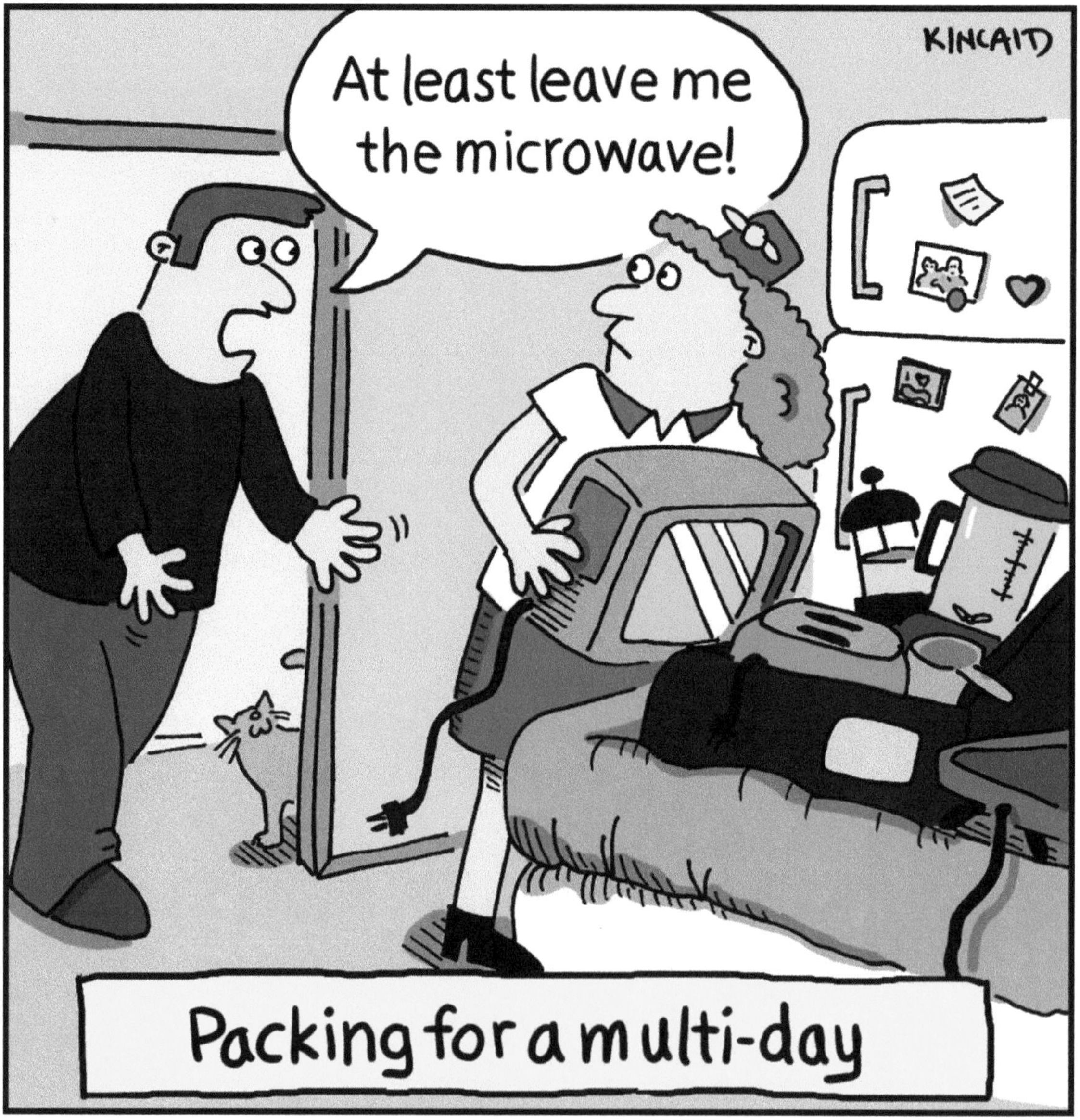
KINCAID
At least leave me the microwave!

Packing for a multi-day

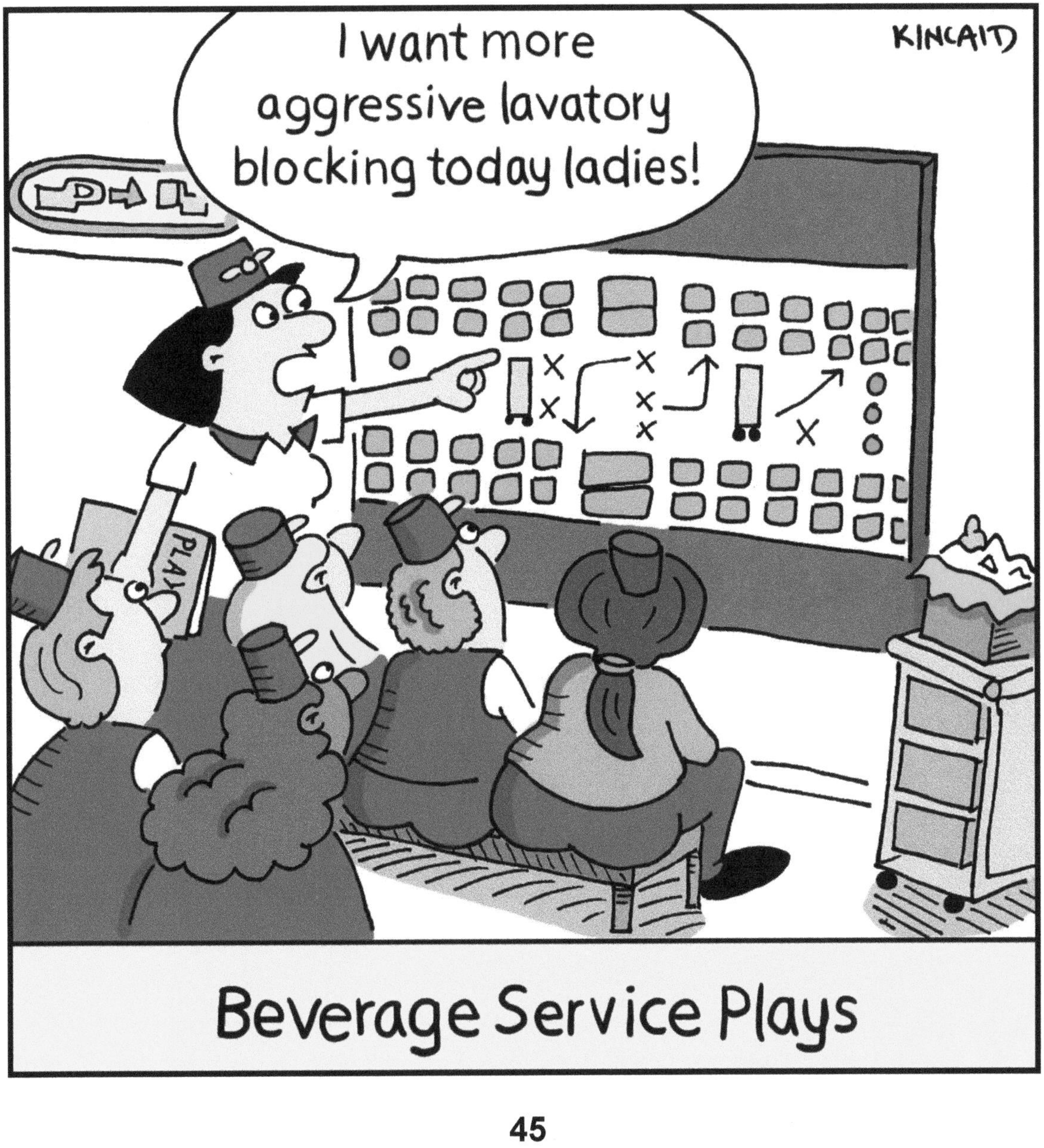
I want more aggressive lavatory blocking today ladies!
KINCAID
PLAY

Beverage Service Plays

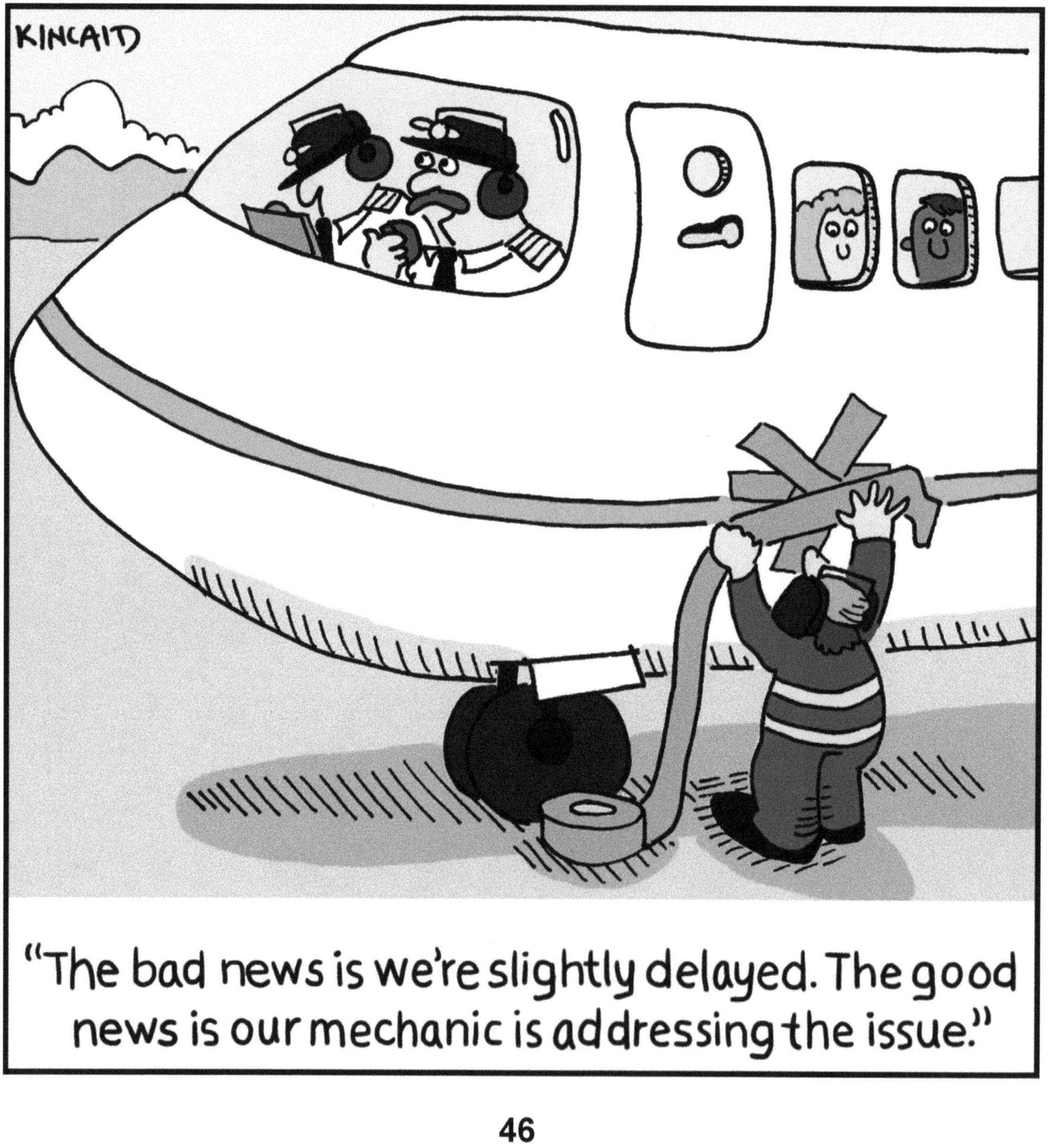
KINCAID

"The bad news is we're slightly delayed. The good news is our mechanic is addressing the issue."

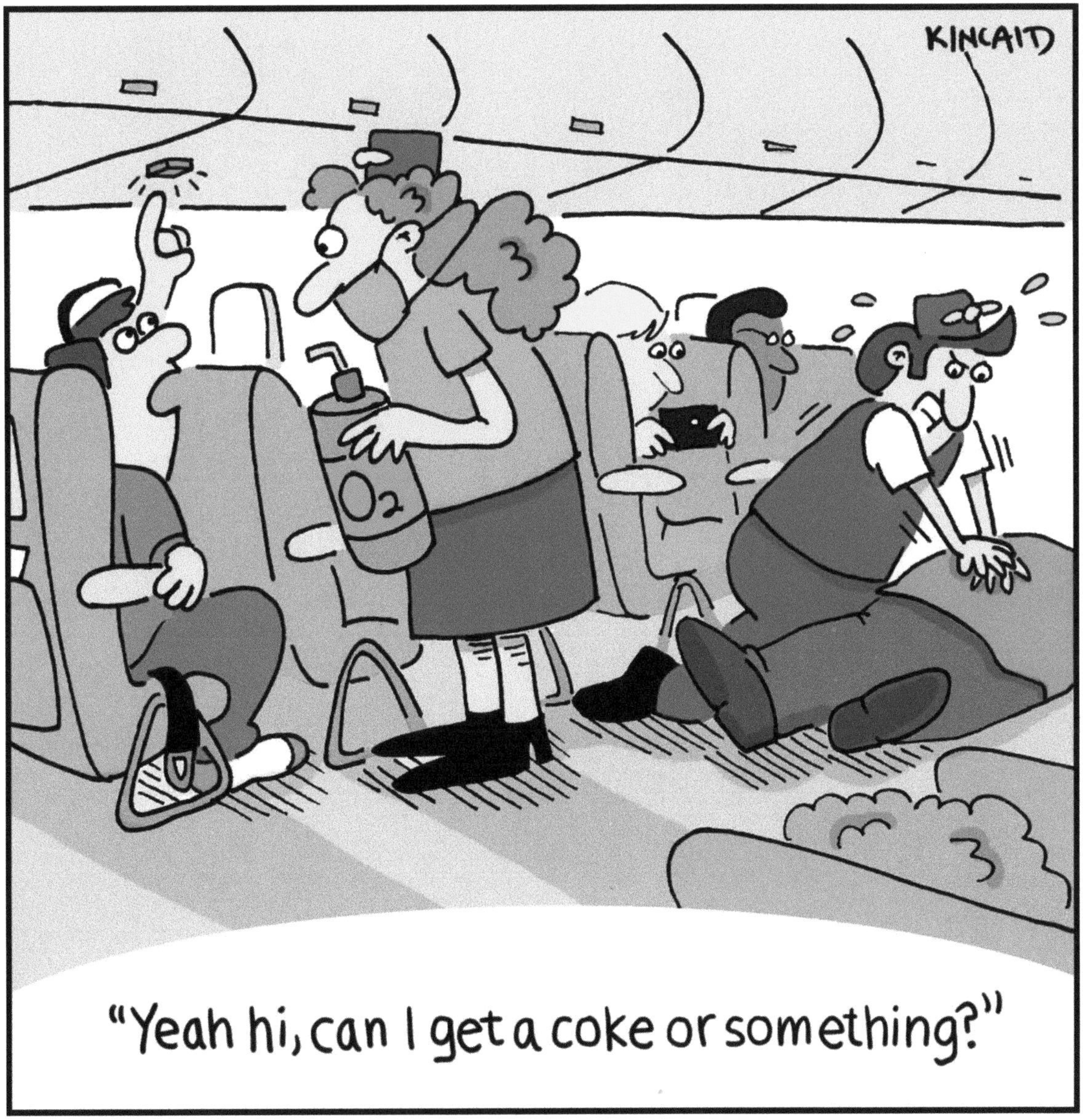
KINCAID
O2

"Yeah hi, can I get a coke or something?"

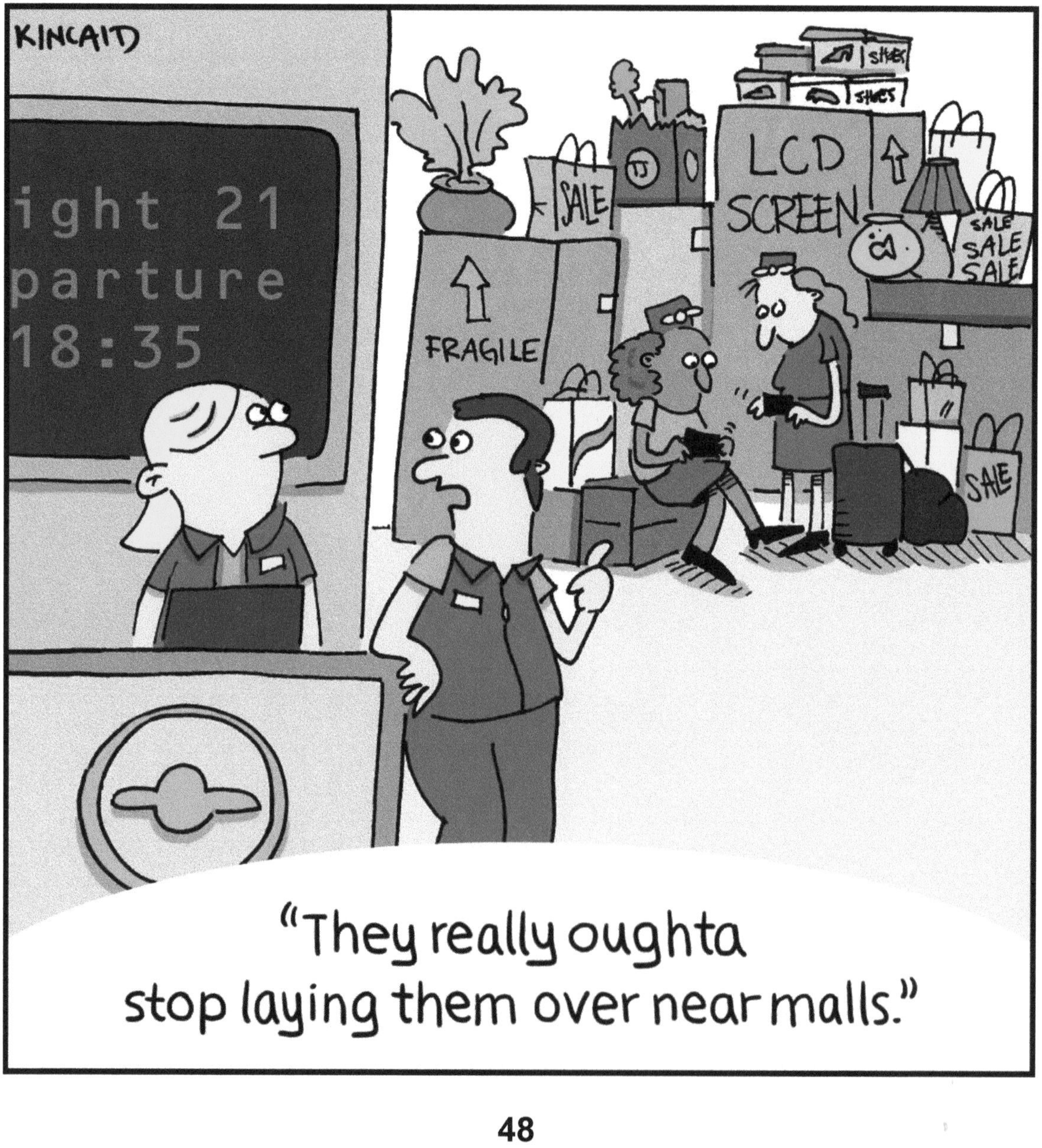
KINCAID
ight 21
parture
18:35
FRAGILE
SALE
LCD
SCREEN
SHOES
SHOES
SALE
SALE
SALE
SALE

"They really oughta stop laying them over near malls."

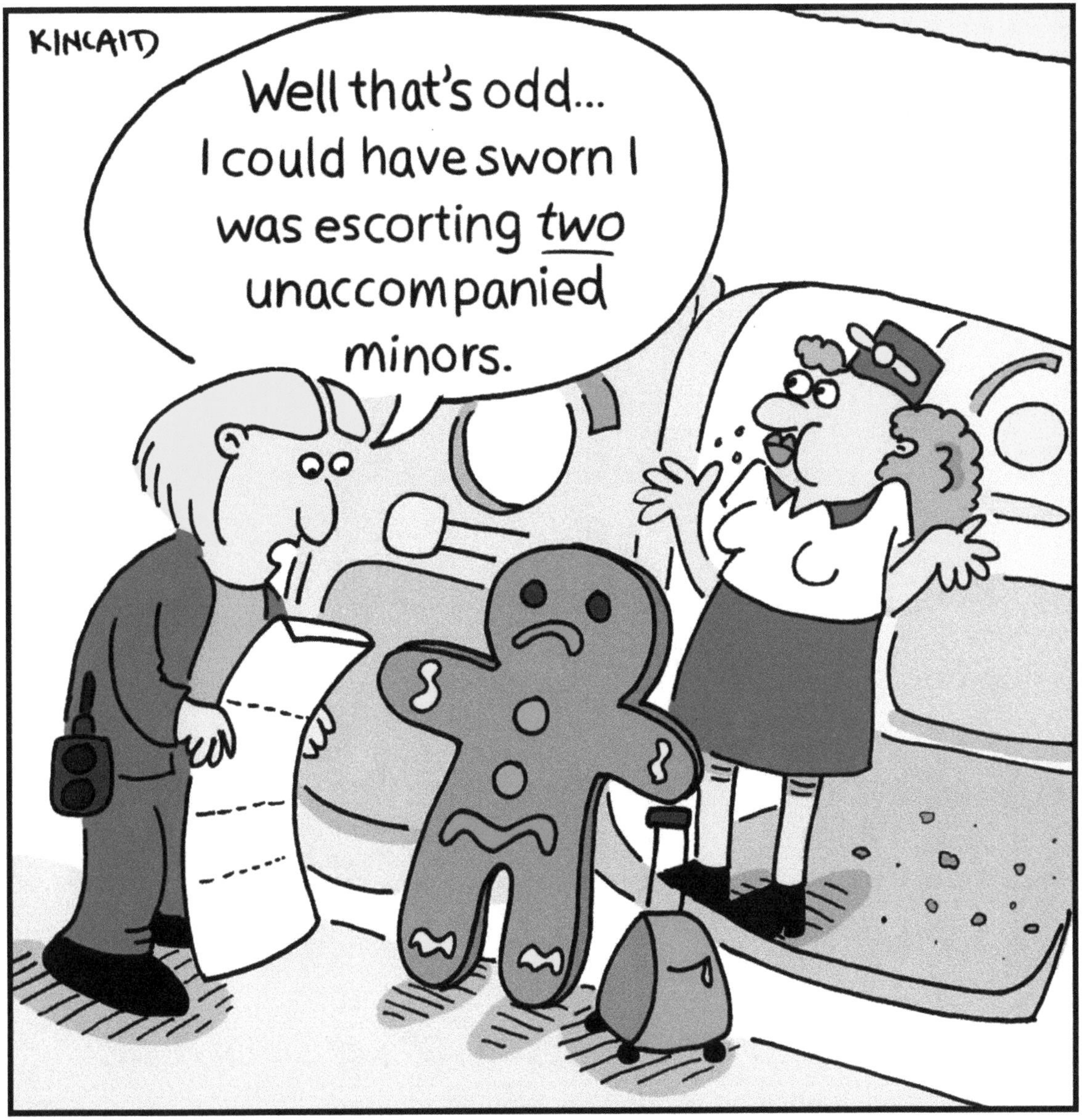
KINCAID
Well that's odd... I could have sworn I was escorting two unaccompanied minors.

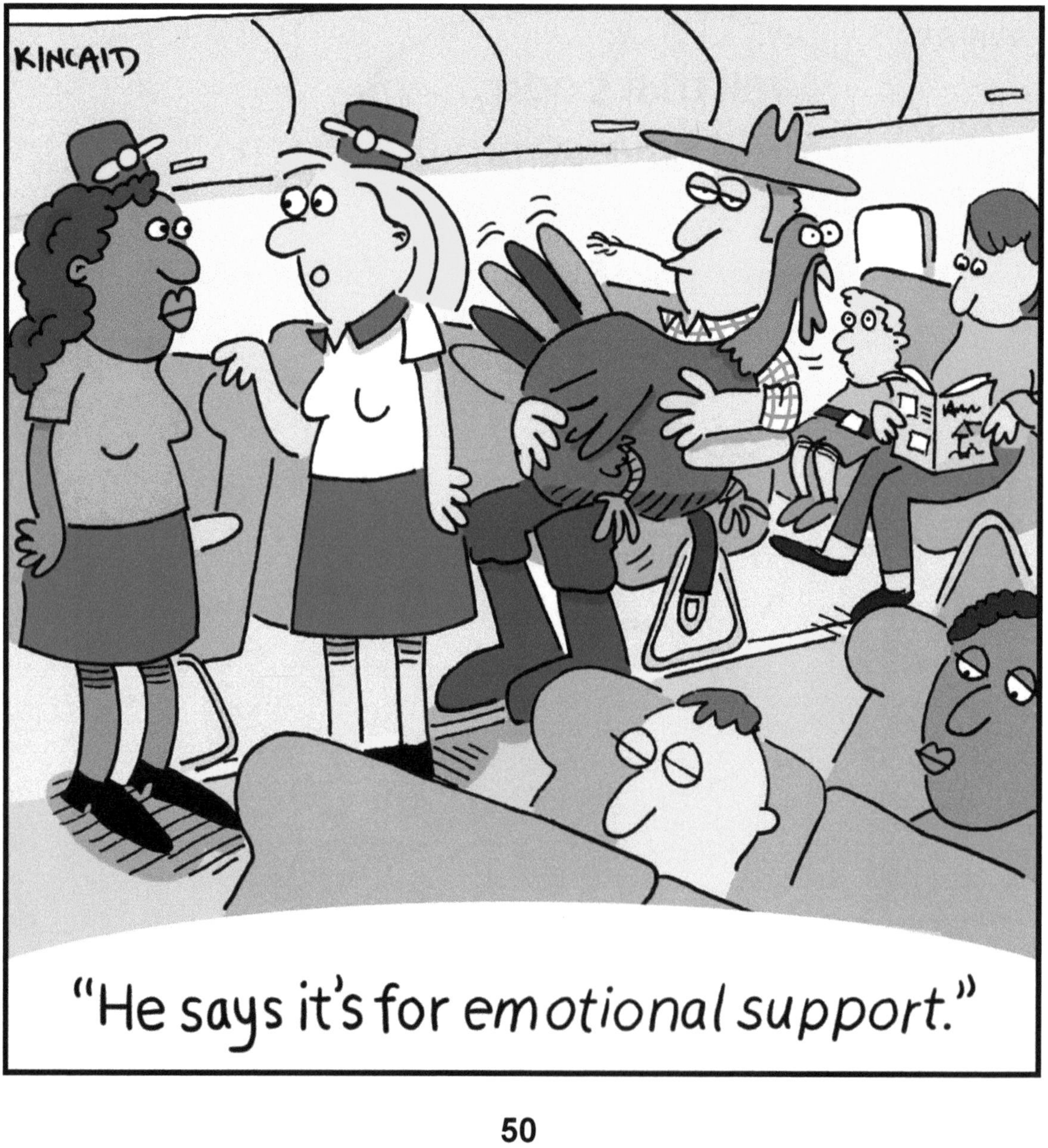
KINCAID

"He says it's for *emotional support.*"

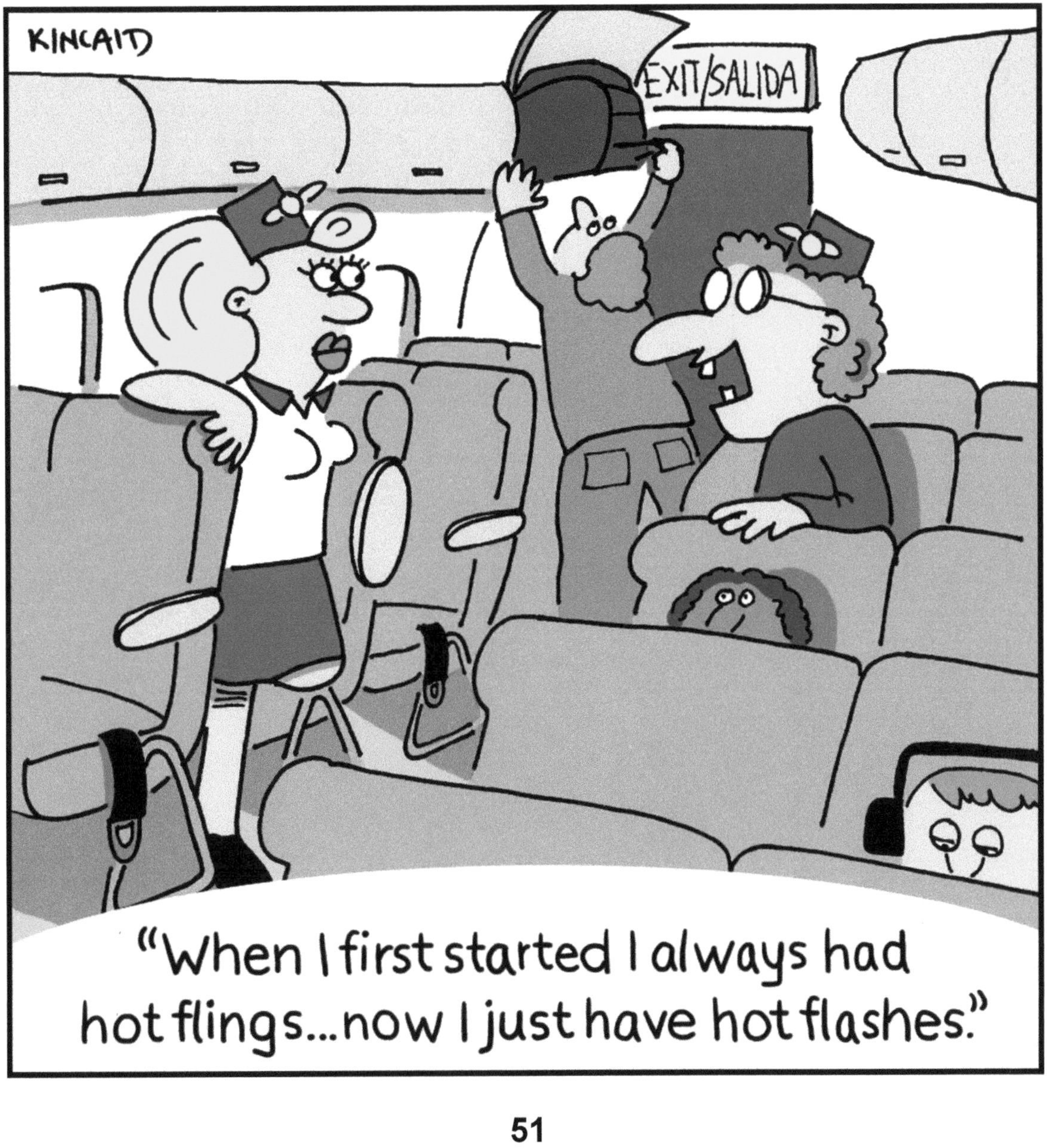
KINCAID
EXIT/SALIDA

"When I first started I always had hot flings...now I just have hot flashes."

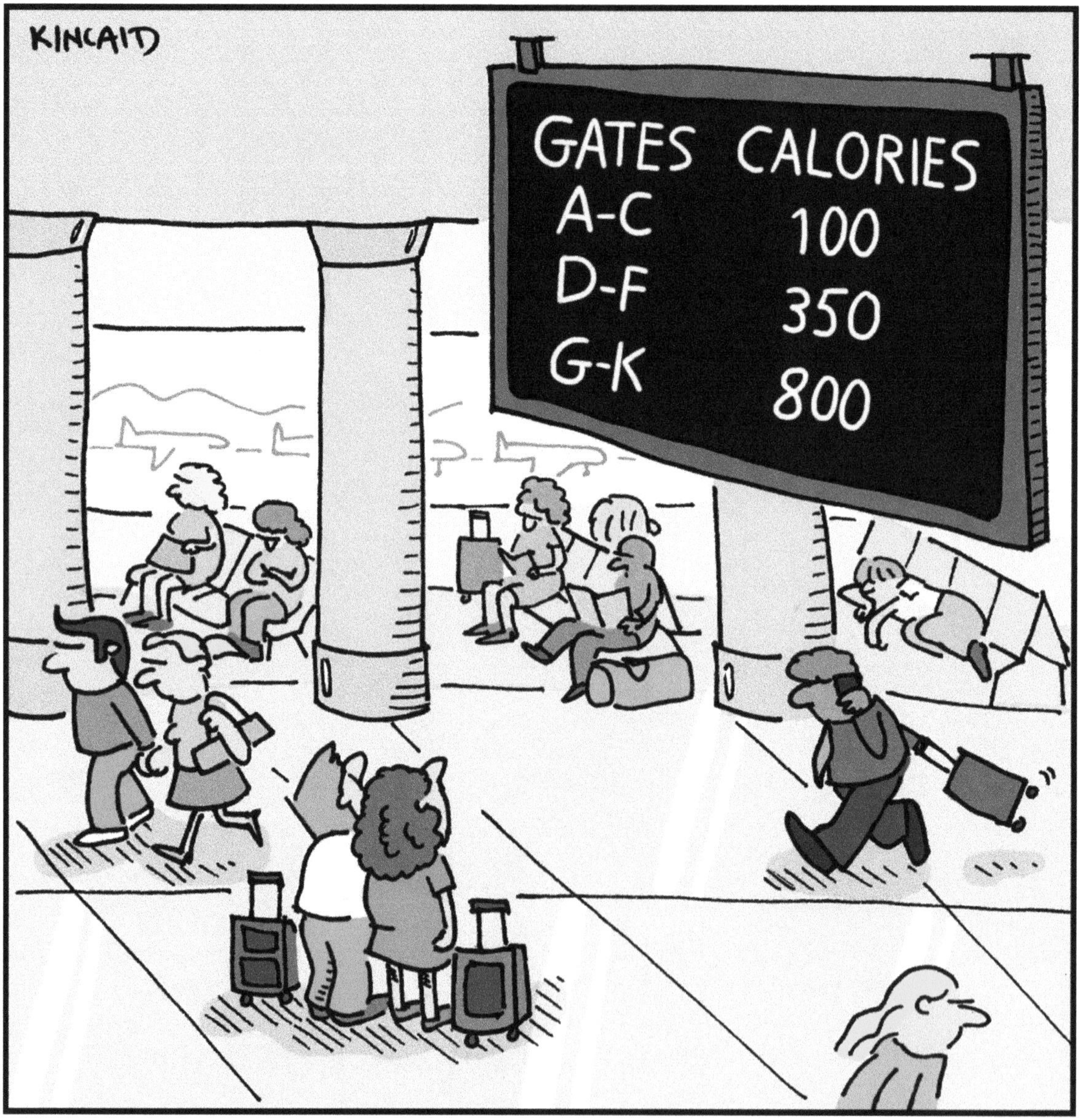
KINCAID
GATES CALORIES
A-C 100
D-F 350
G-K 800

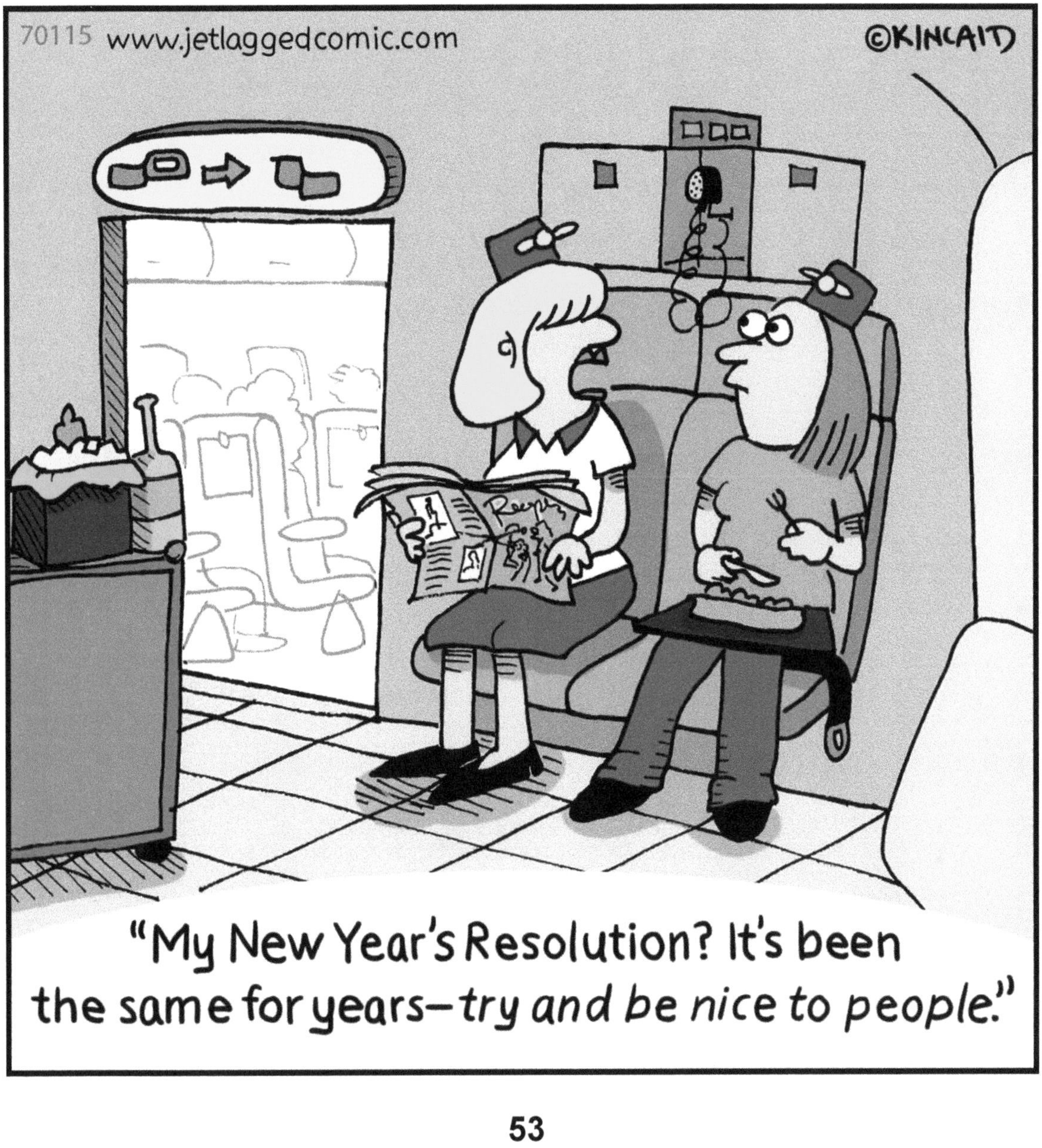
70115 www.jetlaggedcomic.com
©KINCAID

"My New Year's Resolution? It's been the same for years—*try and be nice to people.*"

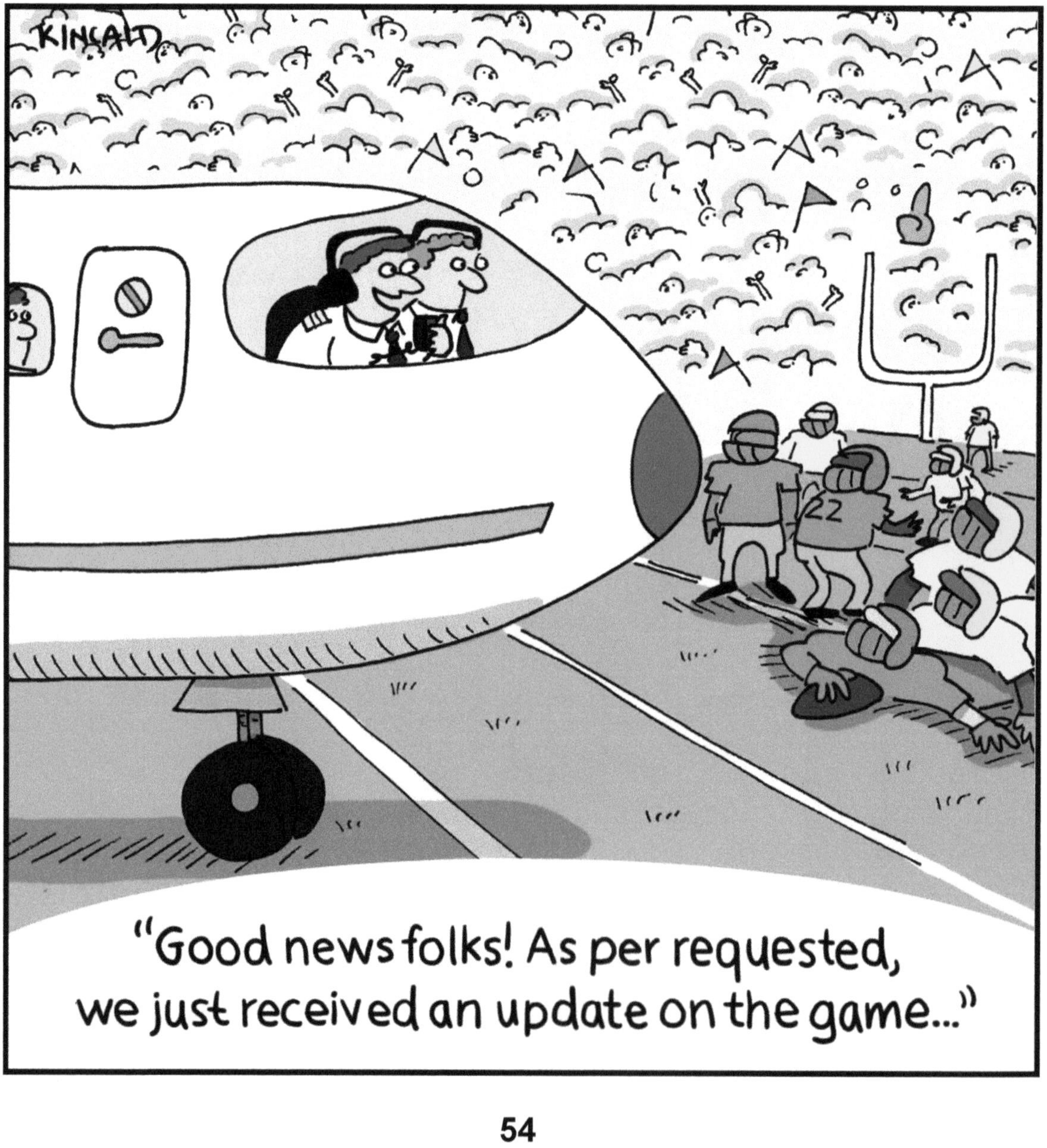
KINCAID
22

"Good news folks! As per requested, we just received an update on the game..."

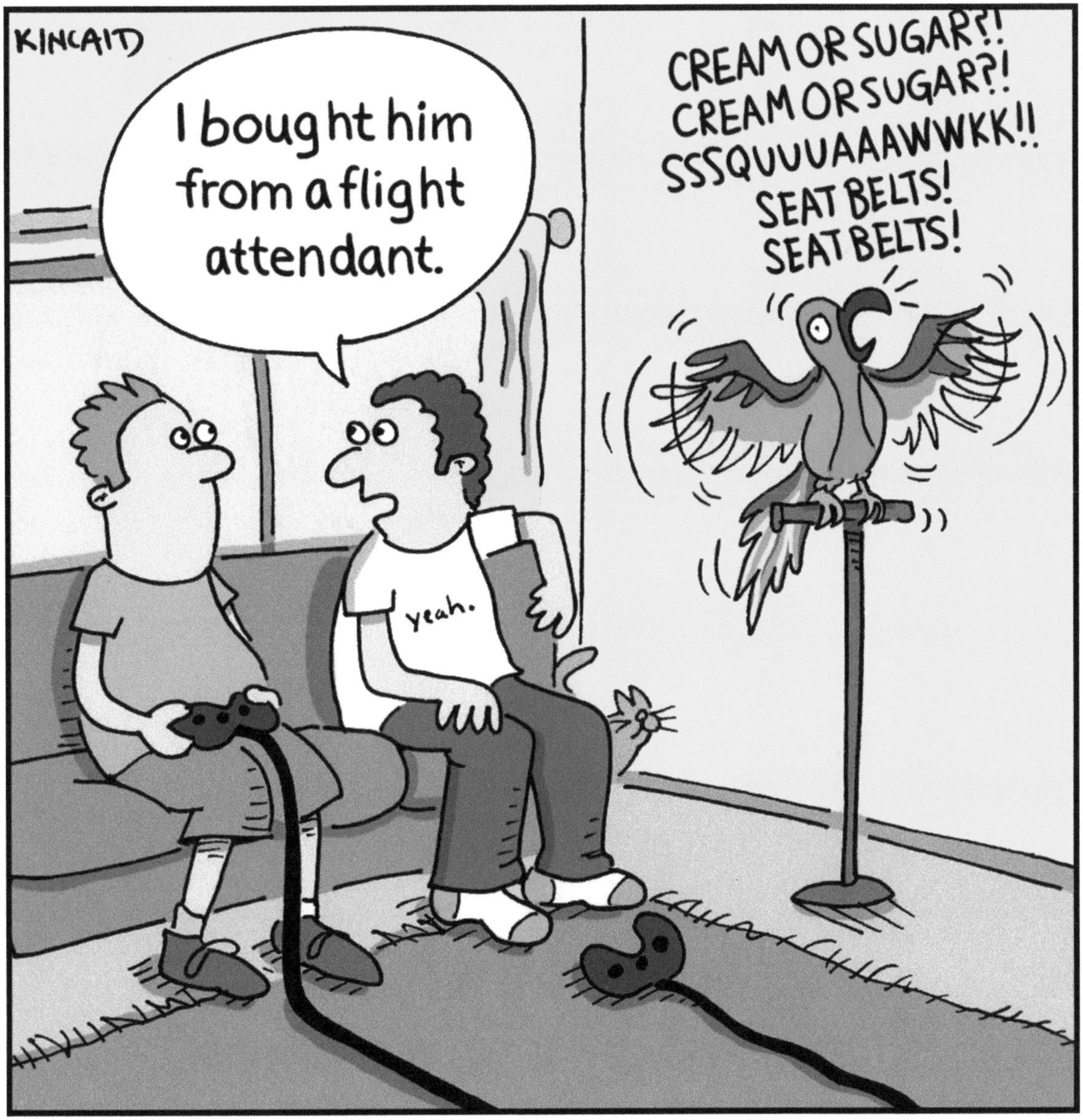
KINCAID
I bought him from a flight attendant.
CREAM OR SUGAR?!
CREAM OR SUGAR?!
SSSQUUUAAAWWKK!!
SEAT BELTS!
SEAT BELTS!
yeah.

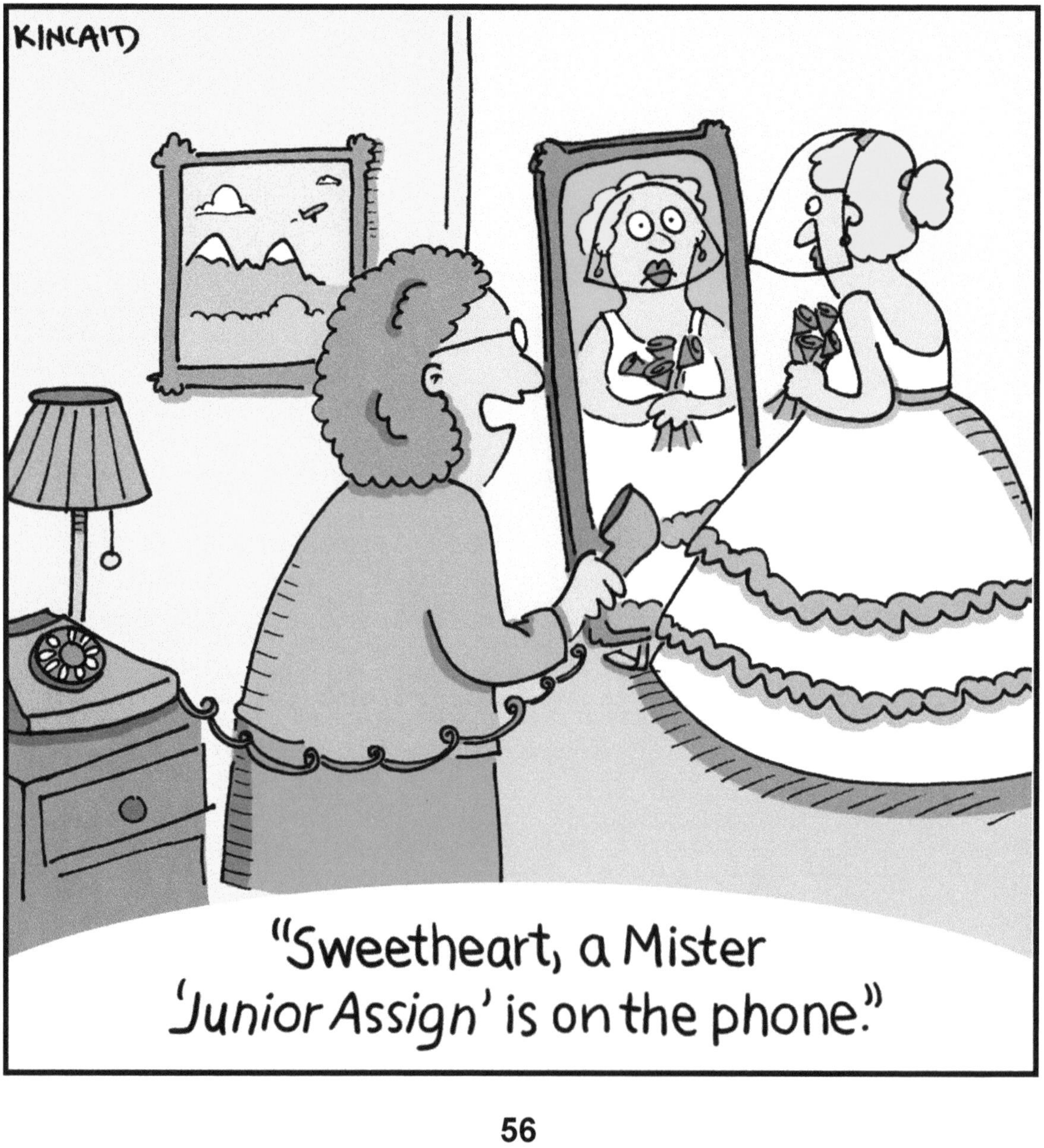
KINCAID

"Sweetheart, a Mister 'Junior Assign' is on the phone."

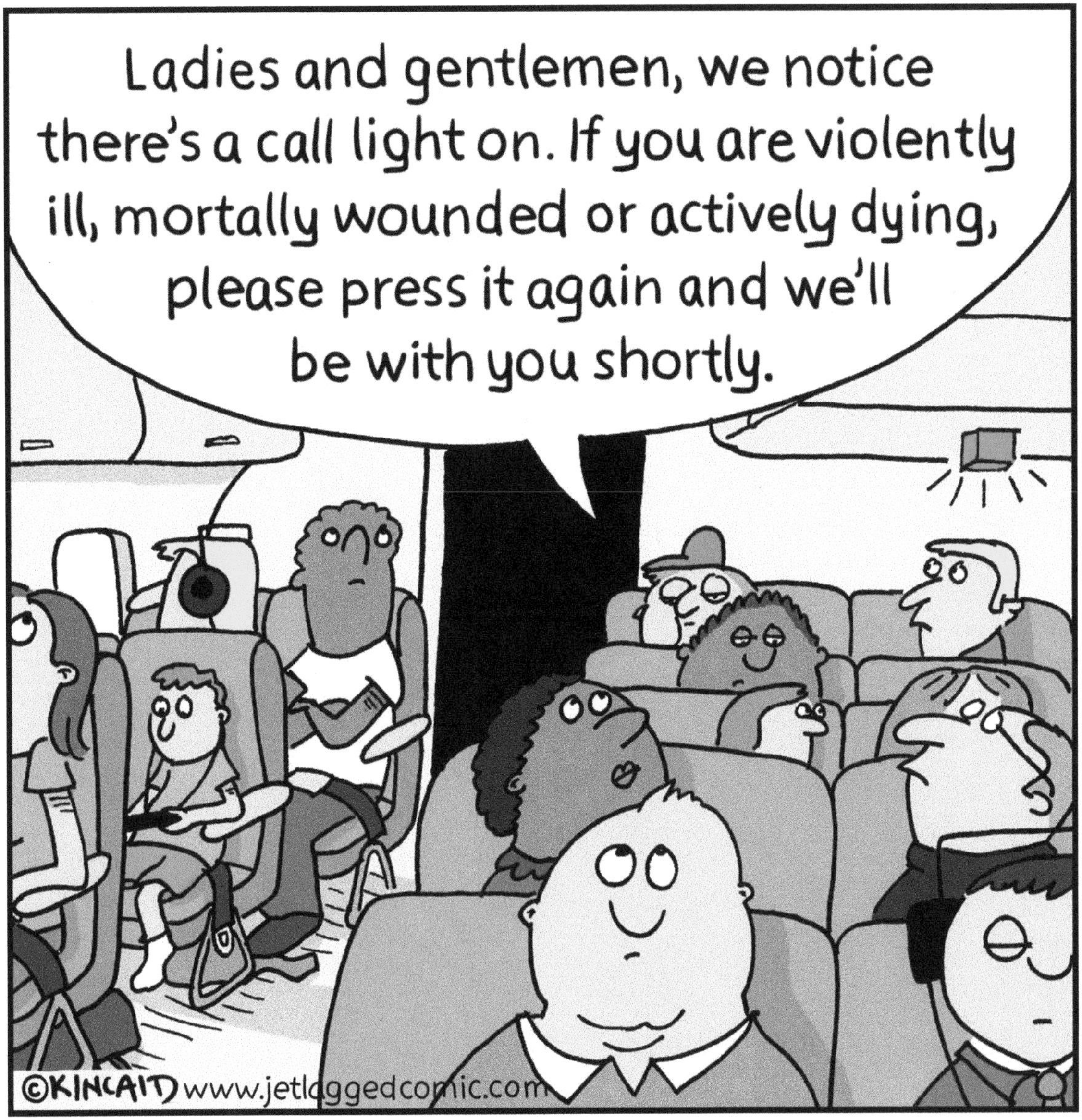
Ladies and gentlemen, we notice there's a call light on. If you are violently ill, mortally wounded or actively dying, please press it again and we'll be with you shortly.
©KINCAID www.jetlaggedcomic.com

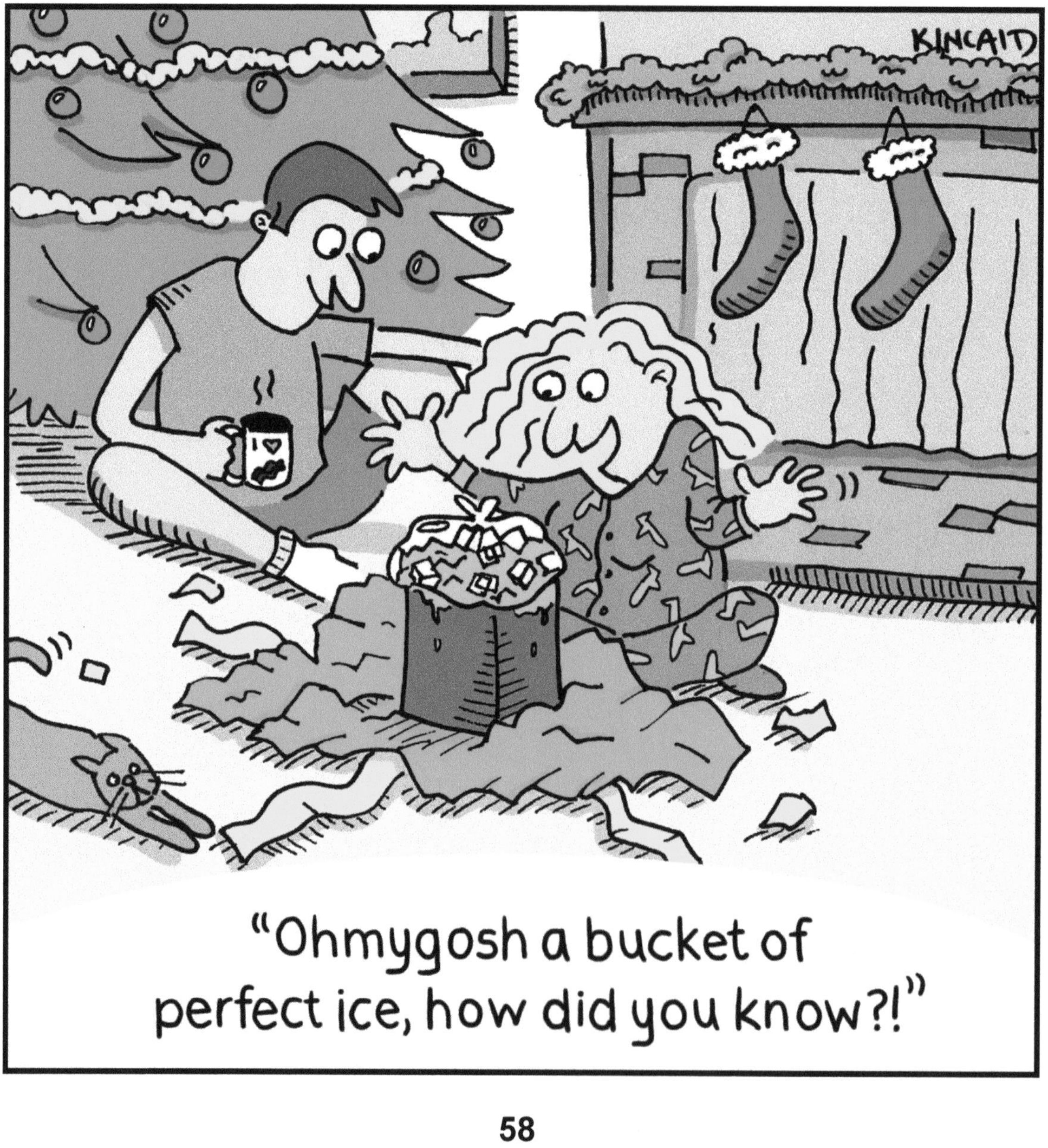
KINCAID

"Ohmygosh a bucket of
perfect ice, how did you know?!"

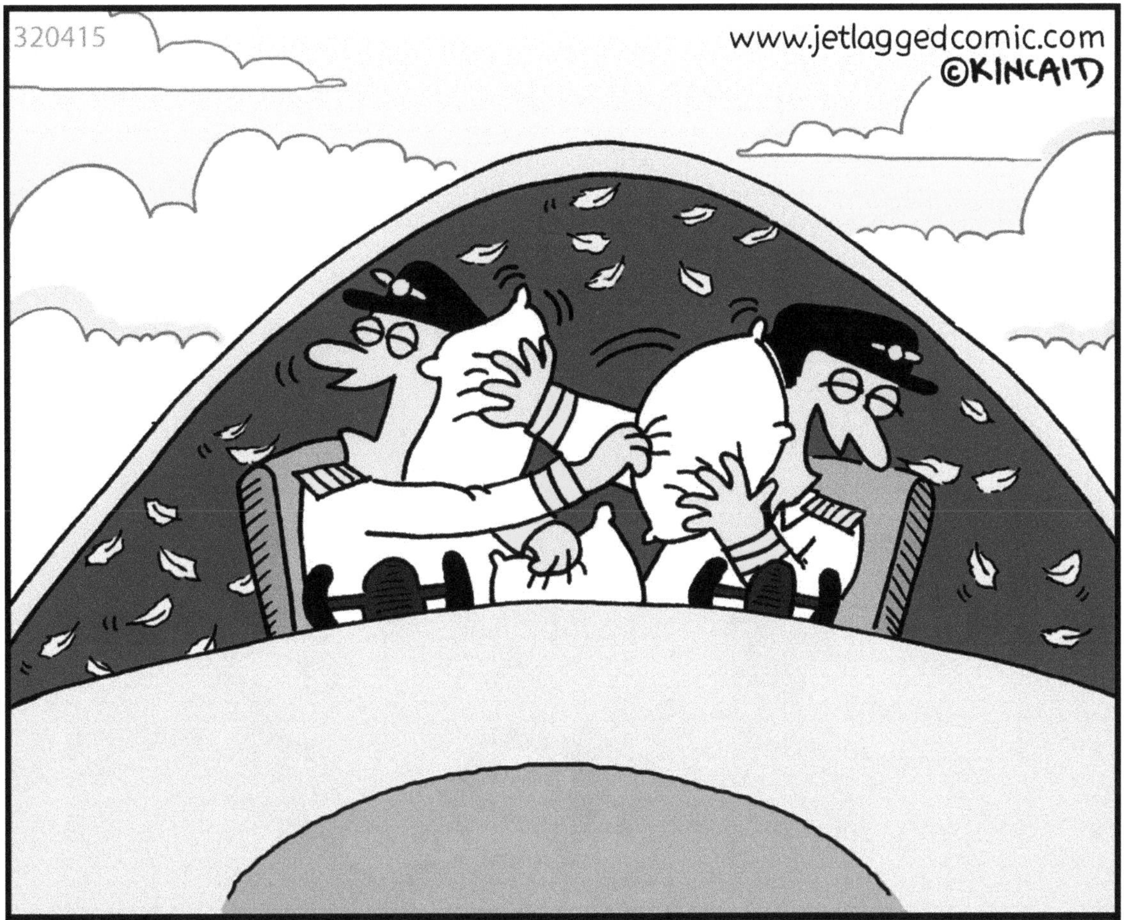
320415
www.jetlaggedcomic.com
©KINCAID

THE REAL REASON AIRLINES DISCONTINUED PILLOWS

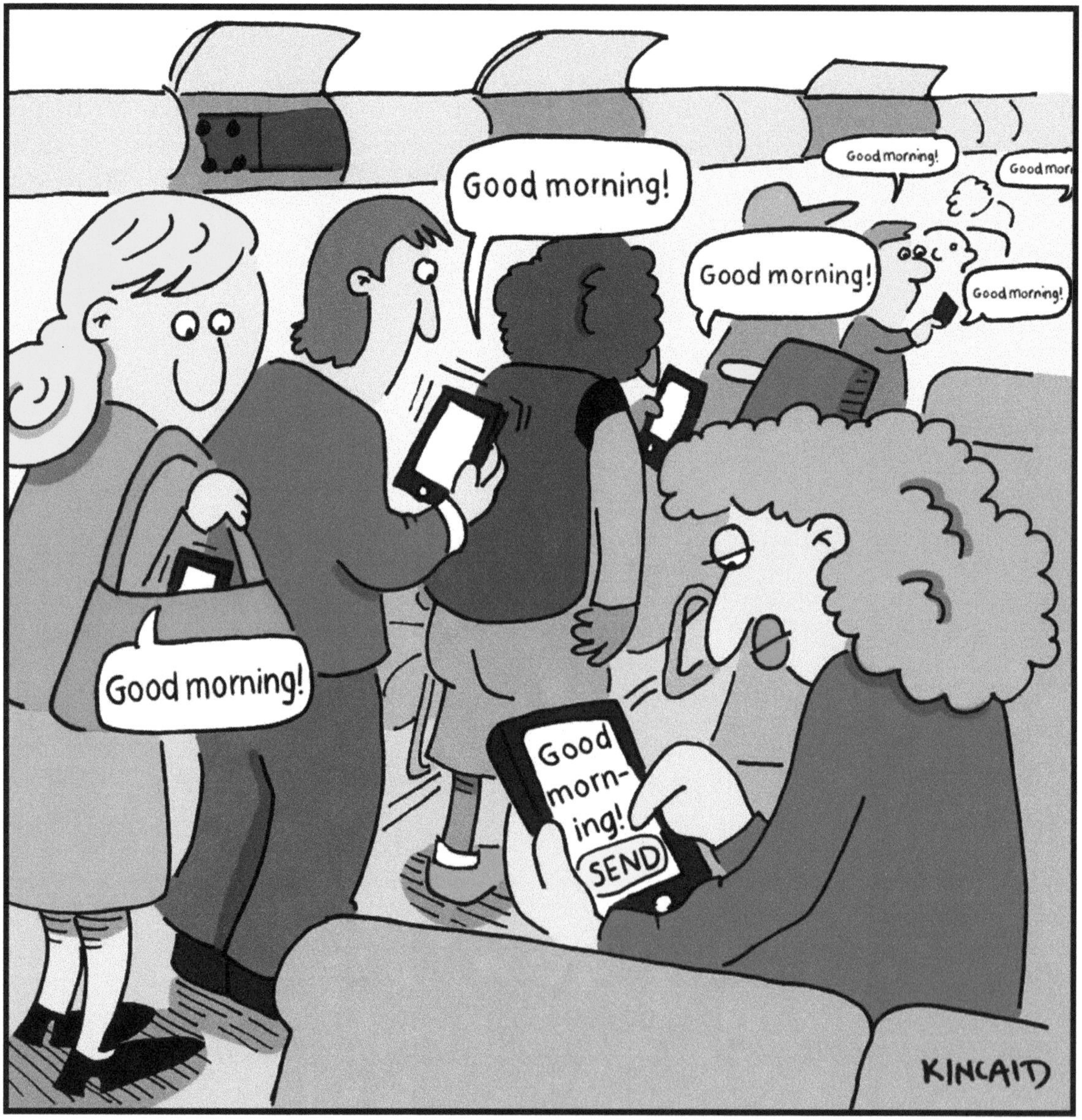
Good morning!
Good morning!
Good morning!
Good morning!
Good morning!
Good morn-
ing!
SEND
KINCAID

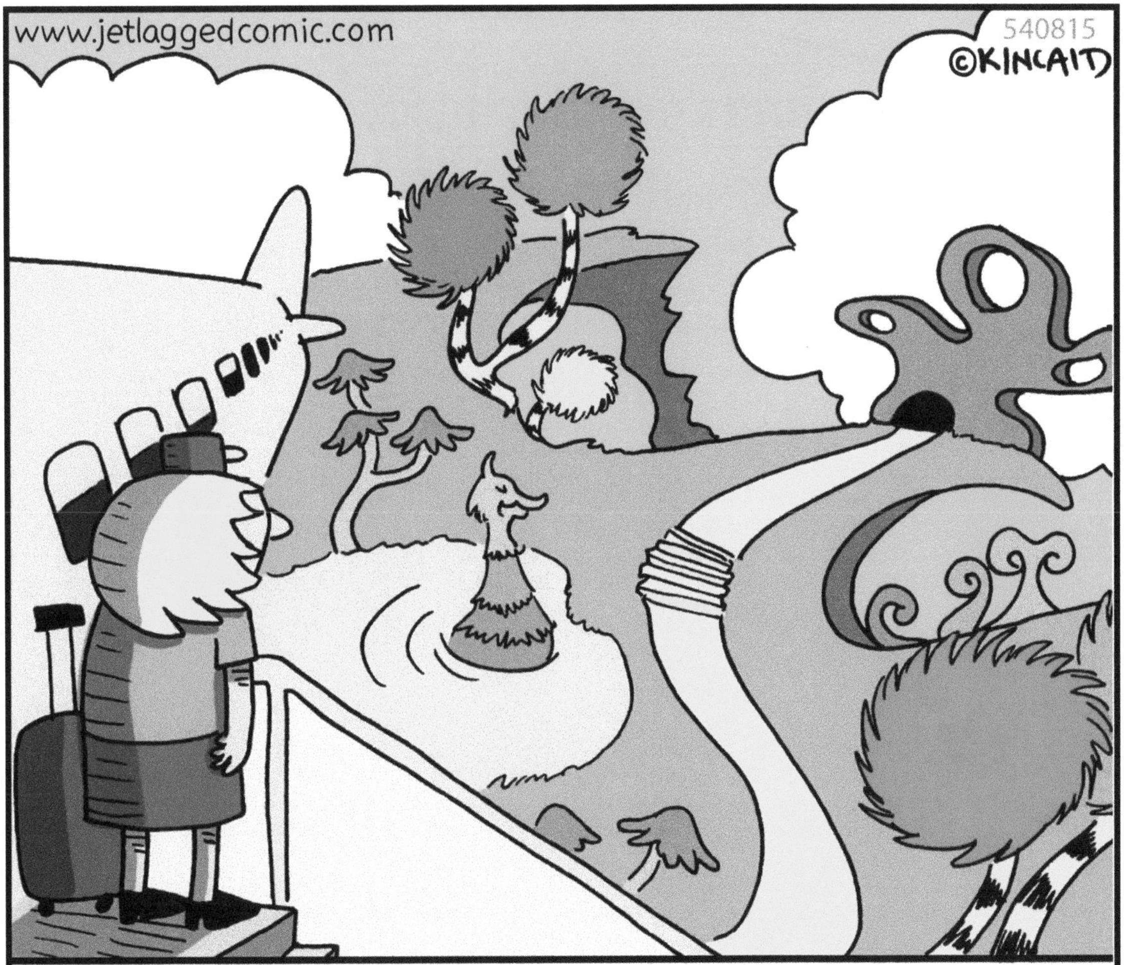
www.jetlaggedcomic.com
540815
©KINCAID

That was the last time Bev forgot to bid.

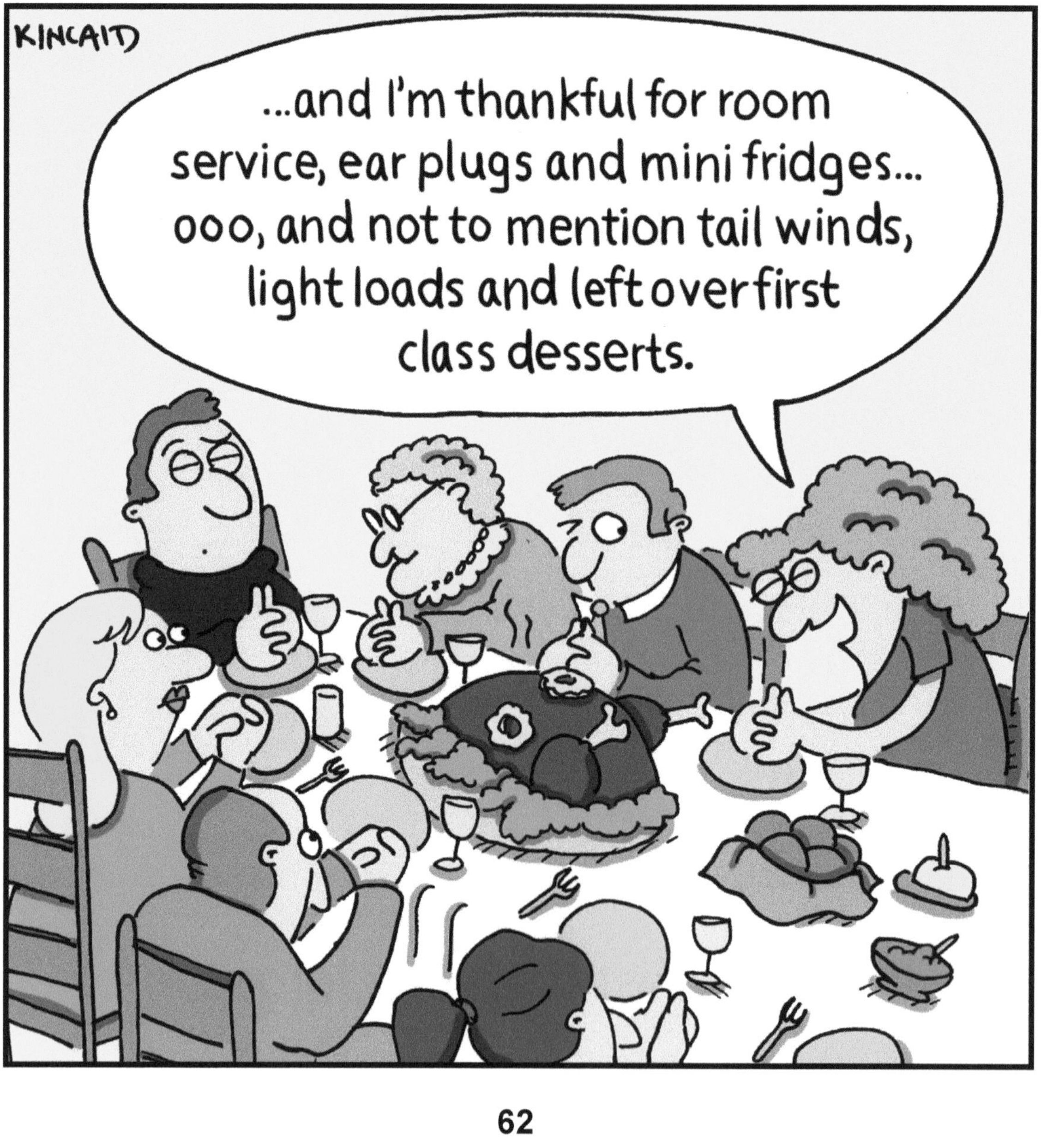
KINCAID
...and I'm thankful for room service, ear plugs and mini fridges... ooo, and not to mention tail winds, light loads and left over first class desserts.

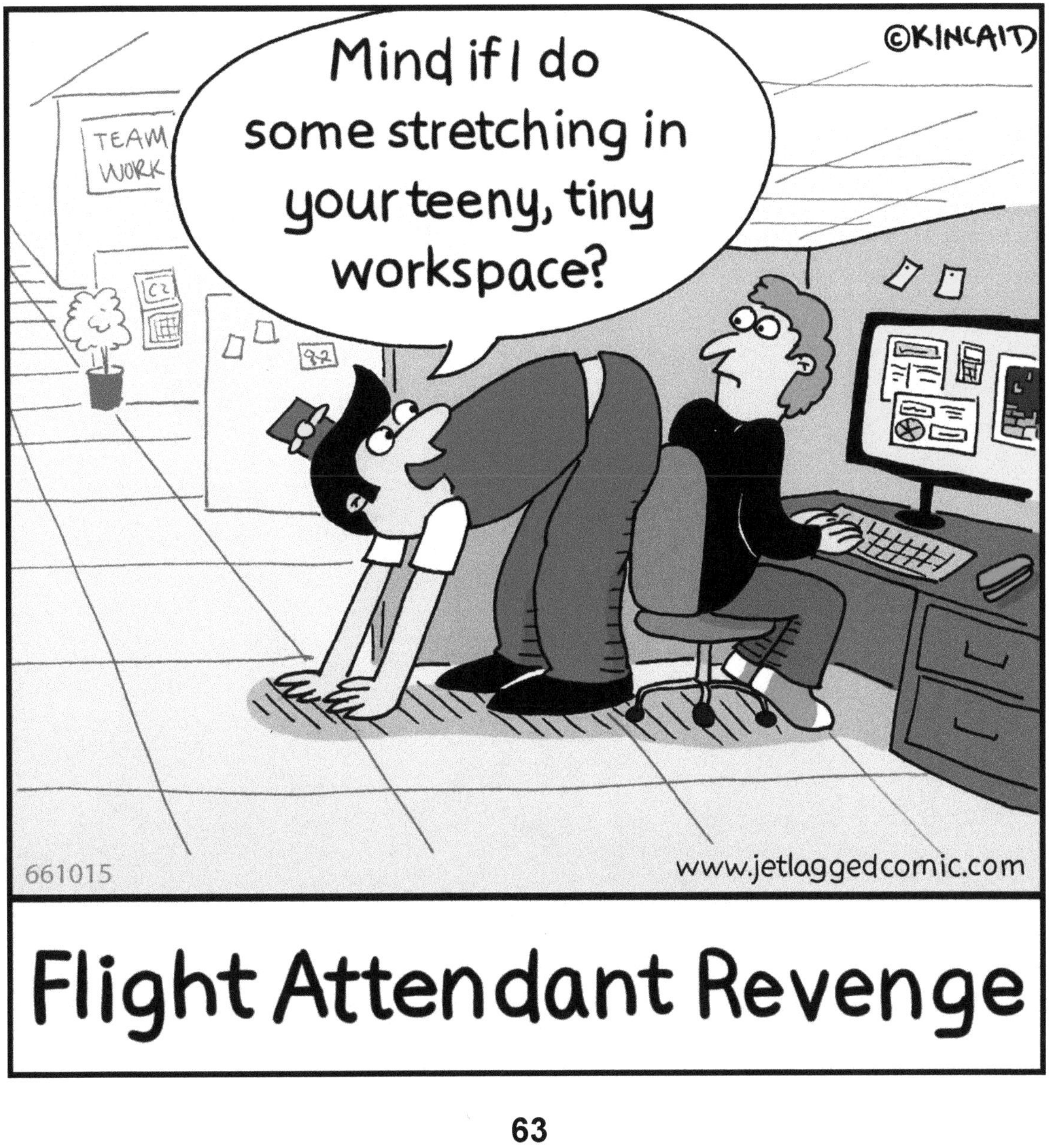
Mind if I do some stretching in your teeny, tiny workspace?
©KINCAID
TEAM WORK
661015
www.jetlaggedcomic.com

Flight Attendant Revenge

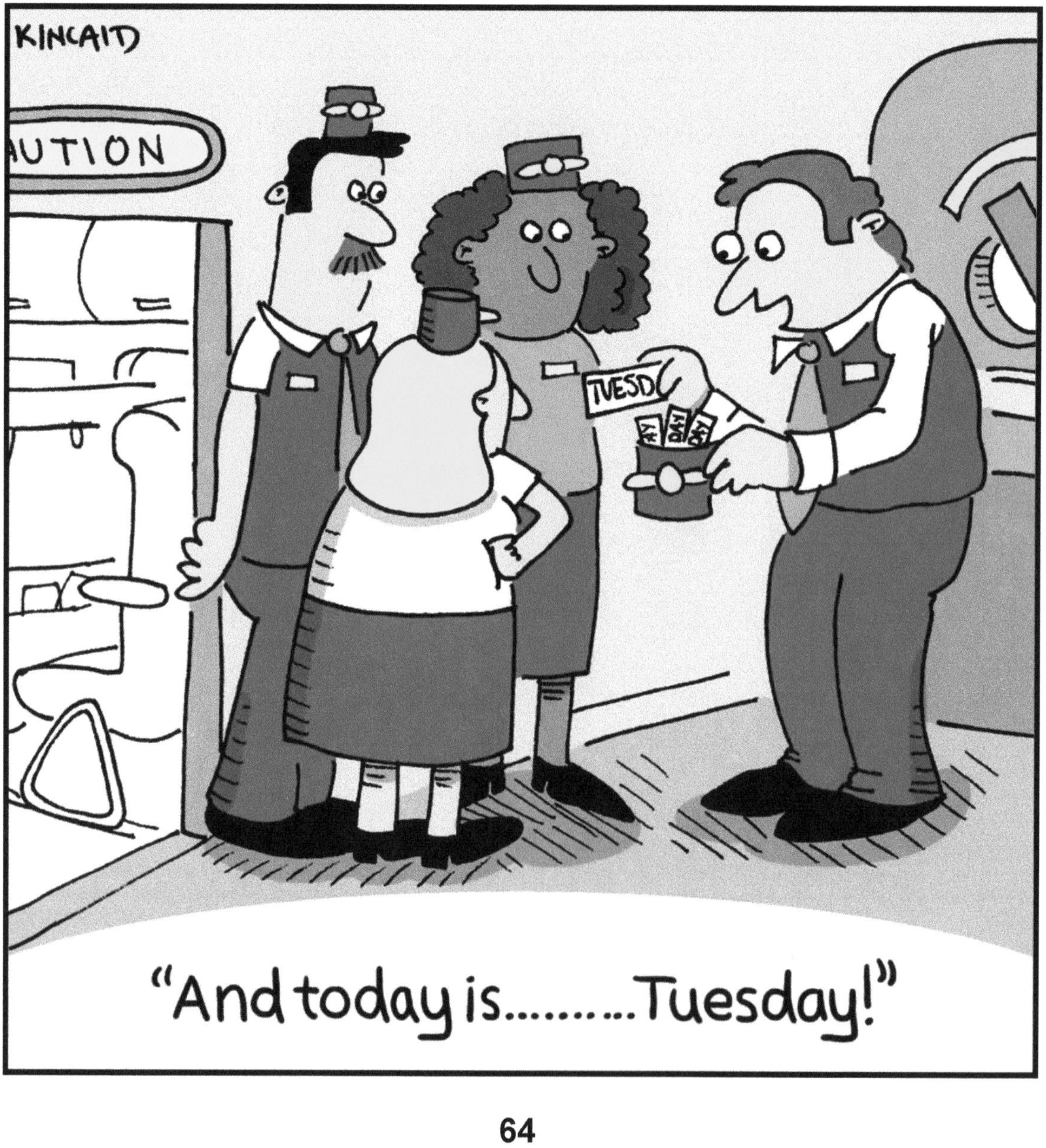
KINCAID
AUTION
TUESD

"And today is..........Tuesday!"

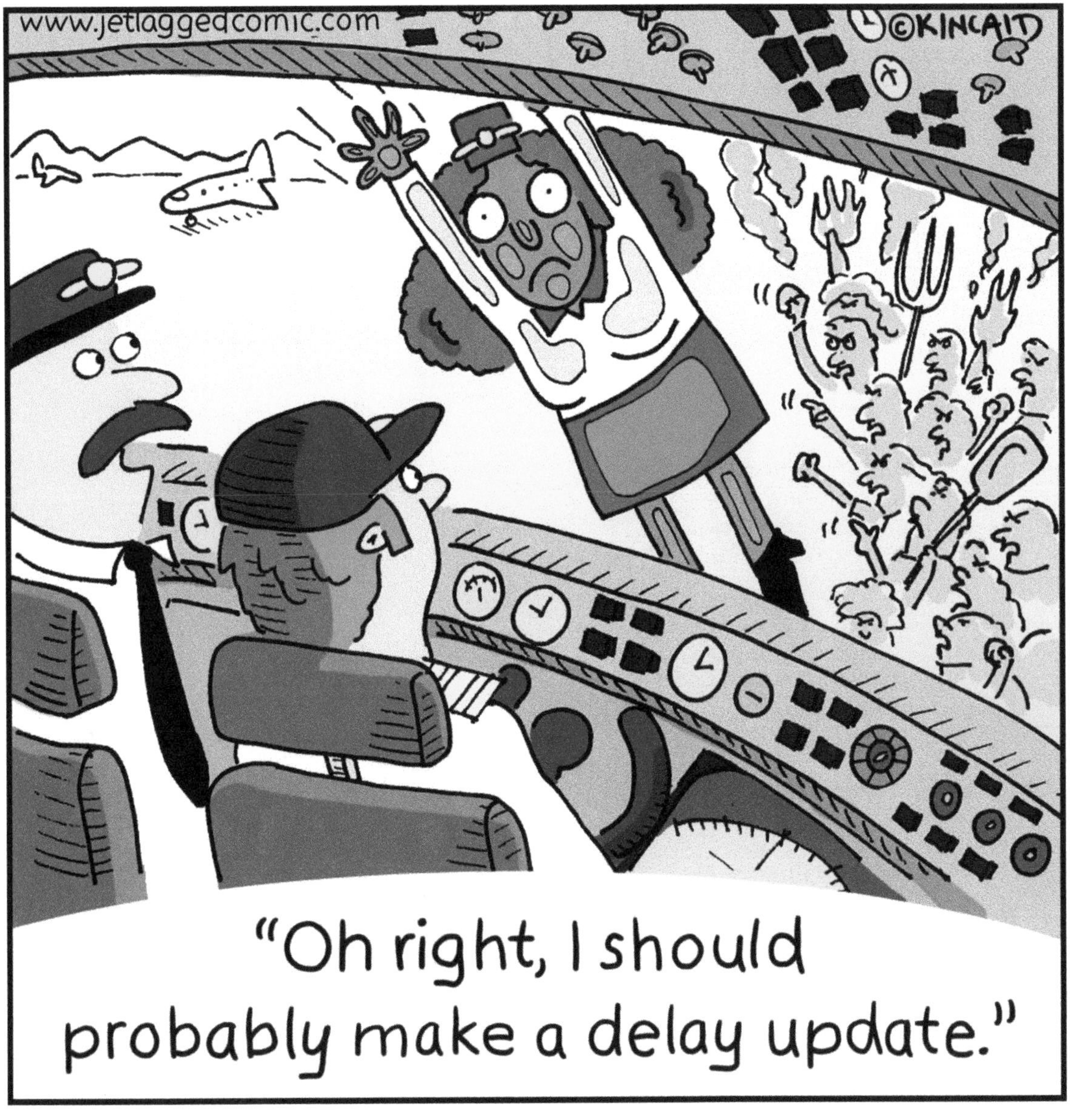
www.jetlaggedcomic.com
©KINCAID

"Oh right, I should probably make a delay update."

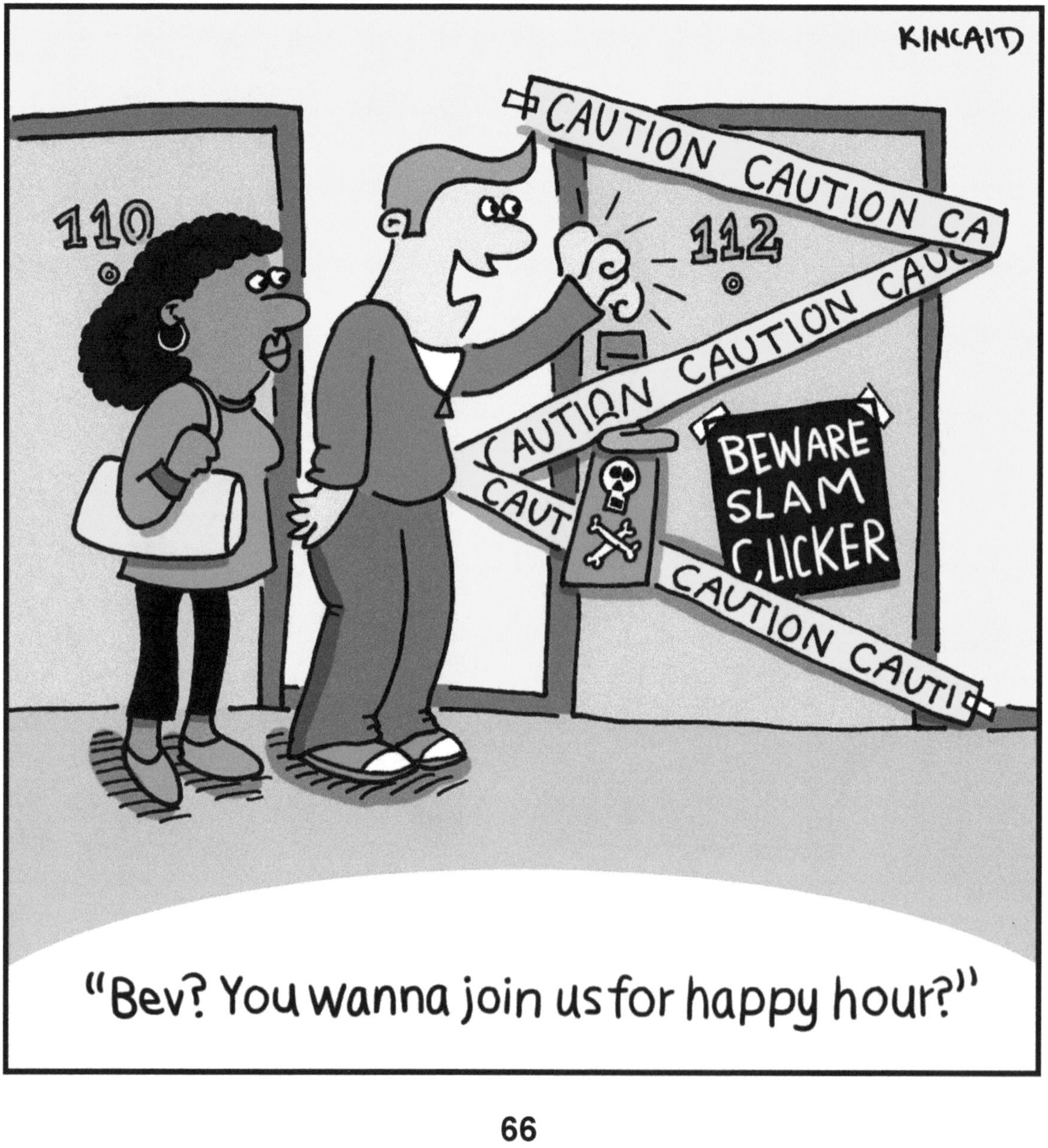
KINCAID
110
112
CAUTION CAUTION CA
CAUTION CAUTION CAU
CAUT
BEWARE SLAM CLICKER
CAUTION CAUTI

"Bev? You wanna join us for happy hour?"

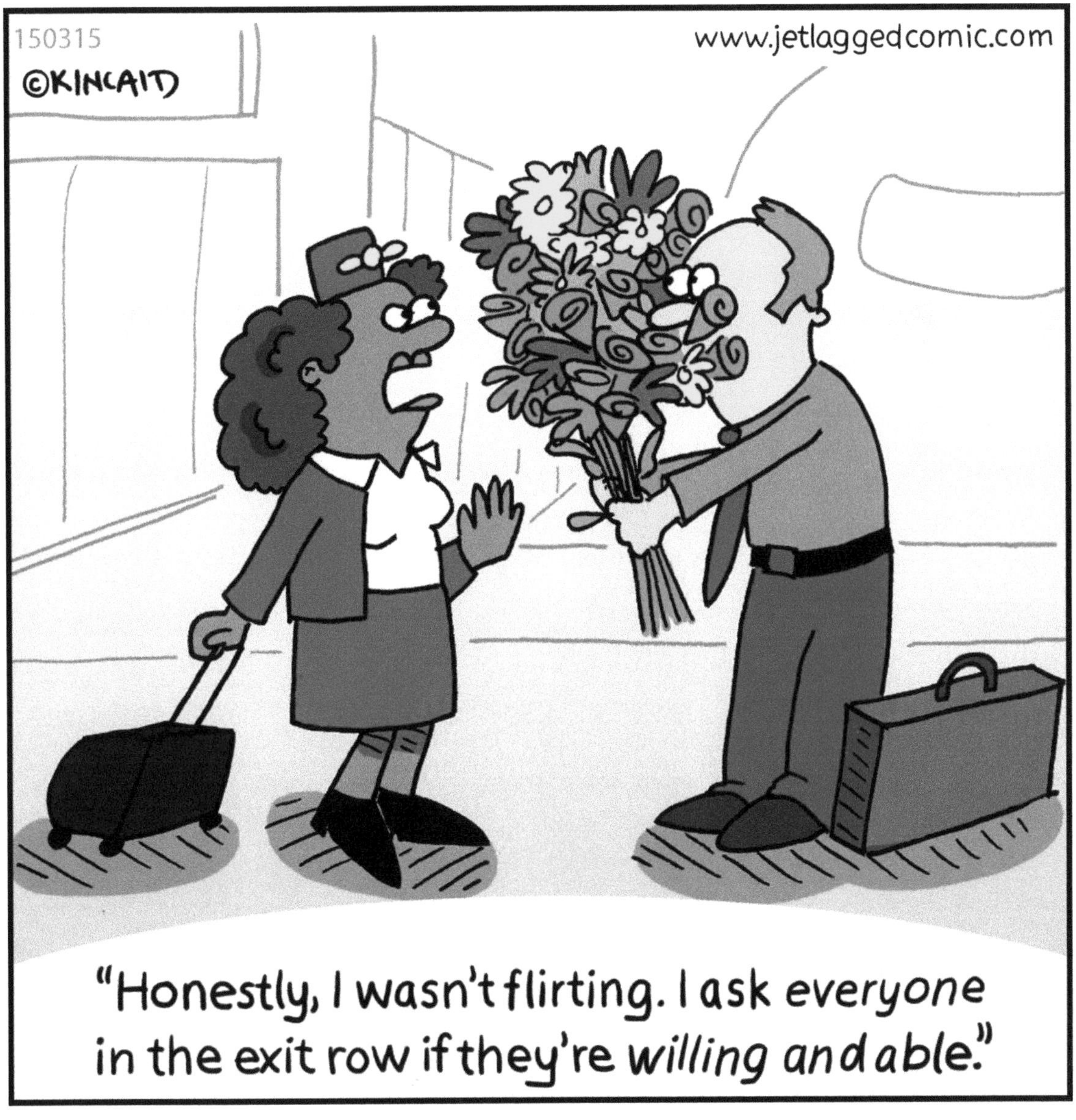
150315
©KINCAID
www.jetlaggedcomic.com
"Honestly, I wasn't flirting. I ask *everyone* in the exit row if they're *willing and able*."

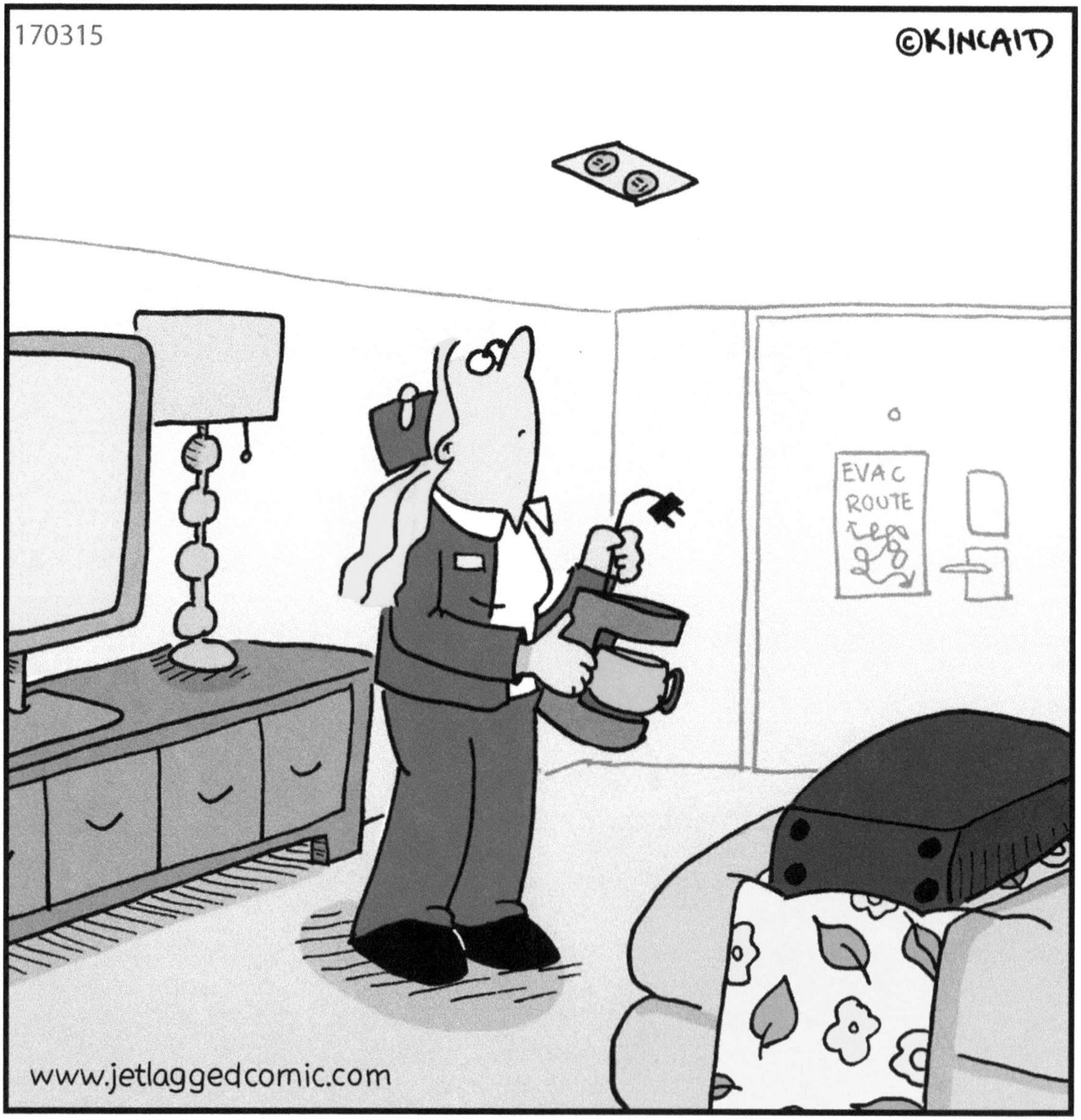

170315
©KINCAID
EVAC
ROUTE
www.jetlaggedcomic.com

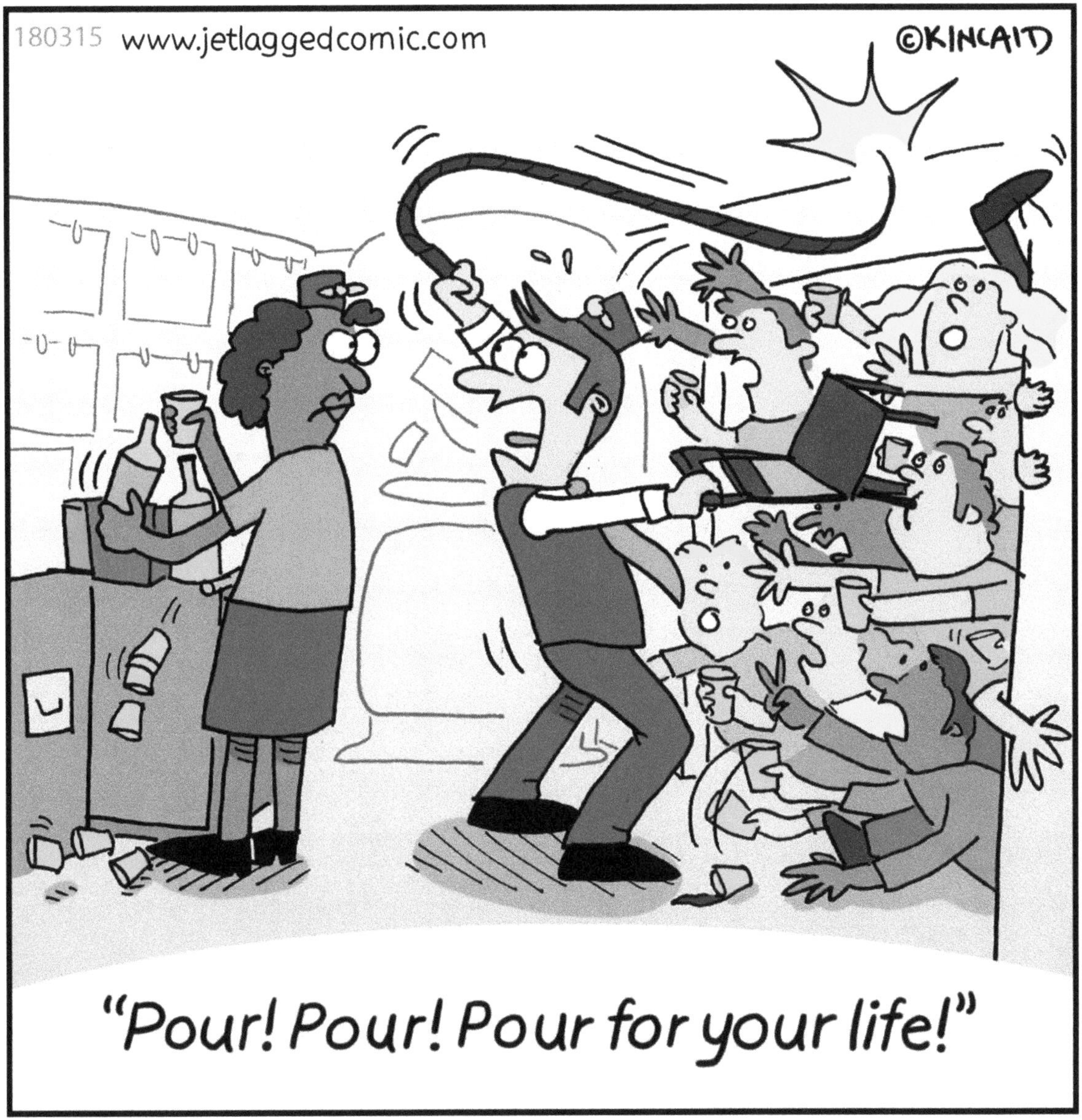
180315 www.jetlaggedcomic.com
©KINCAID

"Pour! Pour! Pour for your life!"

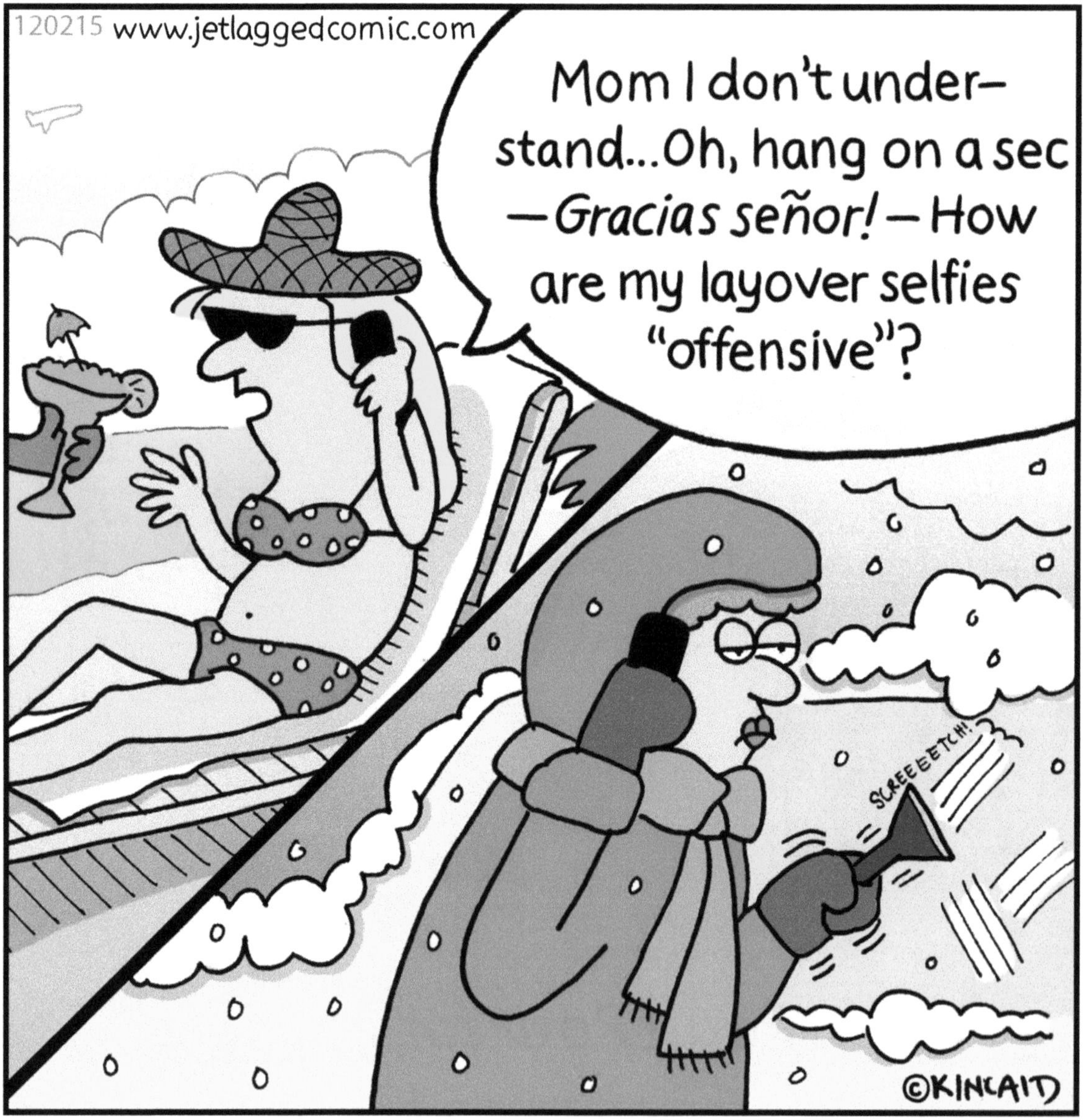
120215 www.jetlaggedcomic.com
Mom I don't under-stand...Oh, hang on a sec —*Gracias señor!*— How are my layover selfies "offensive"?
SCREEEETCH!
©KINCAID

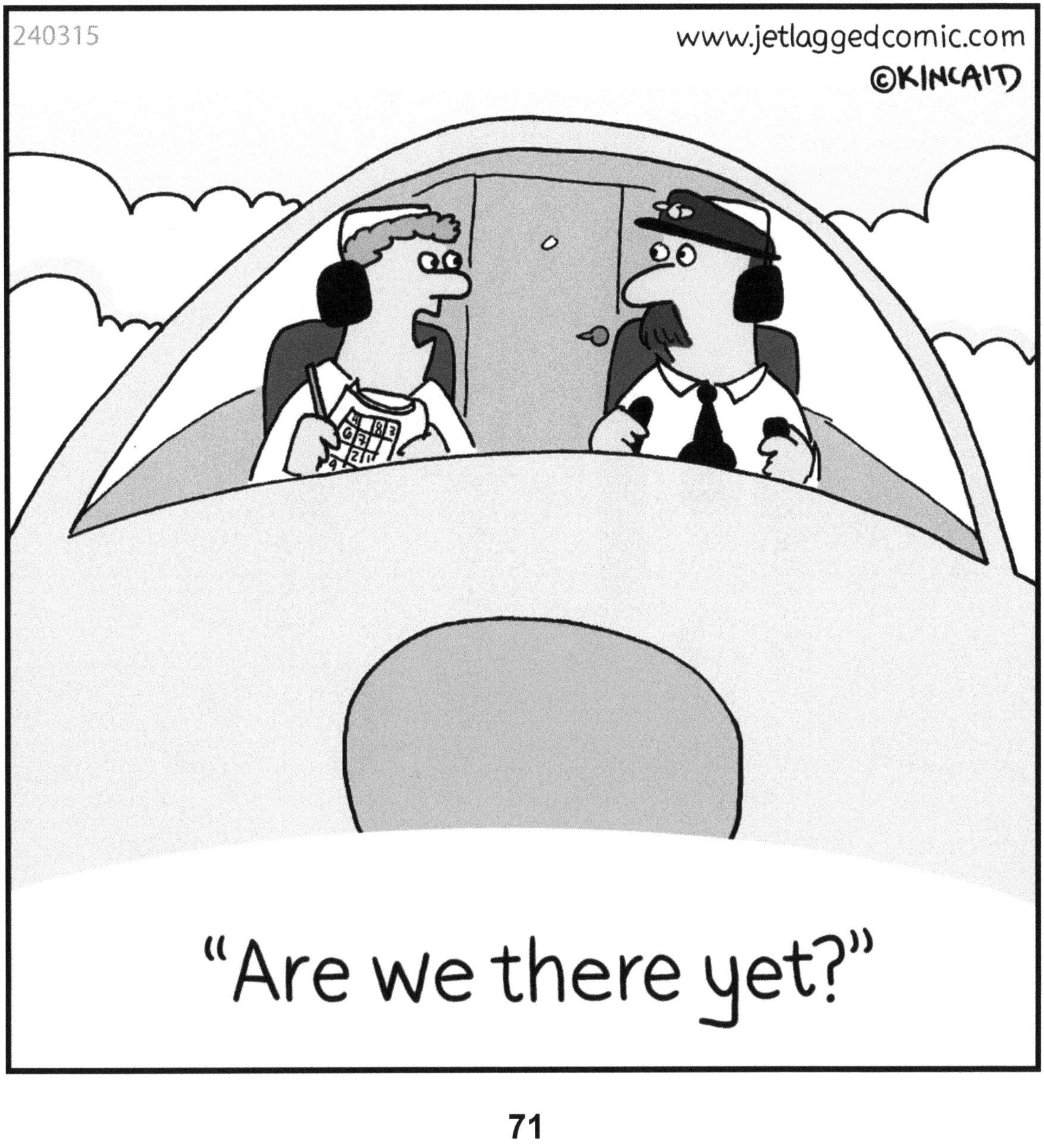
240315
www.jetlaggedcomic.com
©KINCAID

"Are we there yet?"

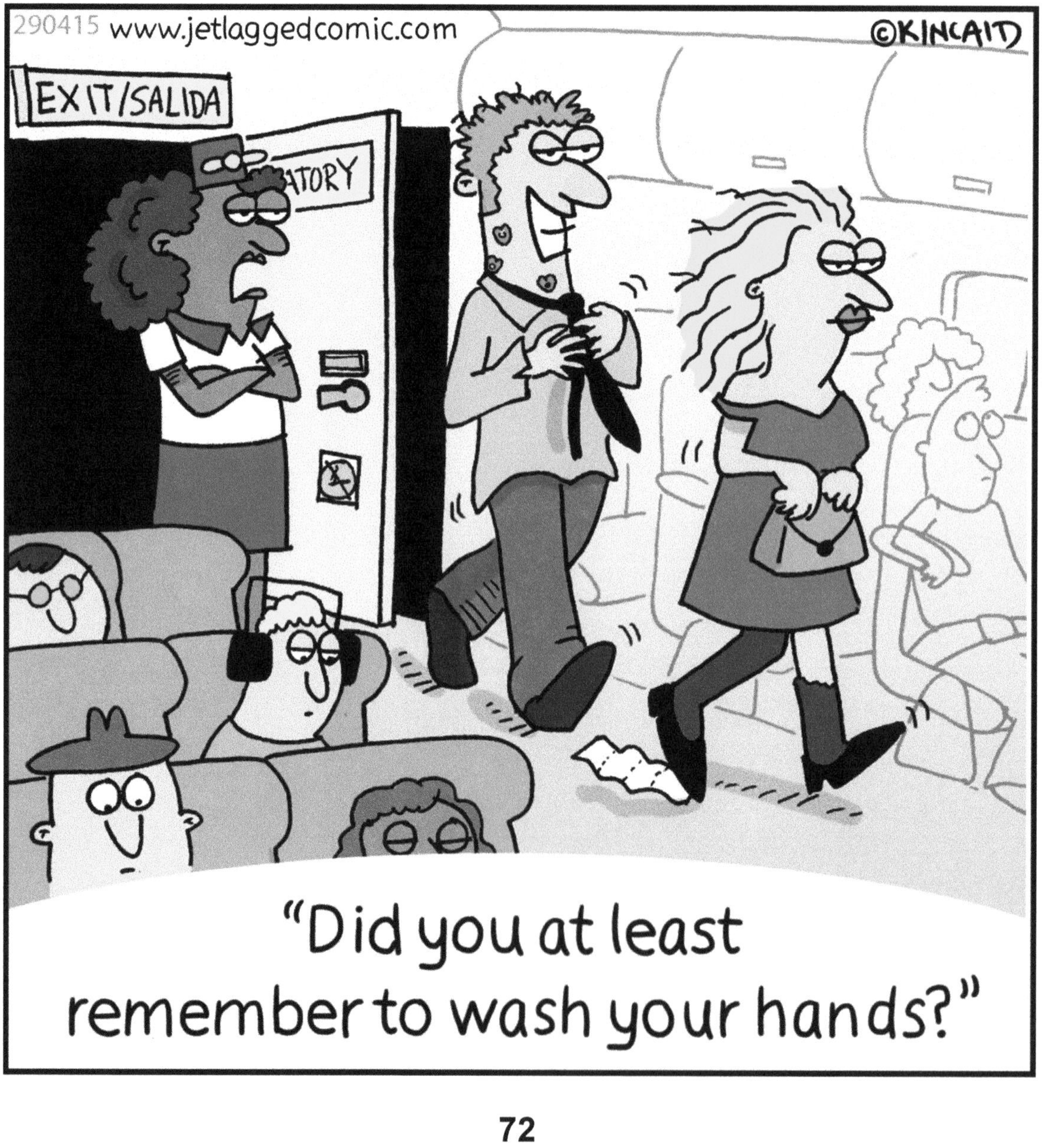
290415 www.jetlaggedcomic.com
©KINCAID
EXIT/SALIDA
ATORY

"Did you at least remember to wash your hands?"

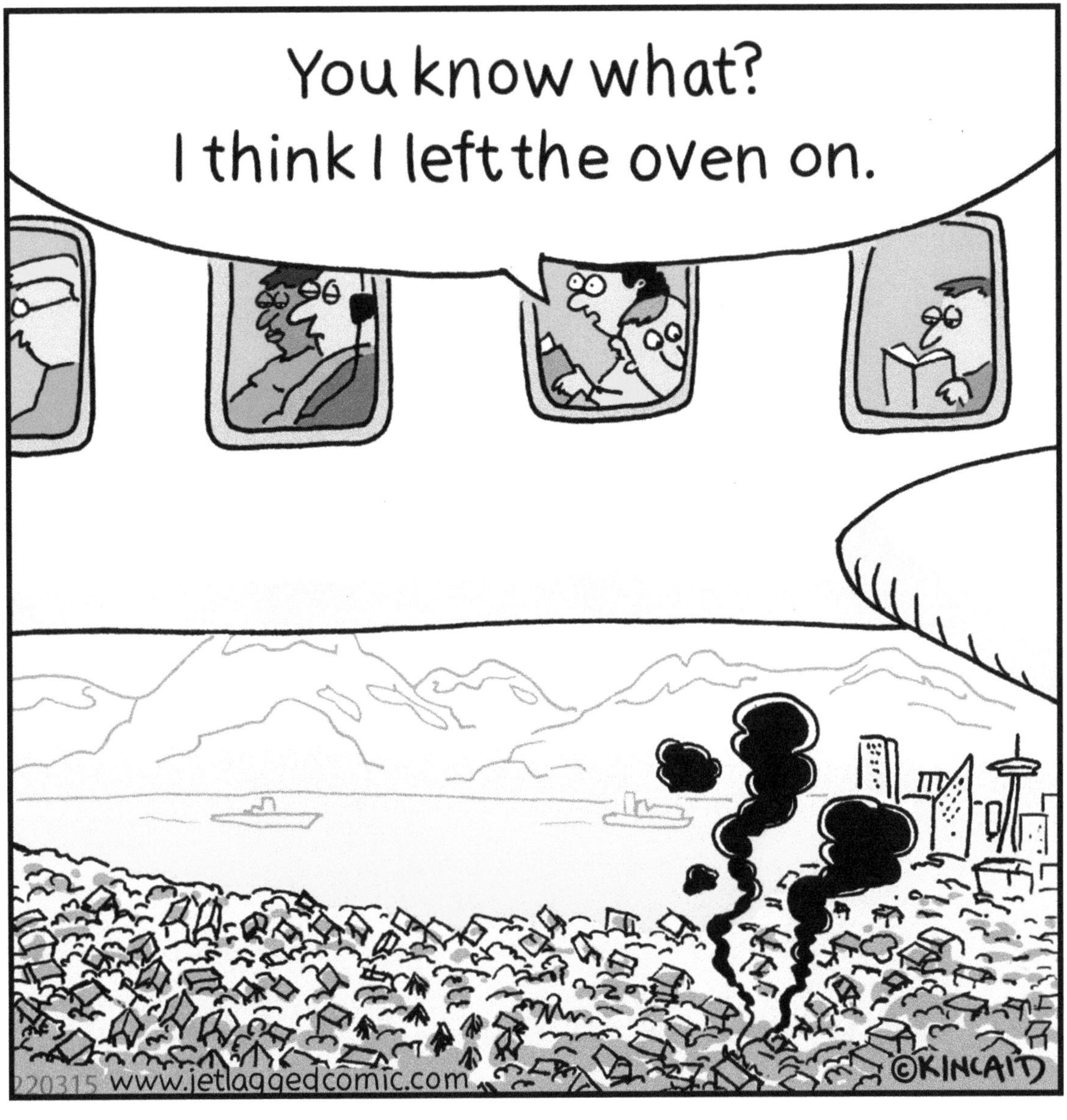
You know what?
I think I left the oven on.
220315 www.jetlaggedcomic.com
©KINCAID

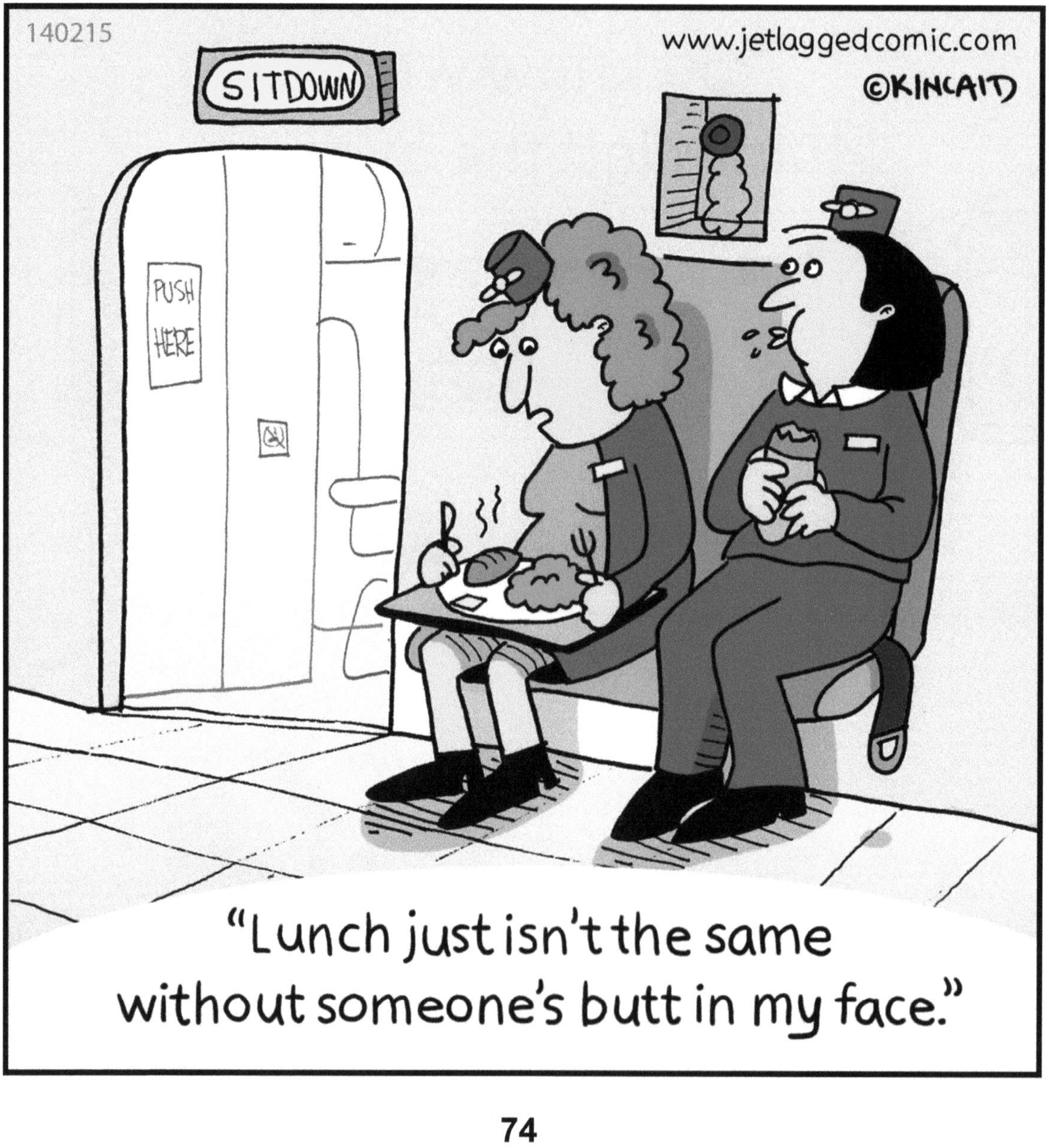

140215
www.jetlaggedcomic.com
©KINCAID
SITDOWN
PUSH HERE

"Lunch just isn't the same without someone's butt in my face."

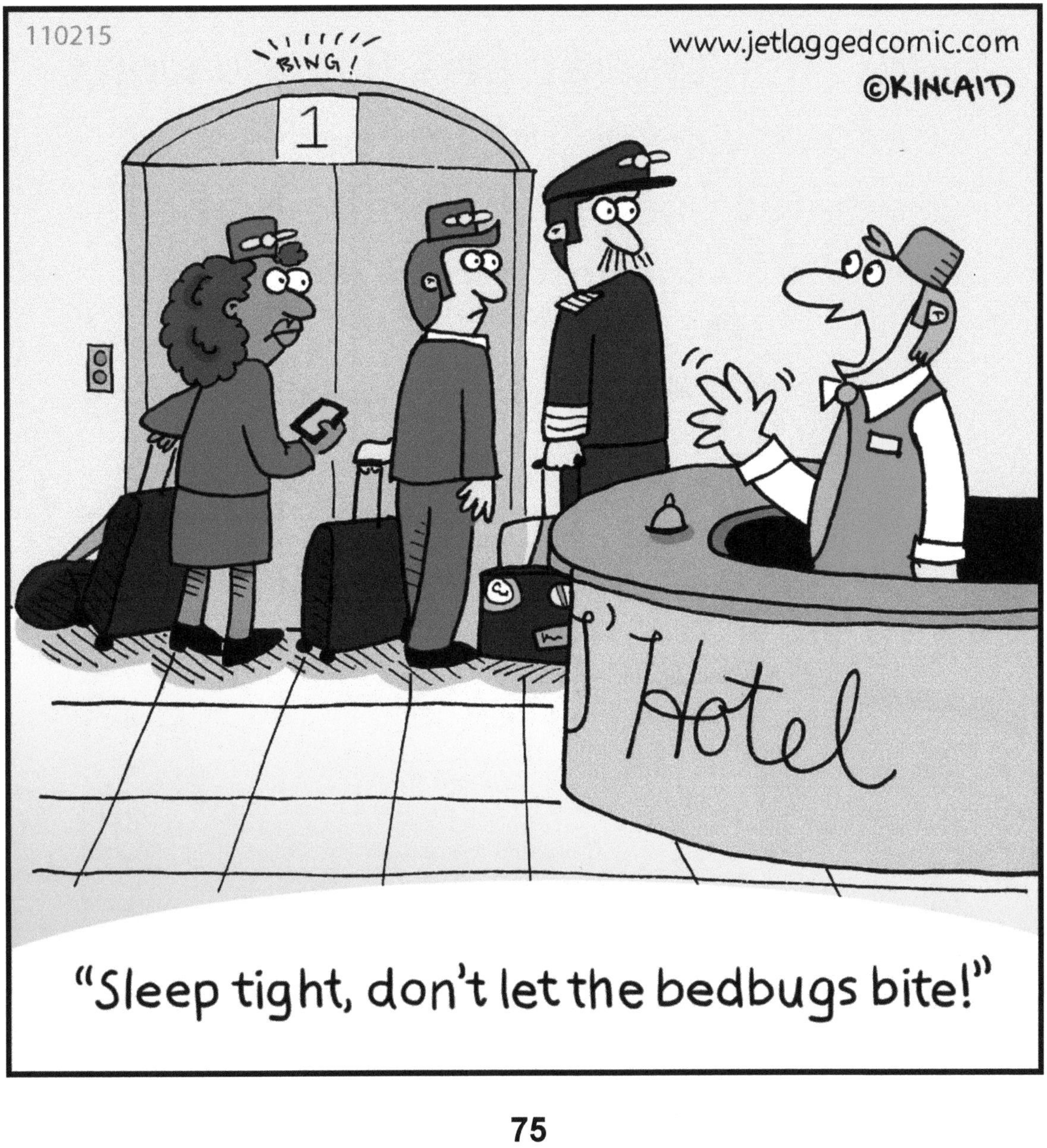
110215
BING!
1
www.jetlaggedcomic.com
©KINCAID
Hotel

"Sleep tight, don't let the bedbugs bite!"

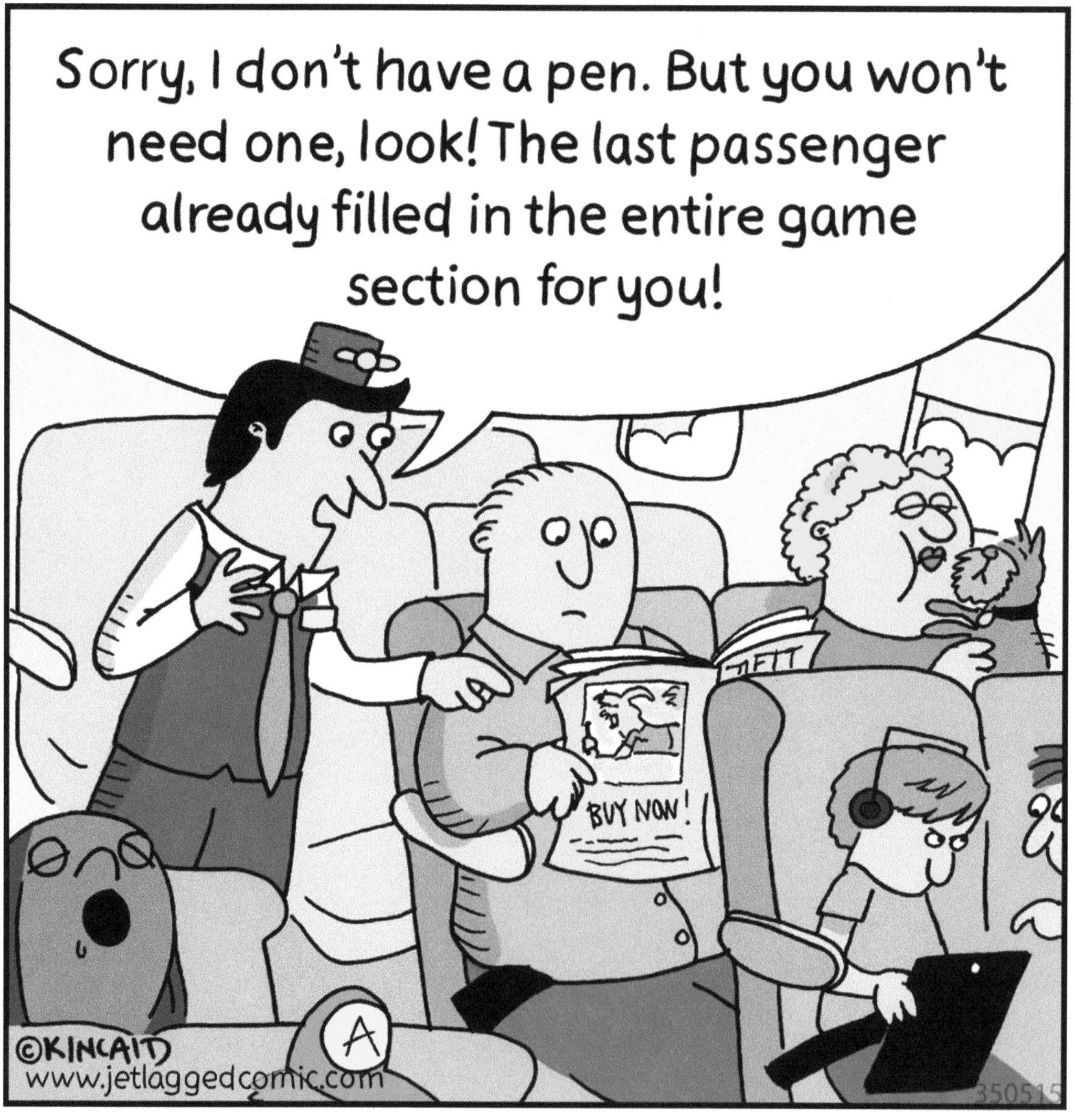
Sorry, I don't have a pen. But you won't need one, look! The last passenger already filled in the entire game section for you!
BUY NOW!
A
©KINCAID
www.jetlaggedcomic.com

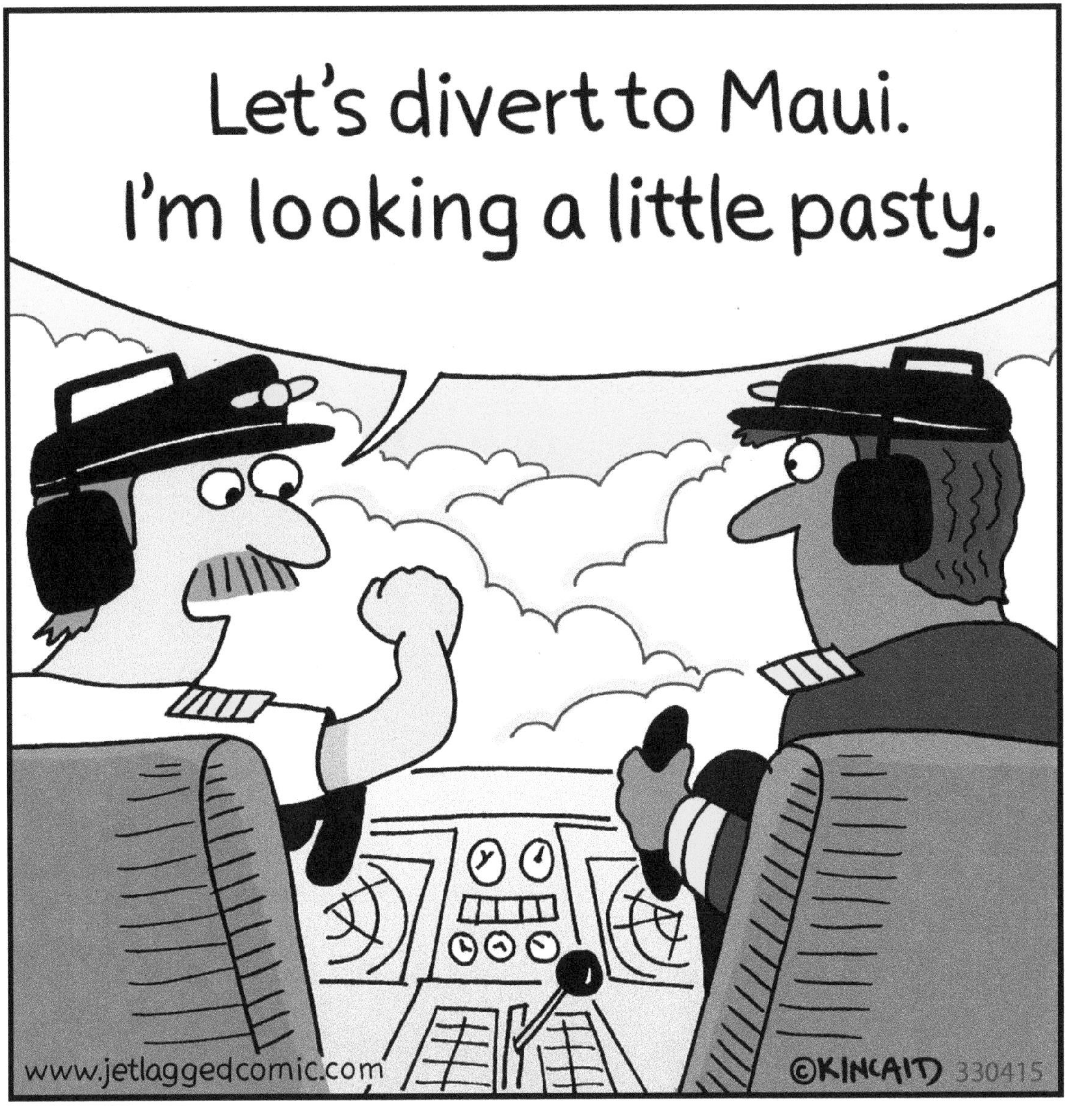
Let's divert to Maui.
I'm looking a little pasty.
www.jetlaggedcomic.com
©KINCAID 330415

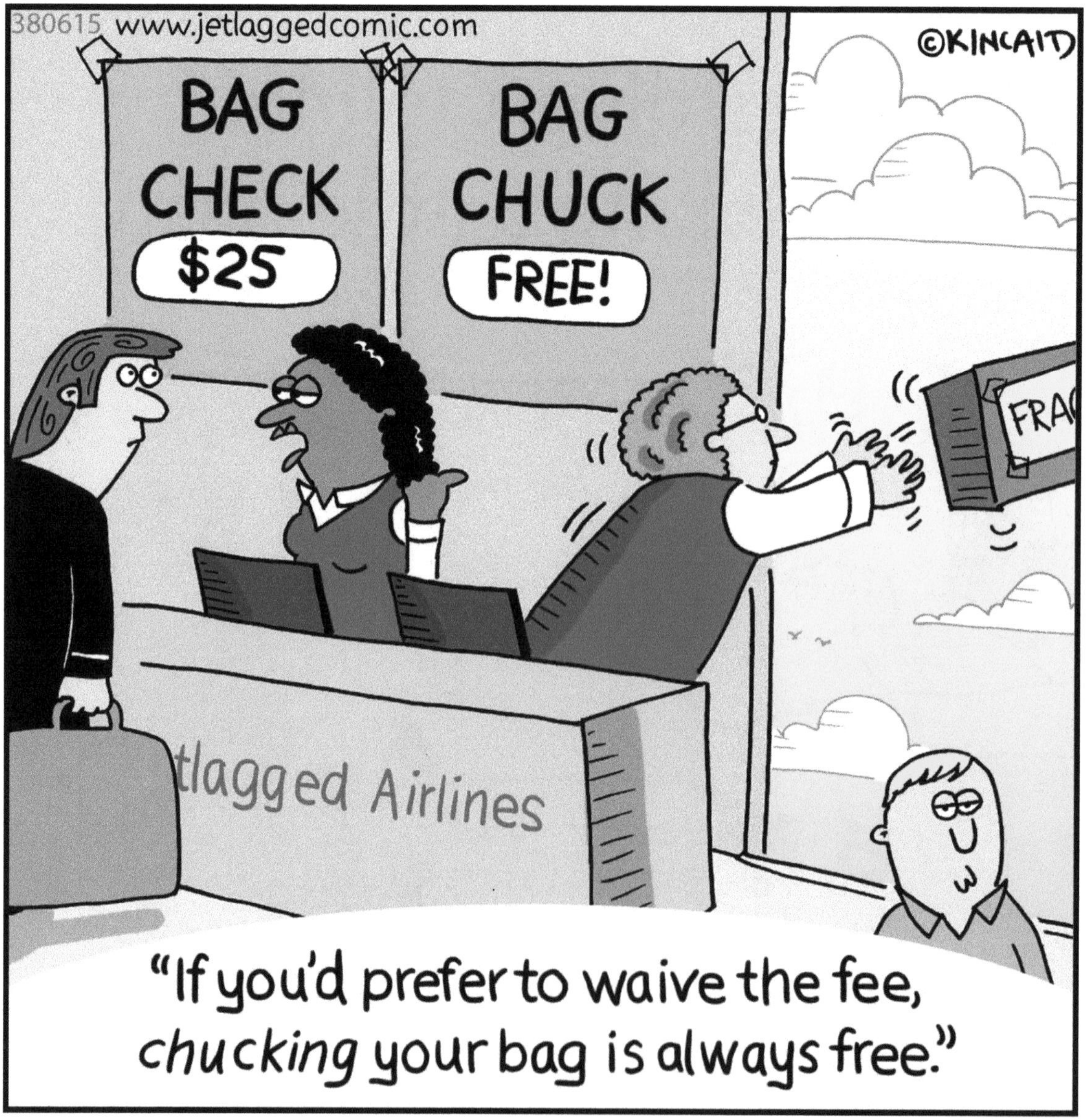
380615 www.jetlaggedcomic.com
©KINCAID
BAG CHECK
$25
BAG CHUCK
FREE!

"If you'd prefer to waive the fee, *chucking* your bag is always free."

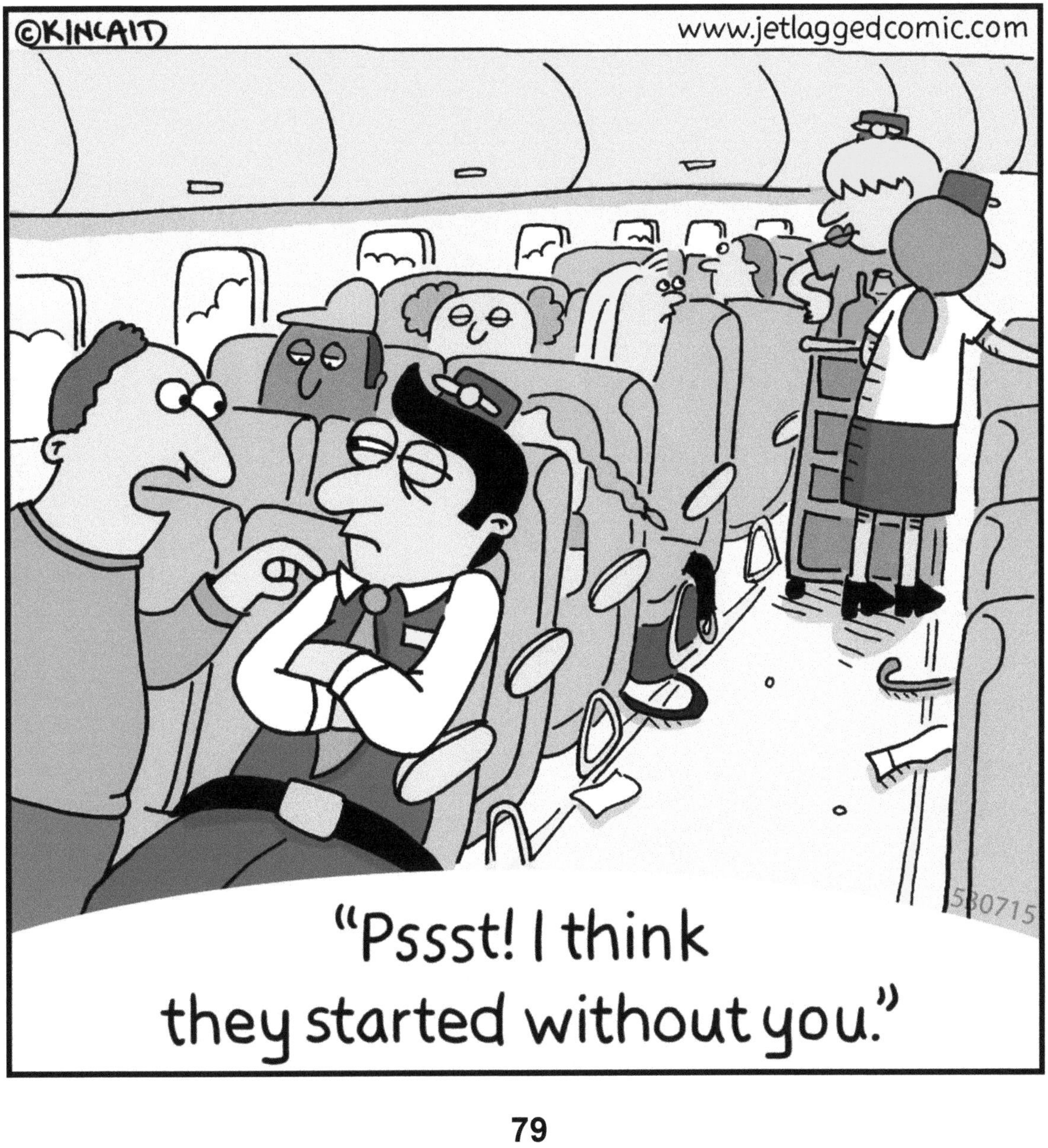
©KINCAID
www.jetlaggedcomic.com

"Pssst! I think they started without you."

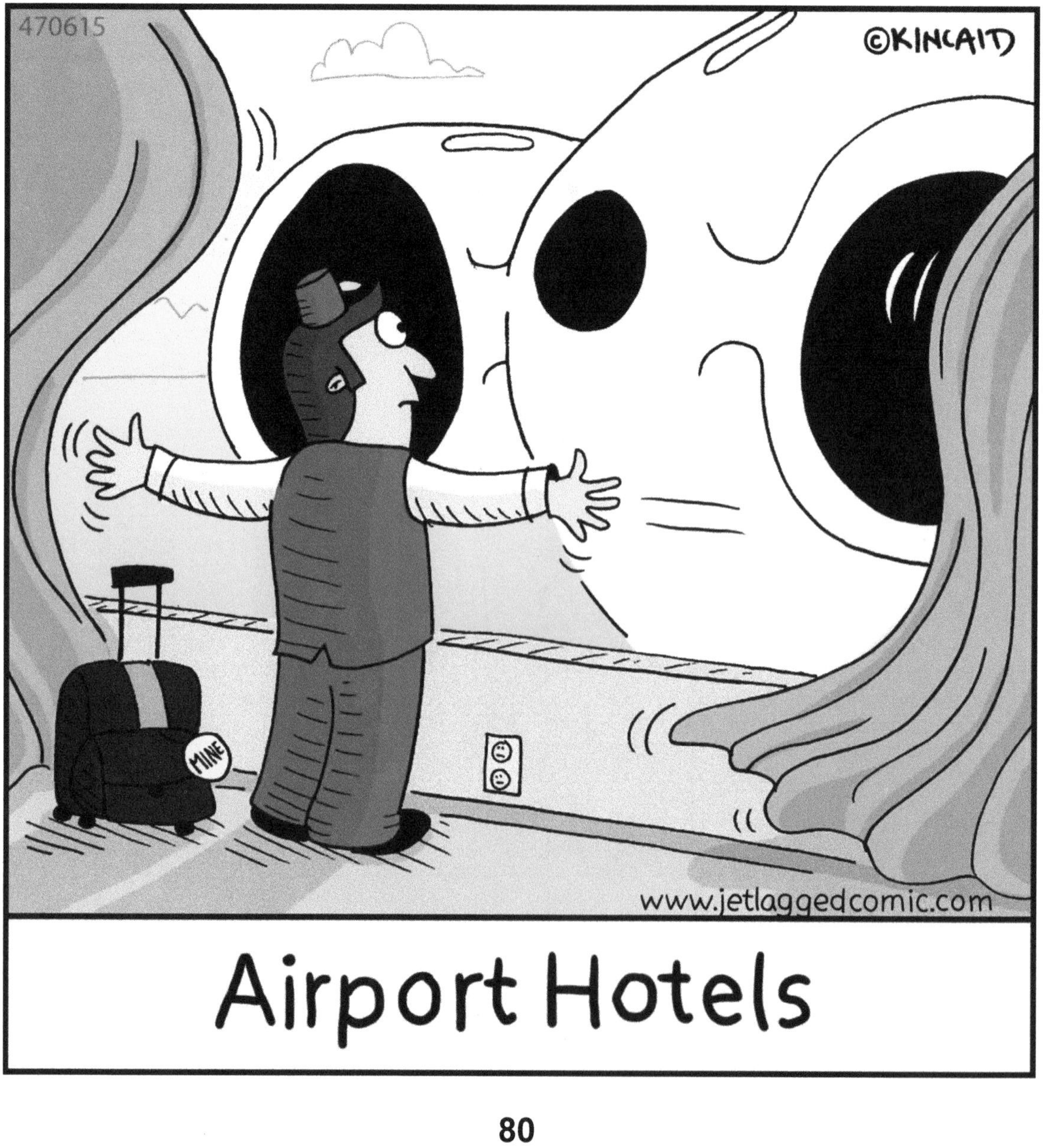
470615
©KINCAID
MINE
www.jetlaggedcomic.com

Airport Hotels

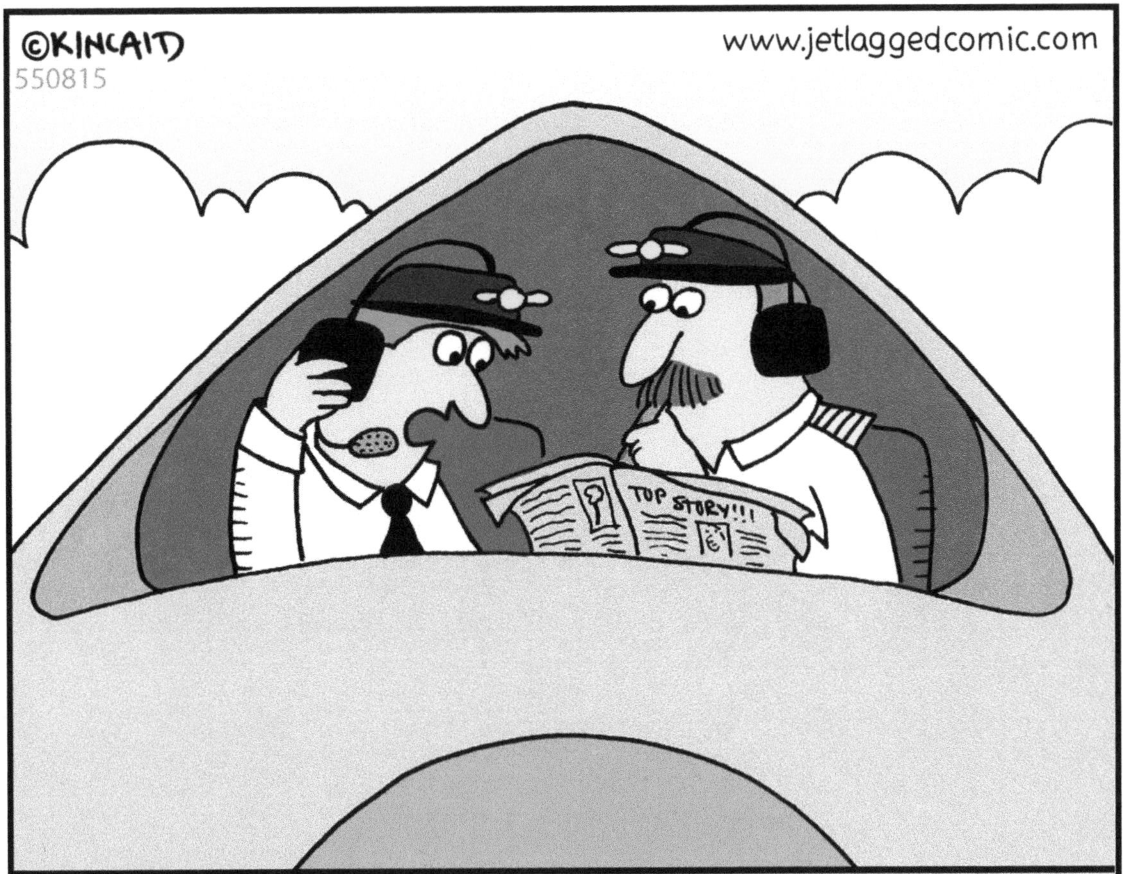
©KINCAID
550815
www.jetlaggedcomic.com
TOP STORY!!!

Flight 87 to Tower! Come in Tower! We are in a real pickle up here—— what's a five letter word for "blue"?

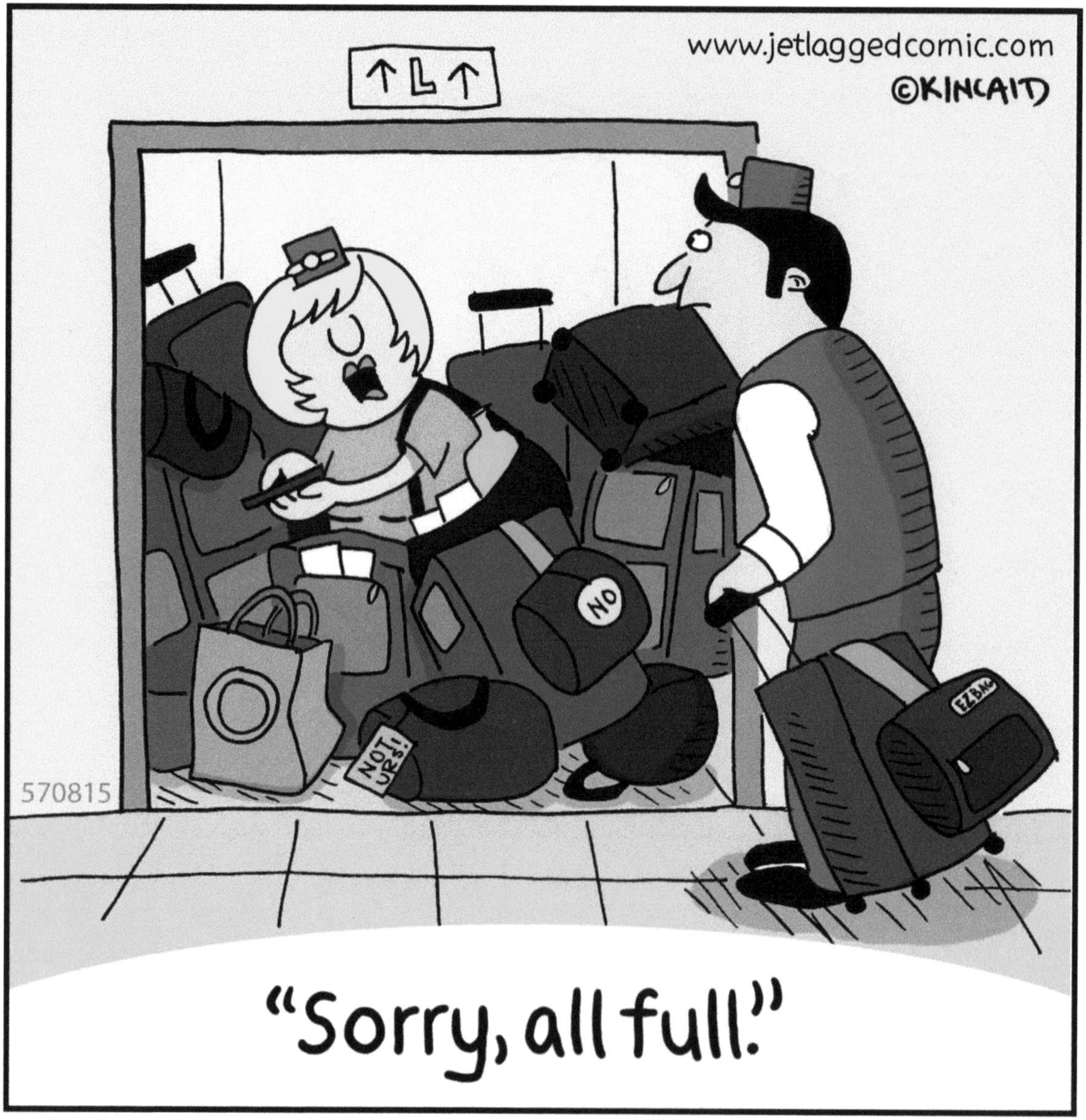
www.jetlaggedcomic.com
©KINCAID
L
NO
NOT URS!
EZ BAG
570815

"Sorry, all full."

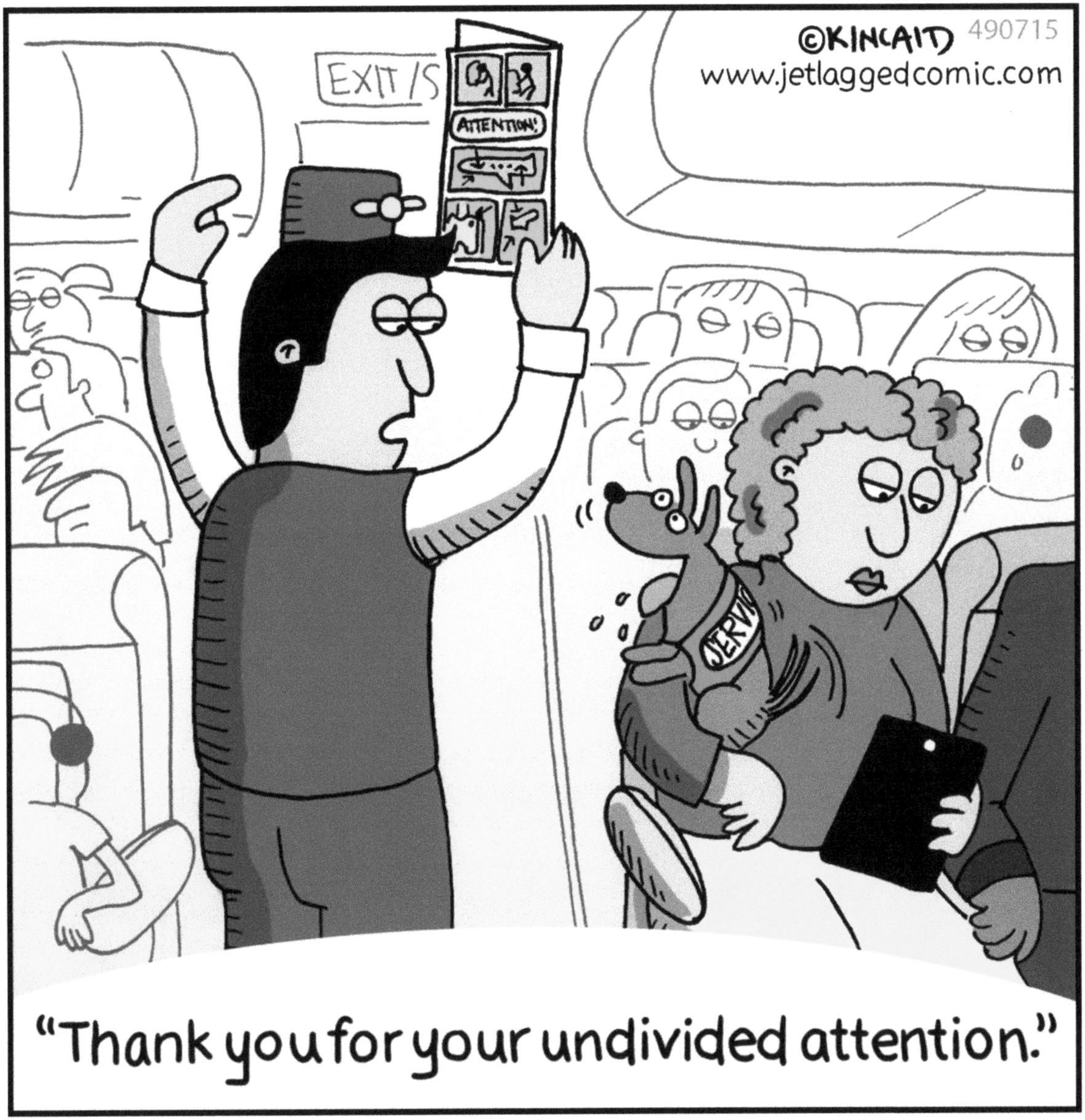
©KINCAID 490715
www.jetlaggedcomic.com
EXIT/S
ATTENTION!
SERVI

"Thank you for your undivided attention."

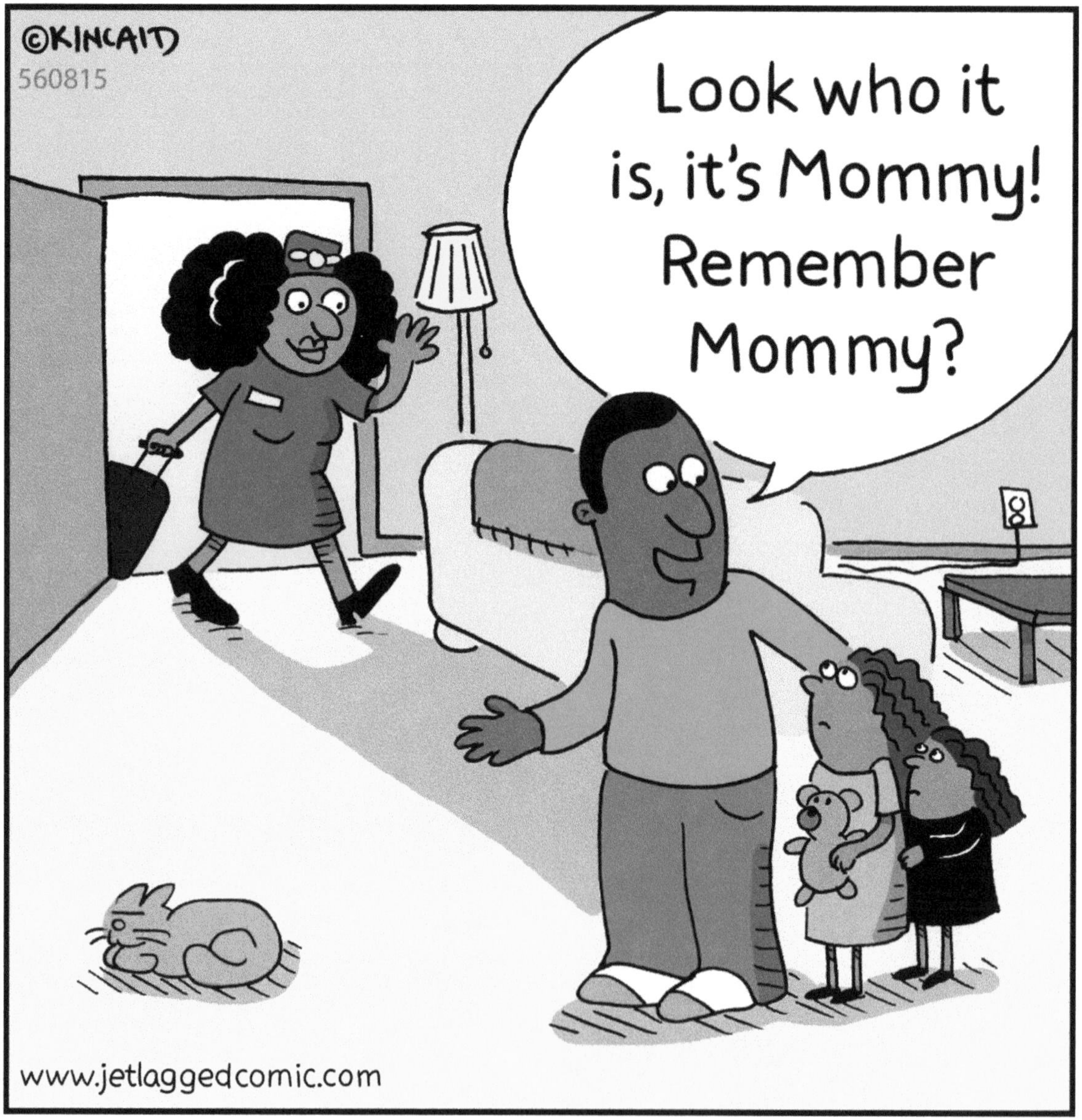
©KINCAID
560815
Look who it is, it's Mommy! Remember Mommy?
www.jetlaggedcomic.com

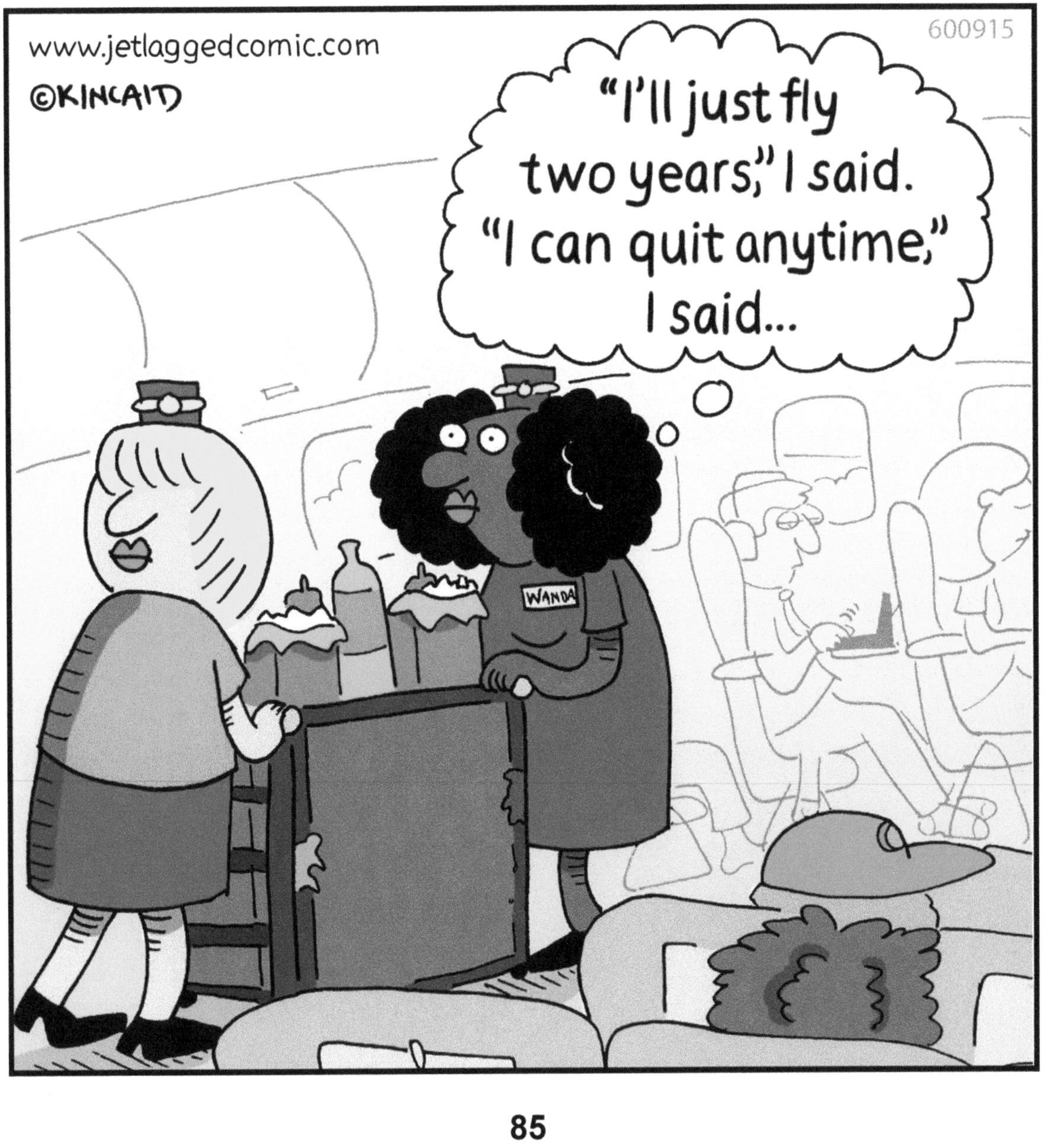
www.jetlaggedcomic.com
©KINCAID
600915
"I'll just fly two years," I said. "I can quit anytime," I said...
WANDA

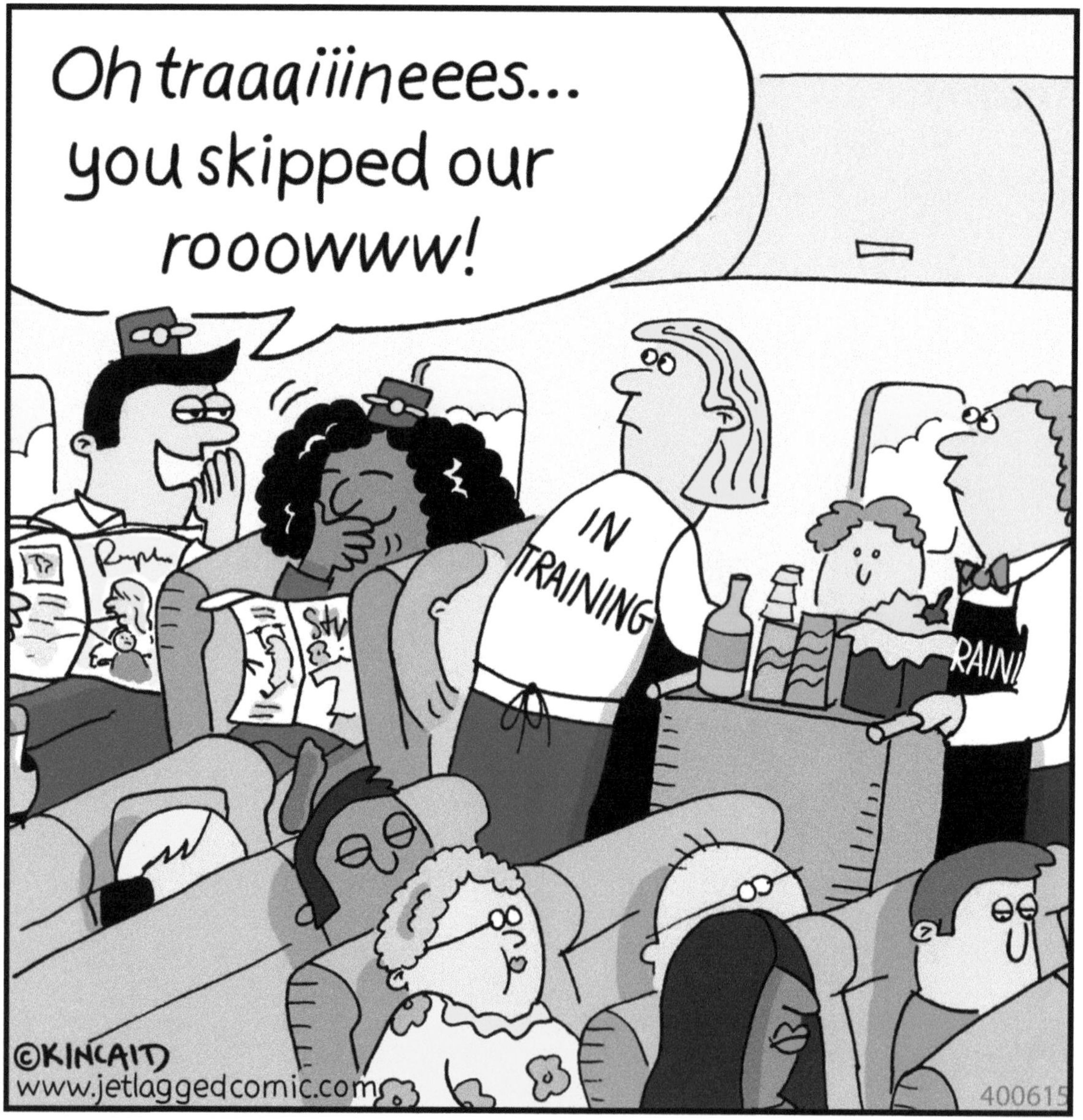
Oh traaaiiineees... you skipped our rooowww!
IN TRAINING
RAINI
©KINCAID
www.jetlaggedcomic.com
400615

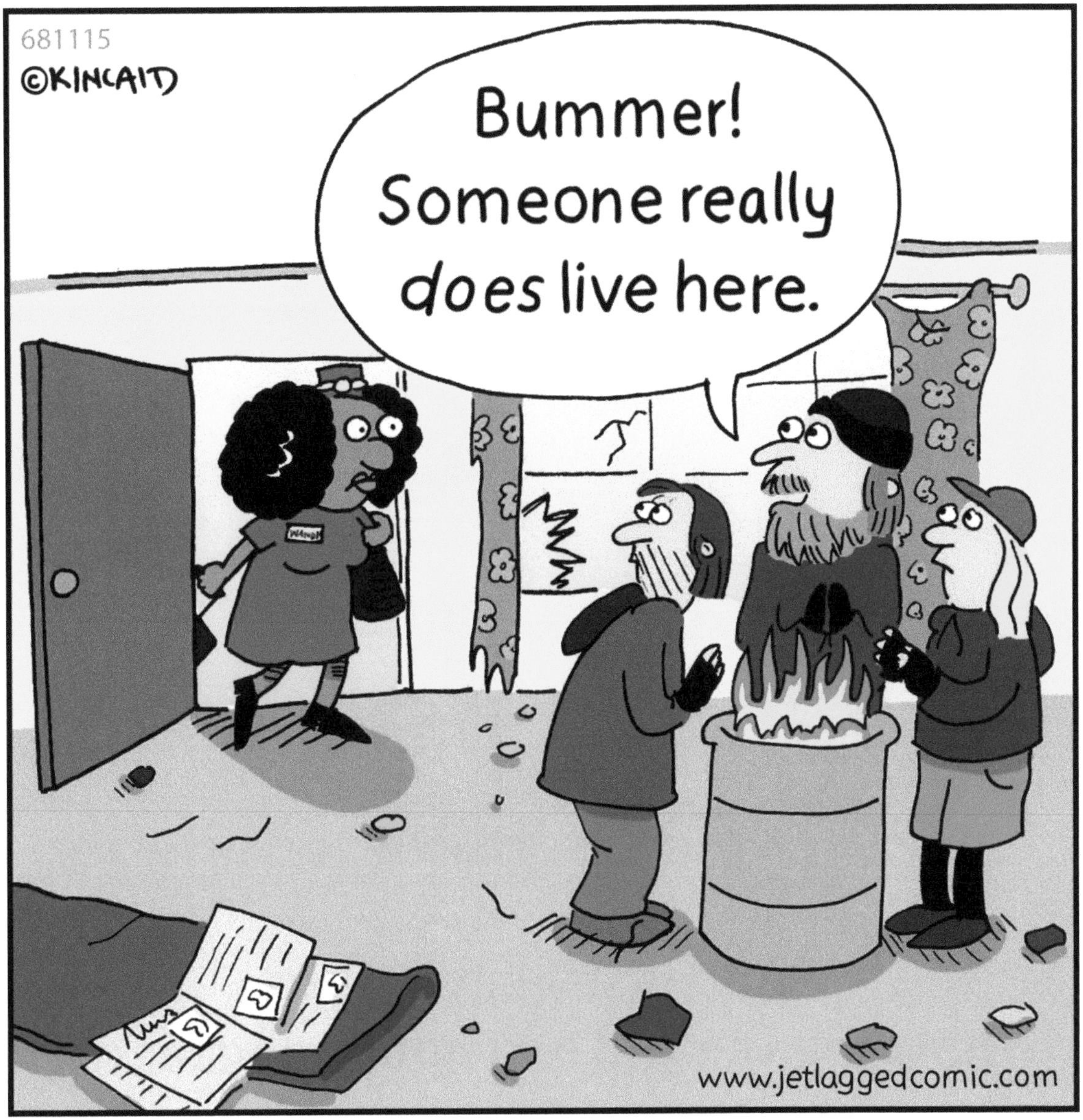
681115
©KINCAID
Bummer! Someone really *does* live here.
www.jetlaggedcomic.com

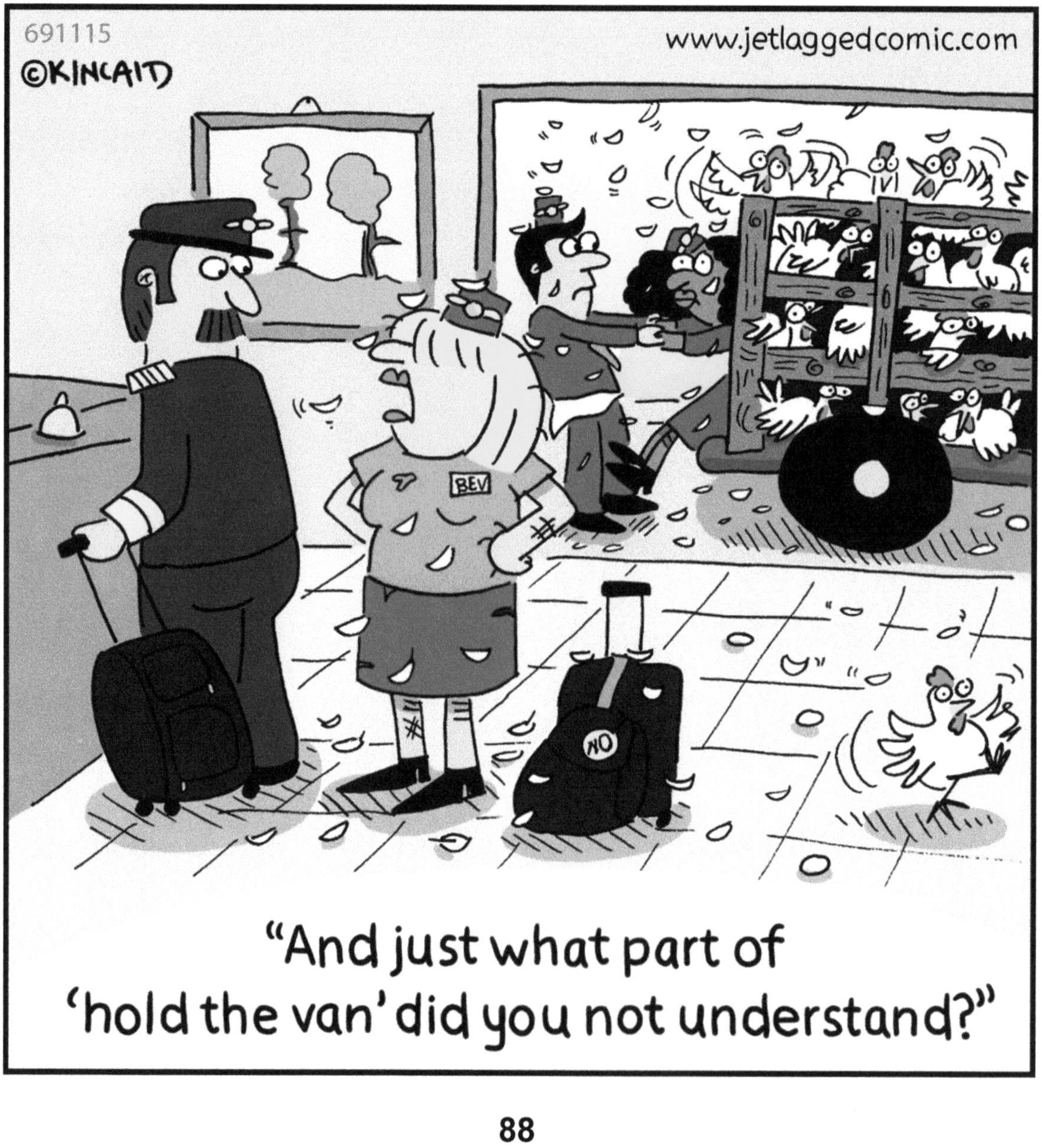
691115
©KINCAID
www.jetlaggedcomic.com
BEV
NO

"And just what part of
'hold the van' did you not understand?"

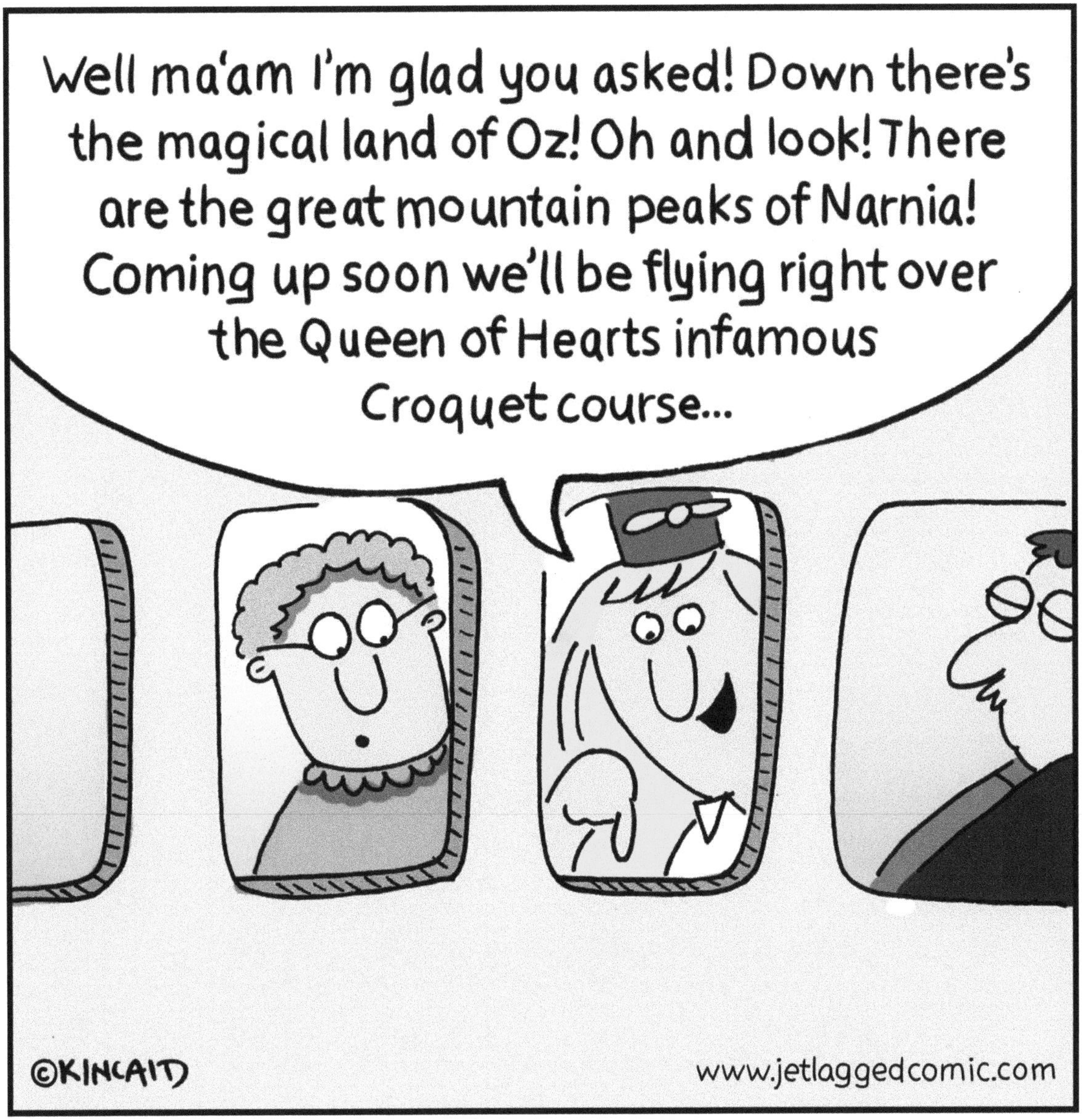
Well ma'am I'm glad you asked! Down there's the magical land of Oz! Oh and look! There are the great mountain peaks of Narnia! Coming up soon we'll be flying right over the Queen of Hearts infamous Croquet course...
©KINCAID
www.jetlaggedcomic.com

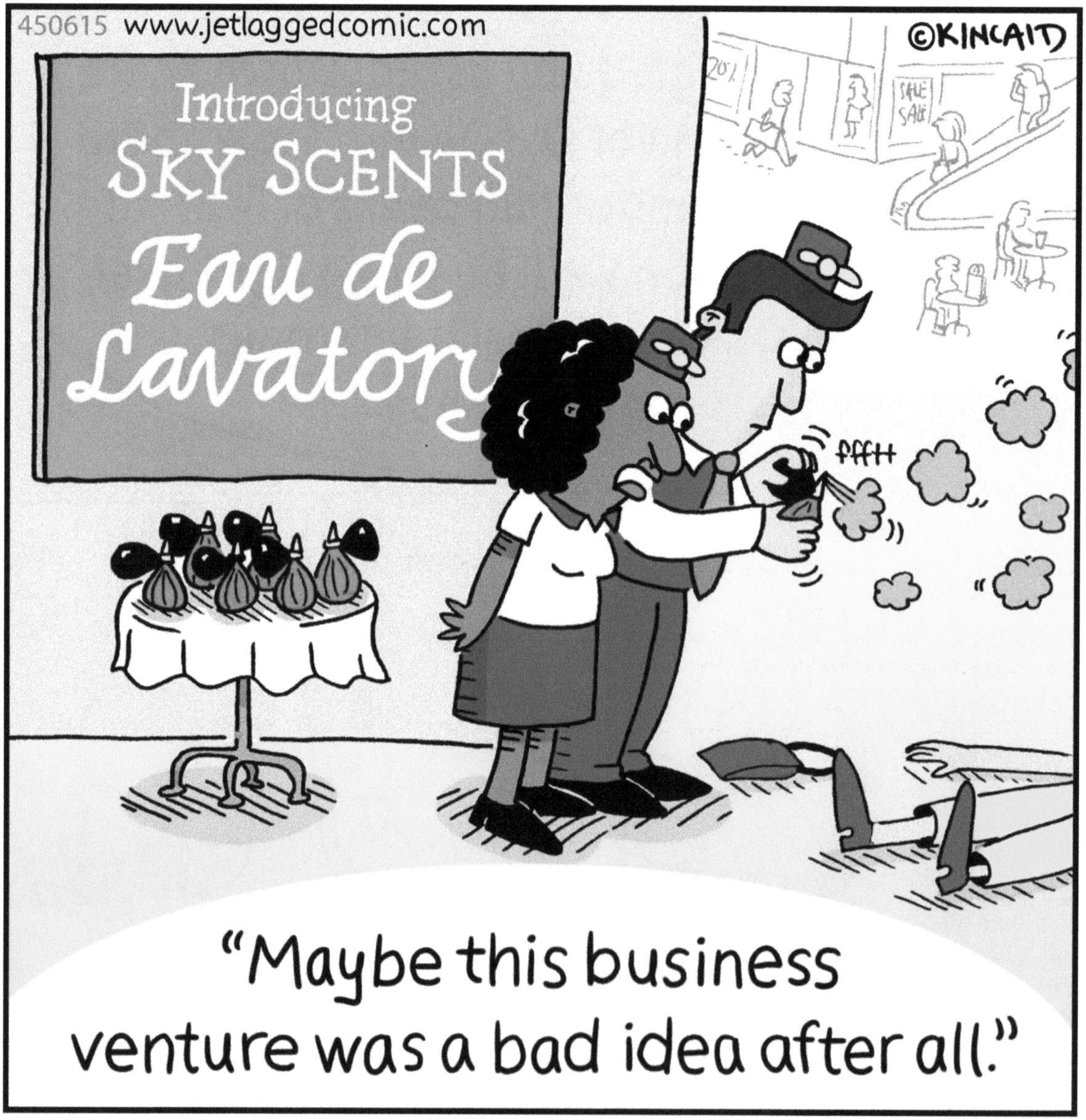
450615 www.jetlaggedcomic.com
©KINCAID
Introducing
SKY SCENTS
Eau de Lavatory
"Maybe this business venture was a bad idea after all."

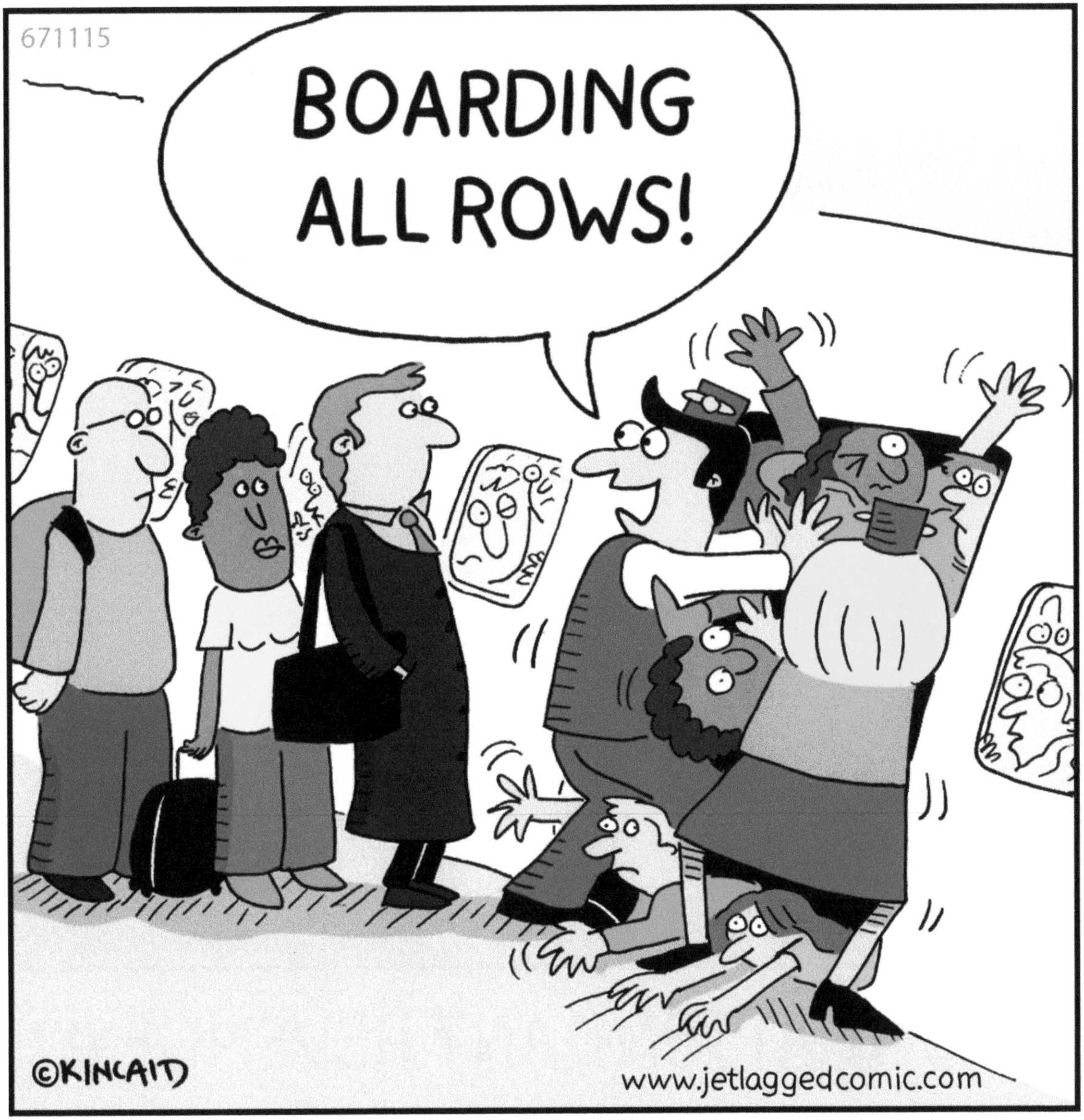
671115
BOARDING ALL ROWS!
©KINCAID
www.jetlaggedcomic.com

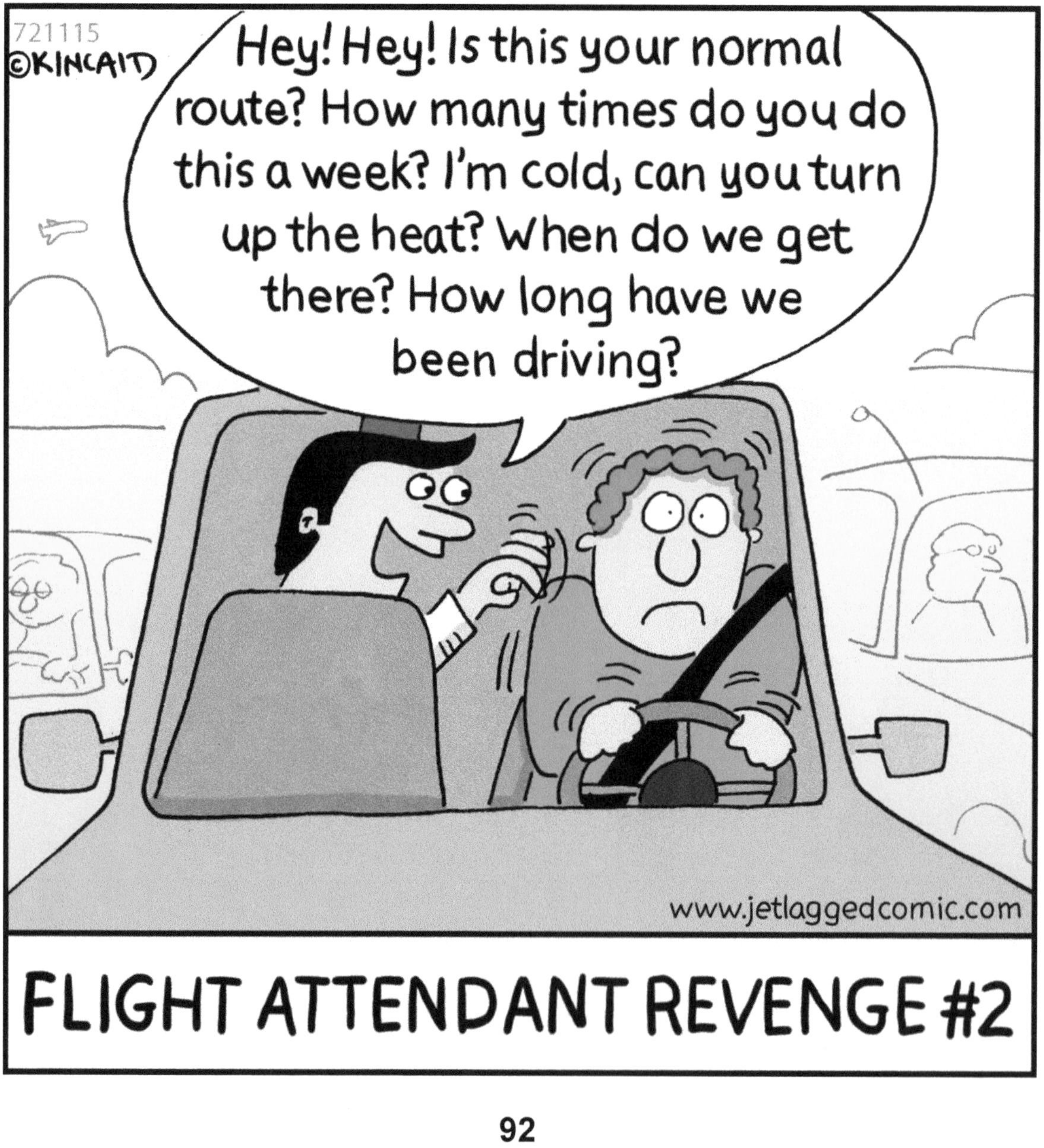
721115
©KINCAID
Hey! Hey! Is this your normal route? How many times do you do this a week? I'm cold, can you turn up the heat? When do we get there? How long have we been driving?
www.jetlaggedcomic.com

FLIGHT ATTENDANT REVENGE #2

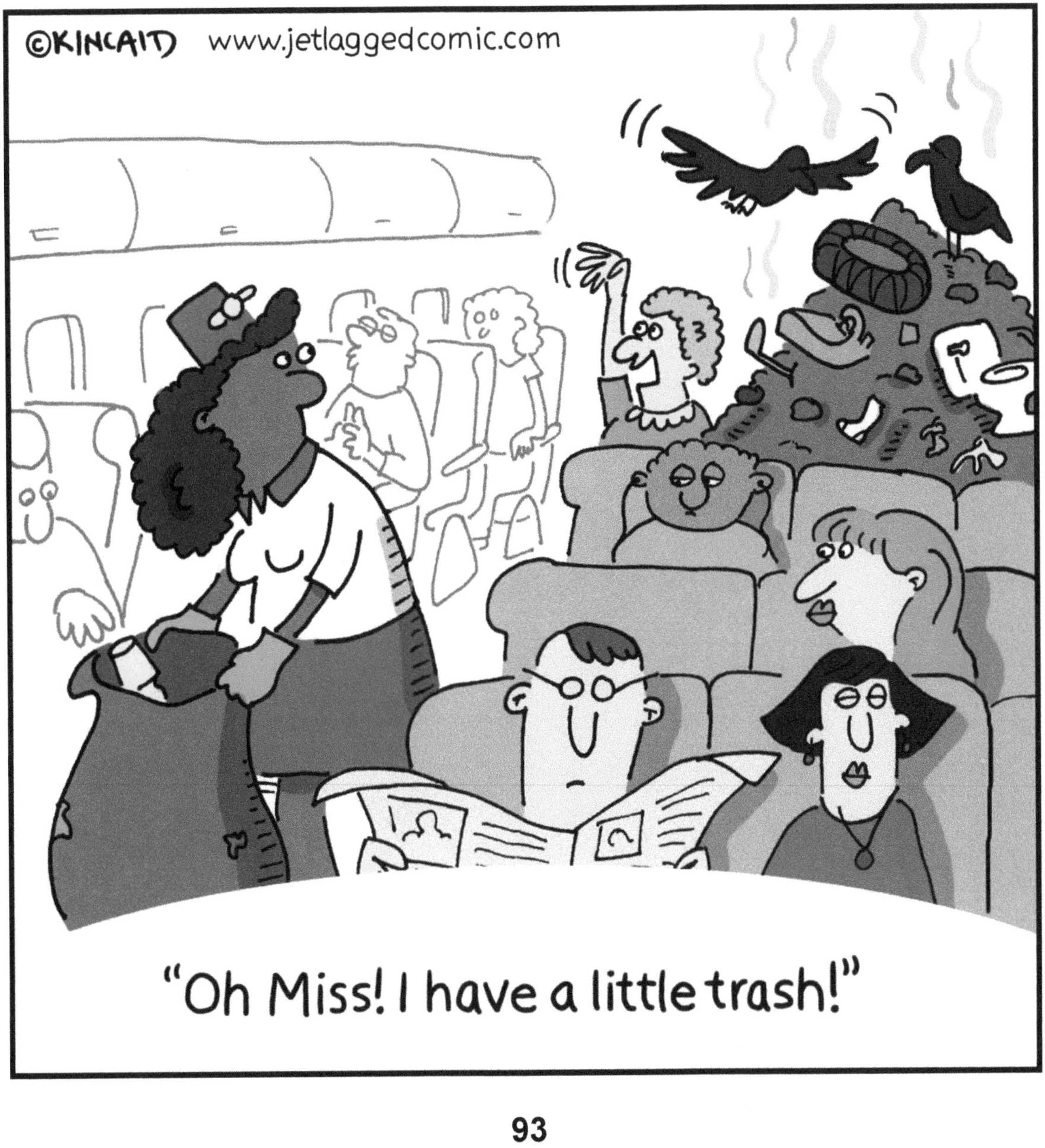
©KINCAID www.jetlaggedcomic.com

"Oh Miss! I have a little trash!"

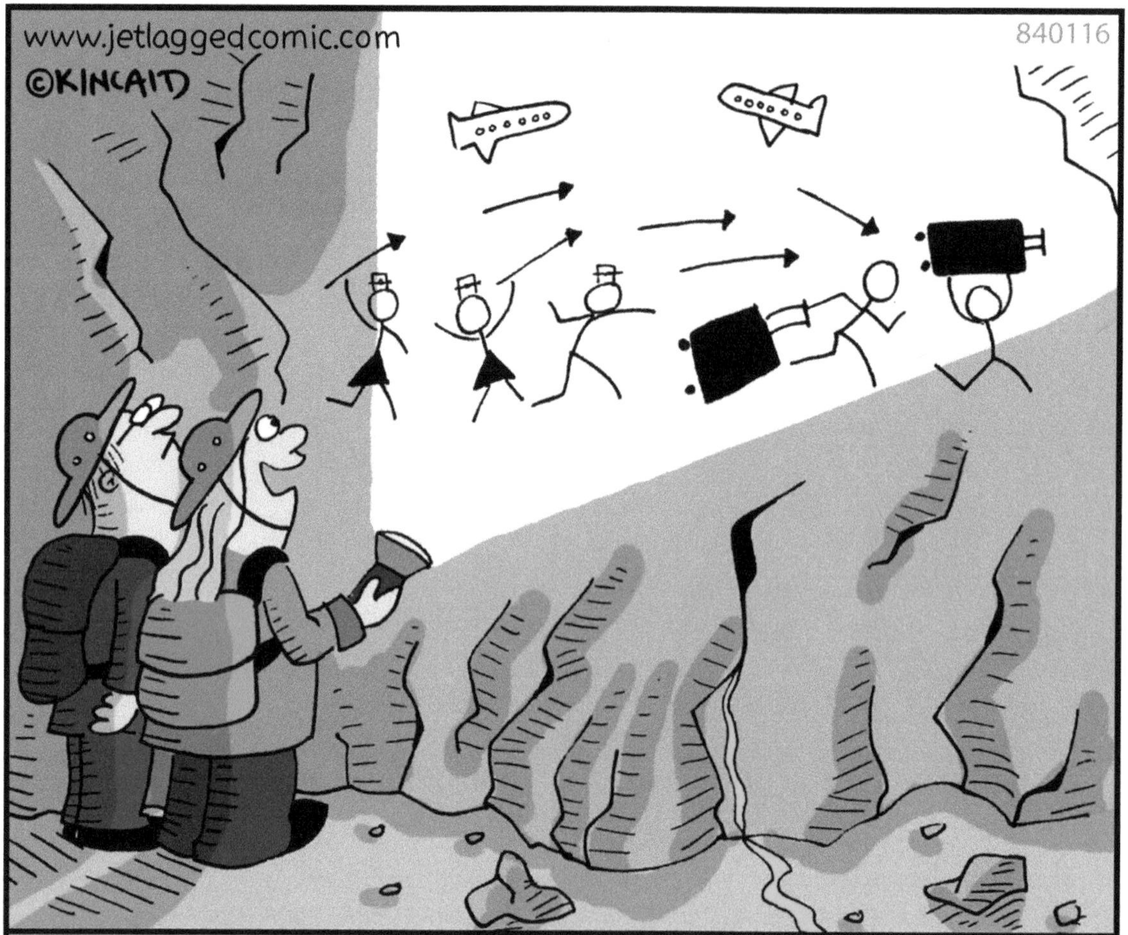
www.jetlaggedcomic.com
©KINCAID
840116

"Fascinating! Dr. Mort, this proves that the early *Flightattenderthal* did in fact impale passengers who brought on oversized carry-on luggage!"

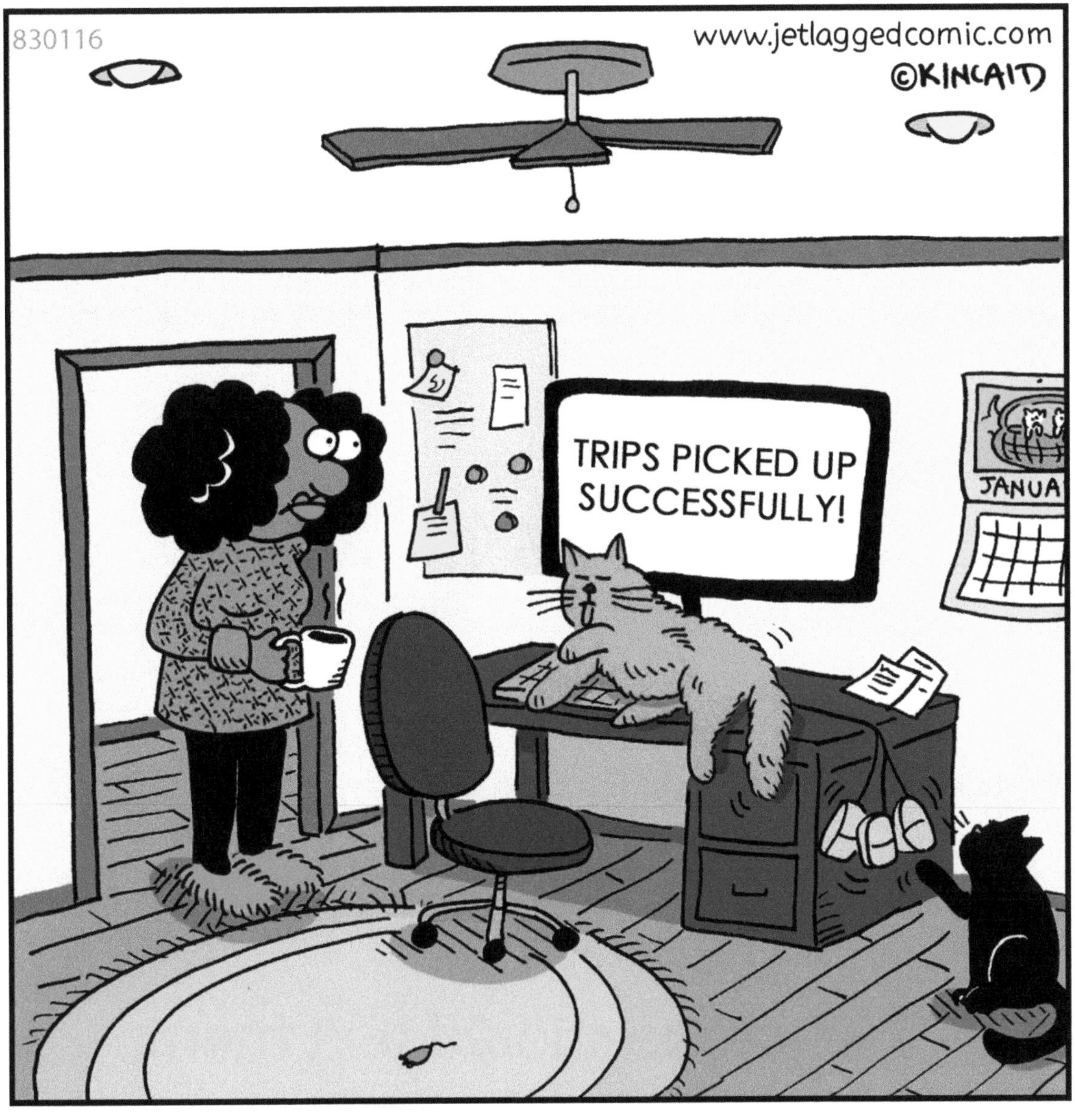
830116
www.jetlaggedcomic.com
©KINCAID
TRIPS PICKED UP
SUCCESSFULLY!
JANUA

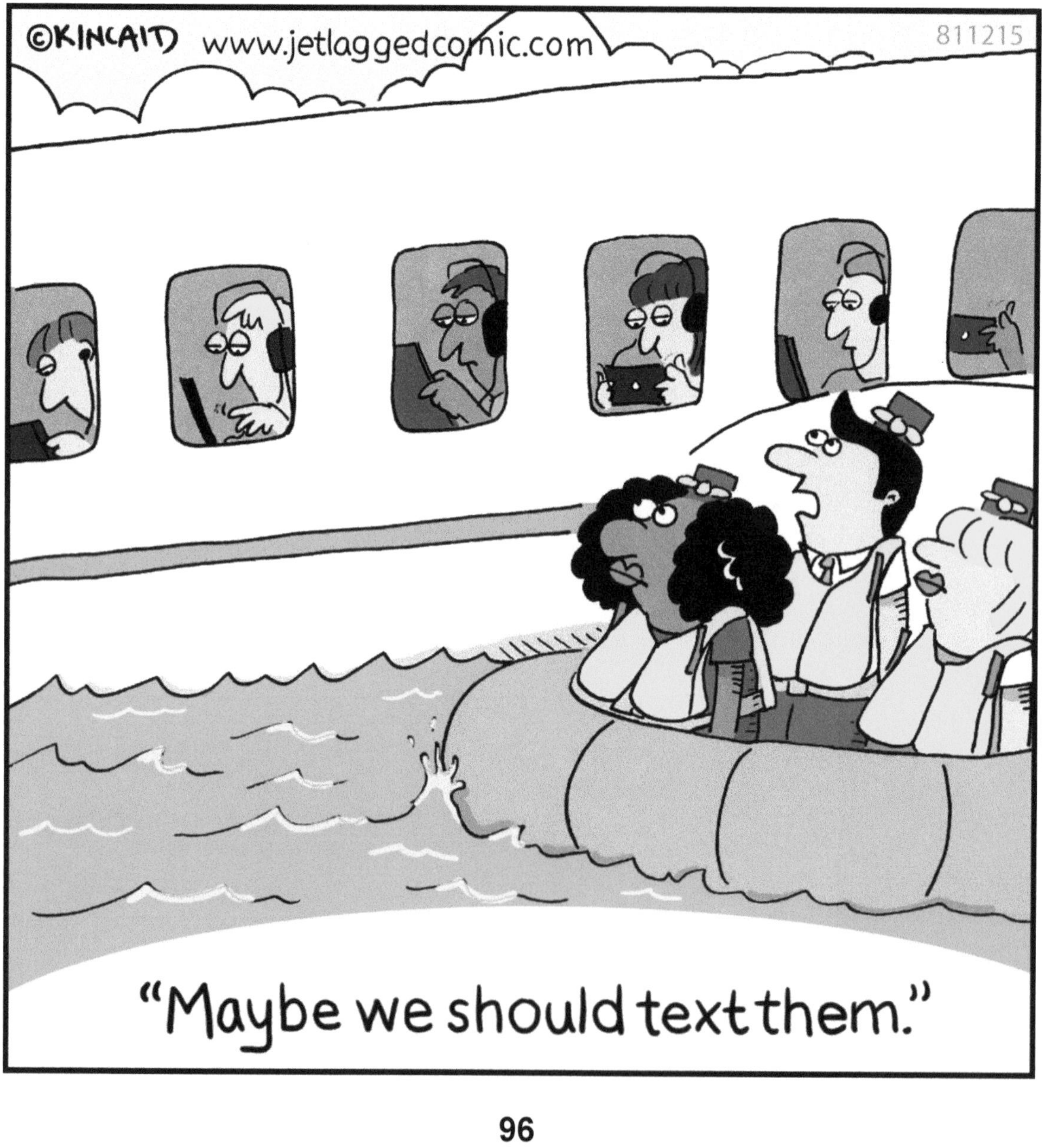
©KINCAID www.jetlaggedcomic.com
811215
"Maybe we should text them."

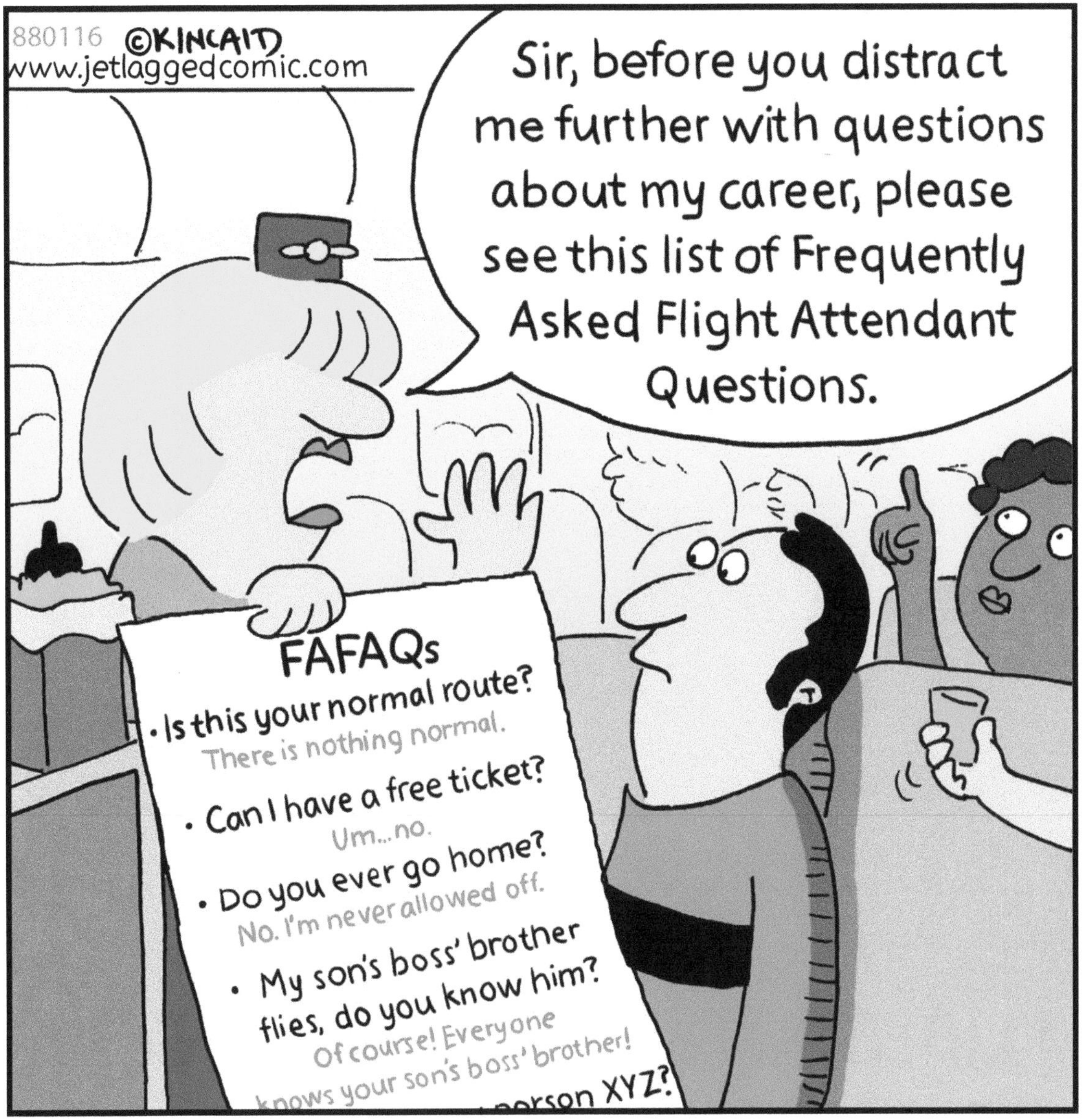
880116 ©KINCAID
www.jetlaggedcomic.com
Sir, before you distract me further with questions about my career, please see this list of Frequently Asked Flight Attendant Questions.
FAFAQs
• Is this your normal route?
There is nothing normal.
• Can I have a free ticket?
Um...no.
• Do you ever go home?
No. I'm never allowed off.
• My son's boss' brother flies, do you know him?
Of course! Everyone knows your son's boss' brother!

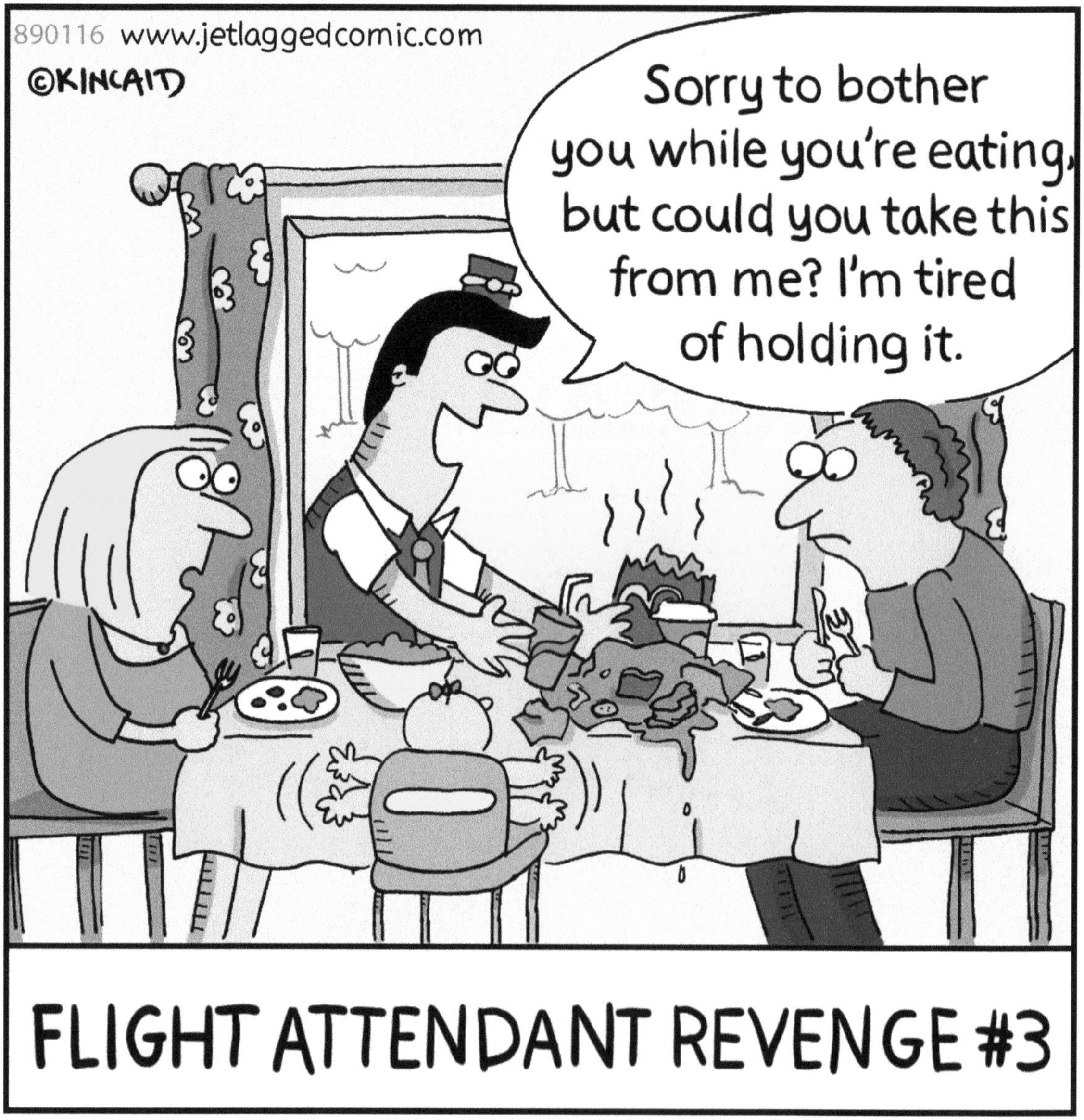
890116 www.jetlaggedcomic.com
©KINCAID
Sorry to bother you while you're eating, but could you take this from me? I'm tired of holding it.
FLIGHT ATTENDANT REVENGE #3

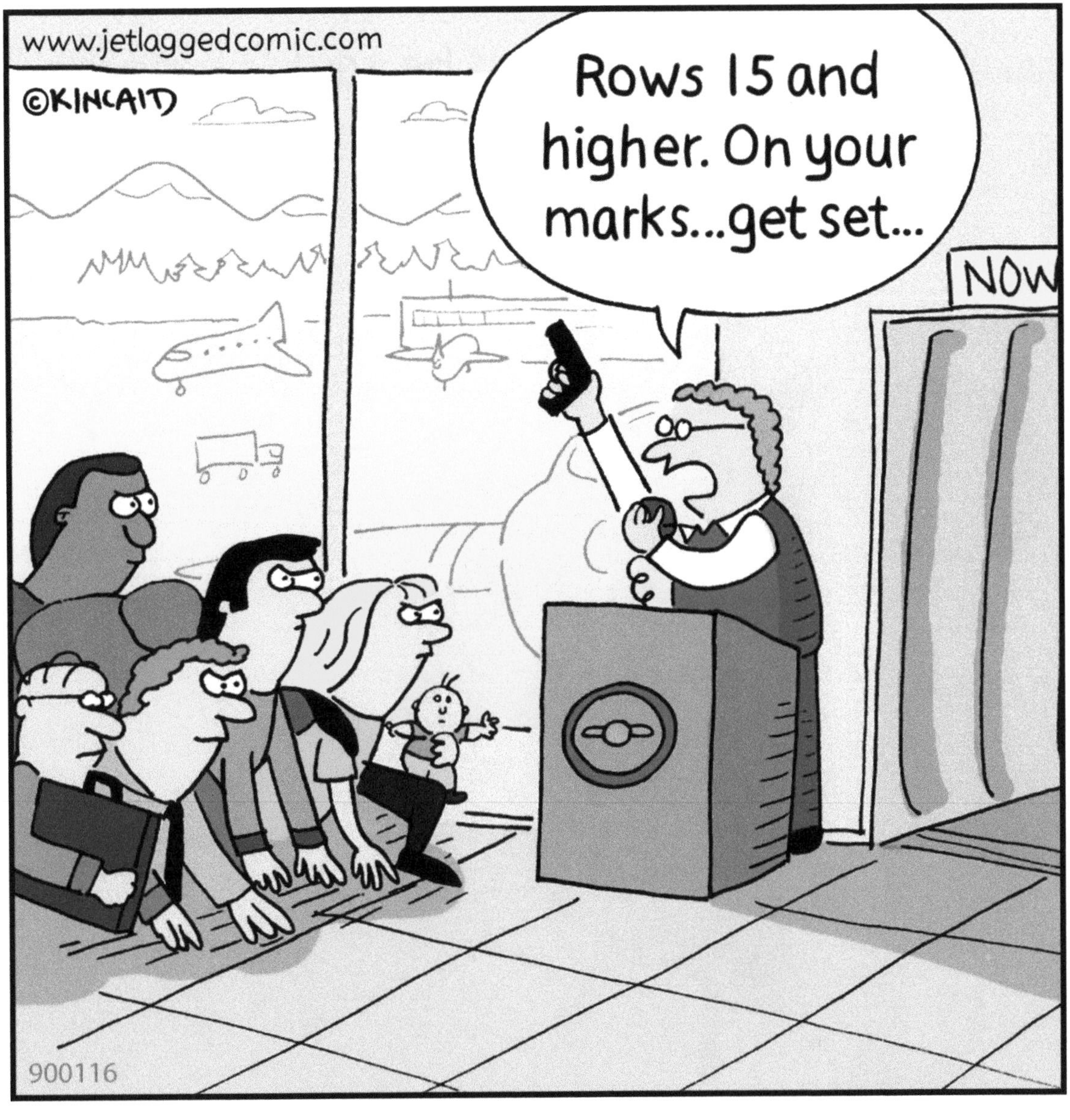
www.jetlaggedcomic.com
©KINCAID
Rows 15 and higher. On your marks...get set...
NOW
900116

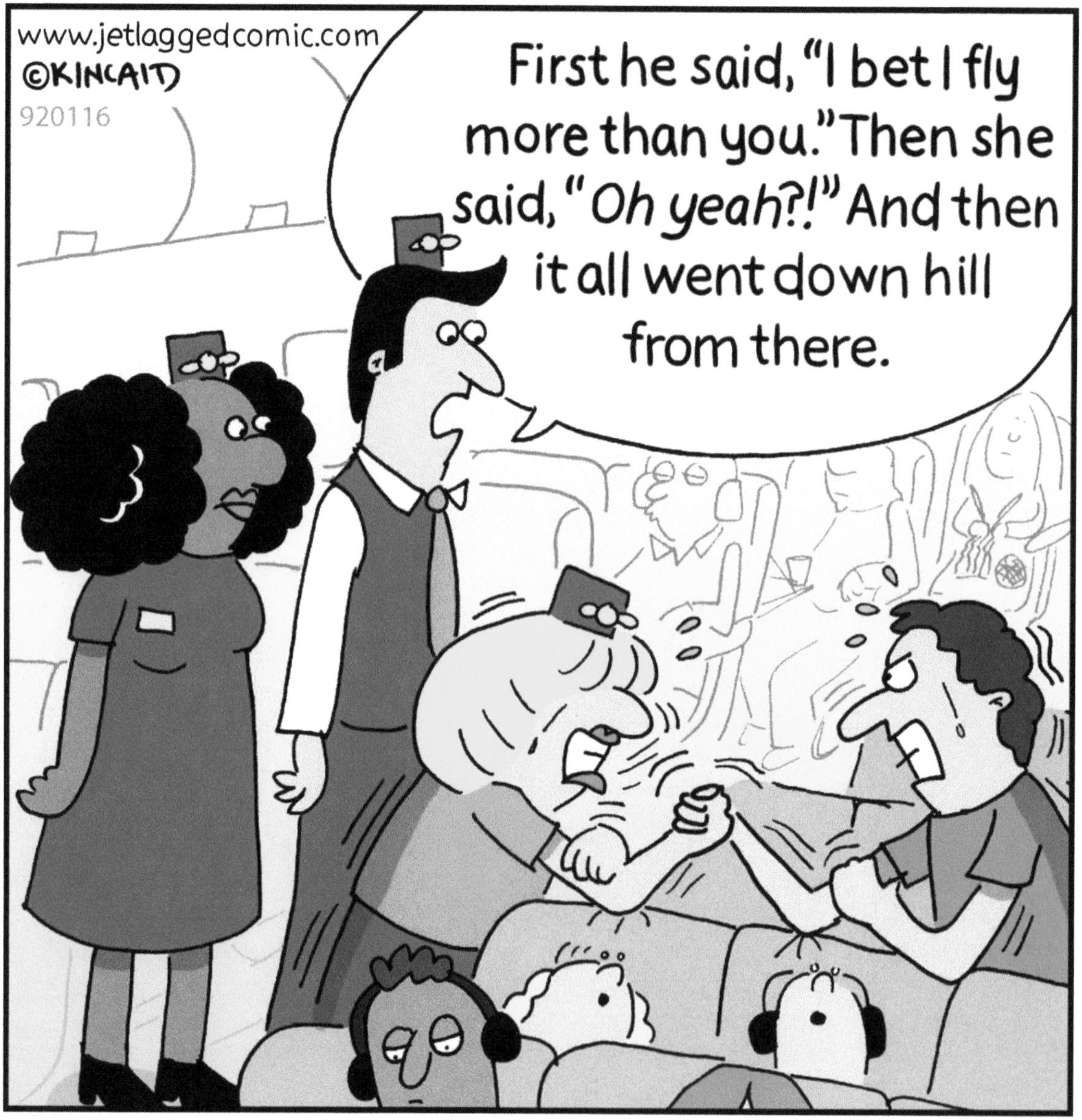
www.jetlaggedcomic.com
©KINCAID
920116
First he said, "I bet I fly more than you." Then she said, "*Oh yeah?!*" And then it all went down hill from there.

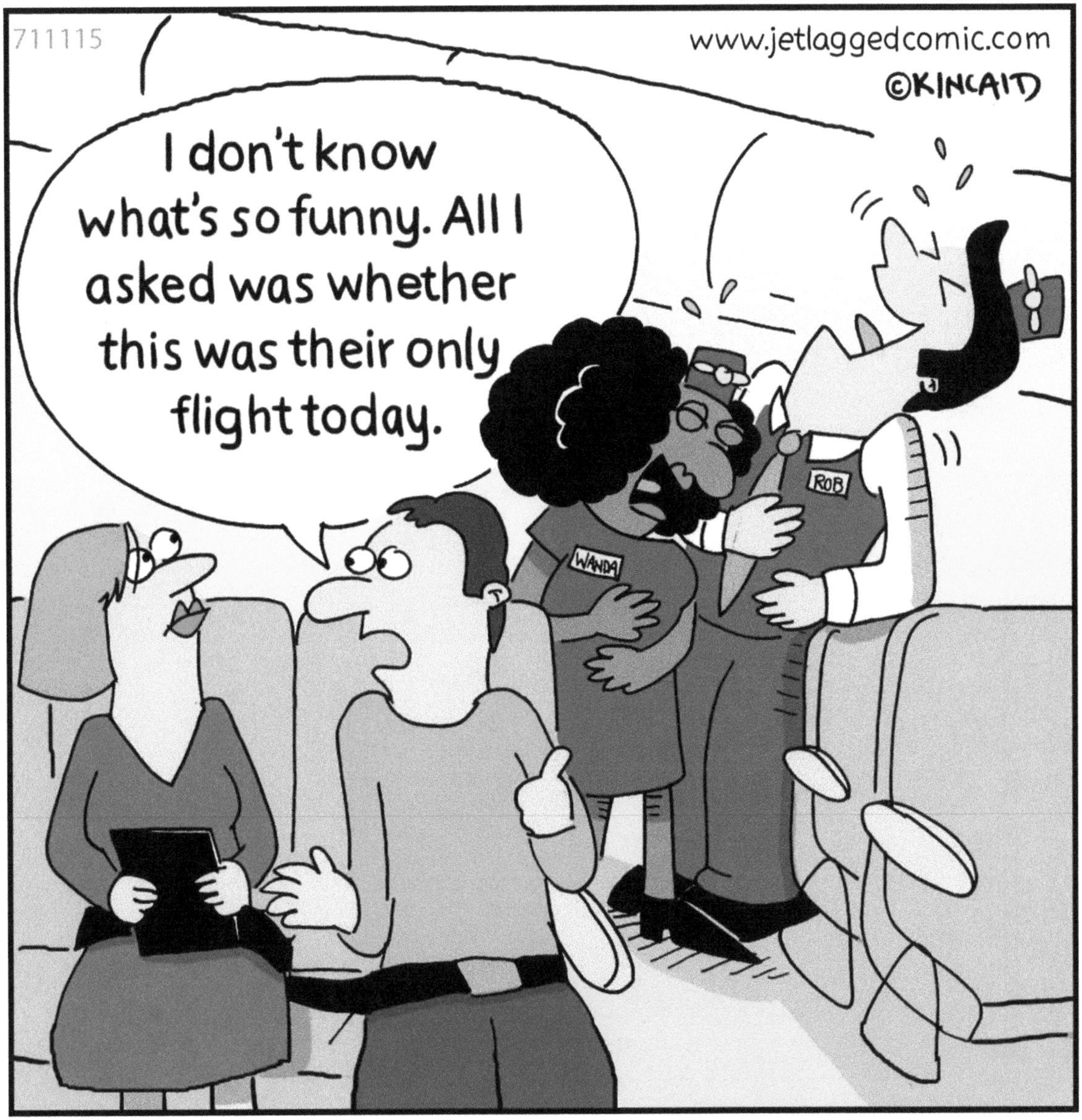
711115
www.jetlaggedcomic.com
©KINCAID
I don't know what's so funny. All I asked was whether this was their only flight today.
WANDA
ROB

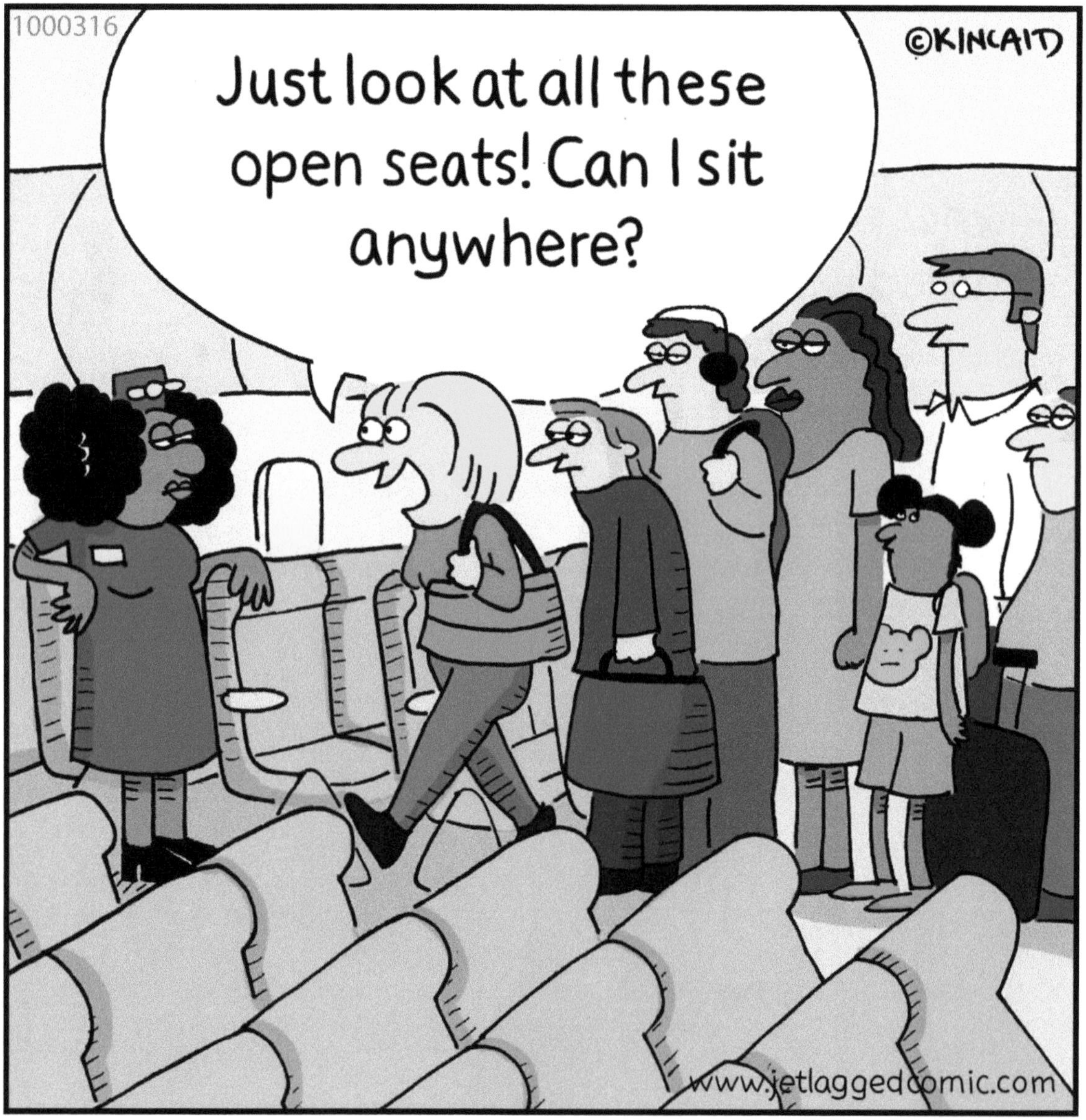
1000316
©KINCAID
Just look at all these open seats! Can I sit anywhere?
www.jetlaggedcomic.com

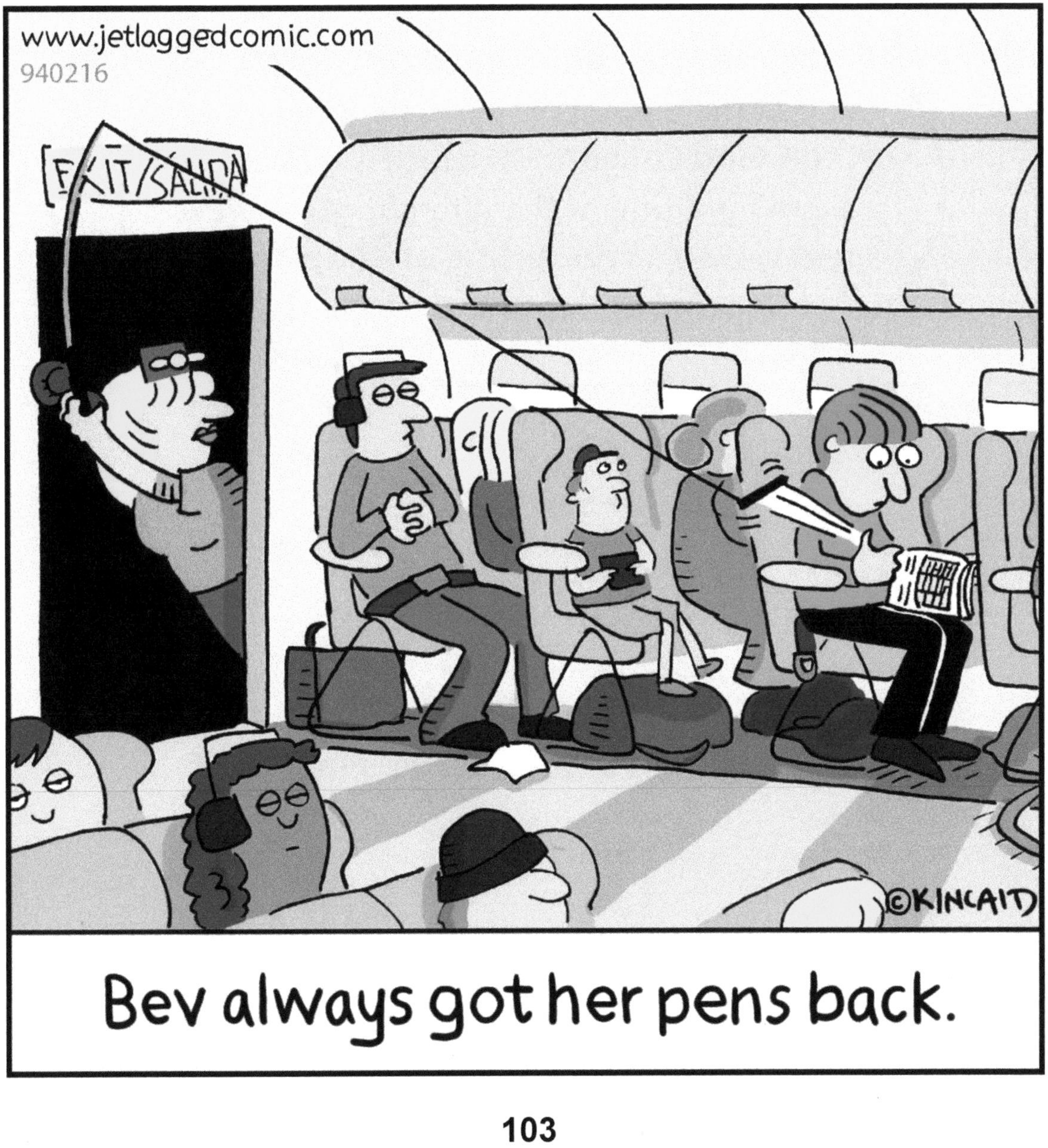
www.jetlaggedcomic.com
940216
EXIT/SALIDA
©KINCAID

Bev always got her pens back.

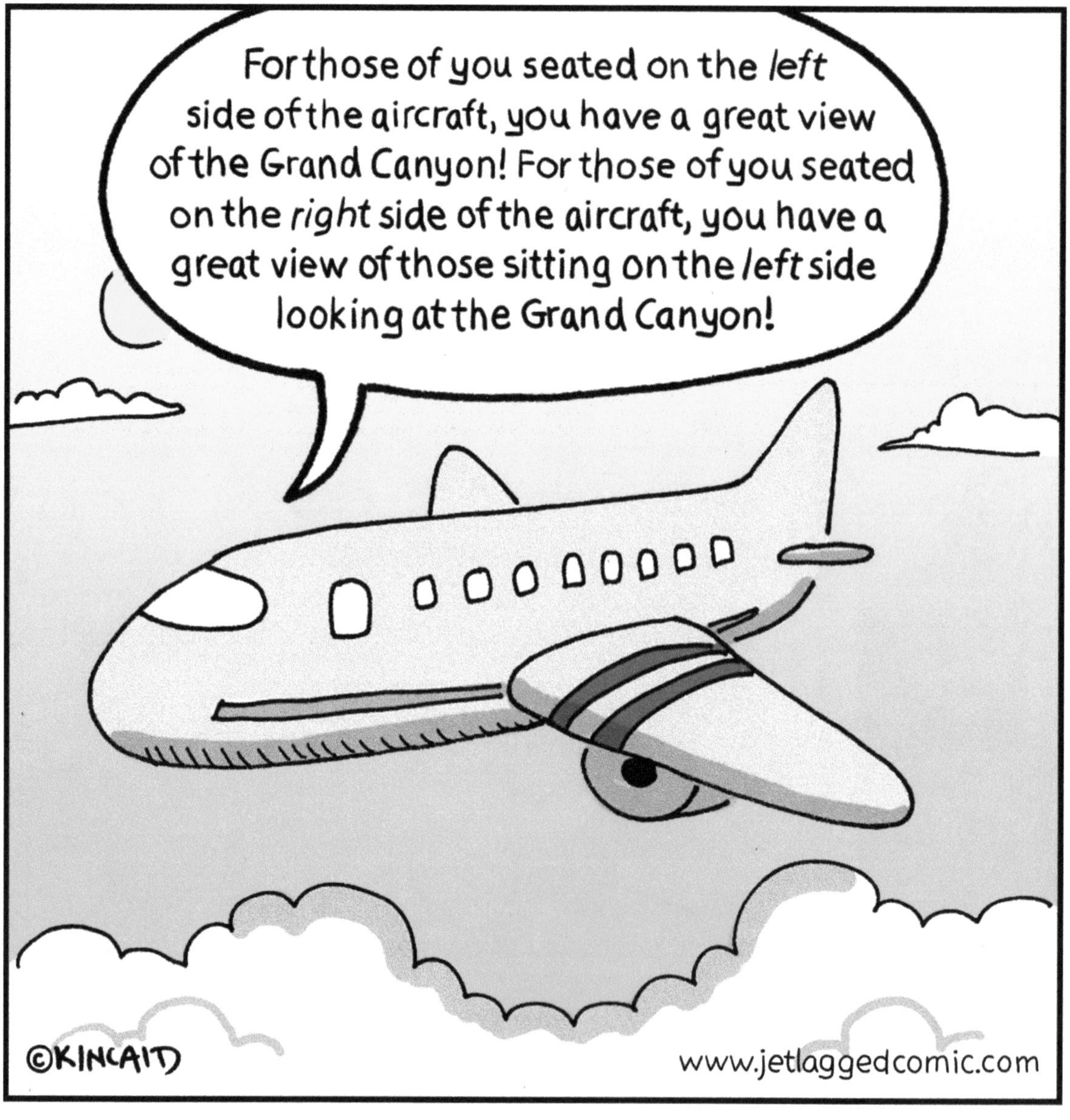
For those of you seated on the *left* side of the aircraft, you have a great view of the Grand Canyon! For those of you seated on the *right* side of the aircraft, you have a great view of those sitting on the *left* side looking at the Grand Canyon!
©KINCAID
www.jetlaggedcomic.com

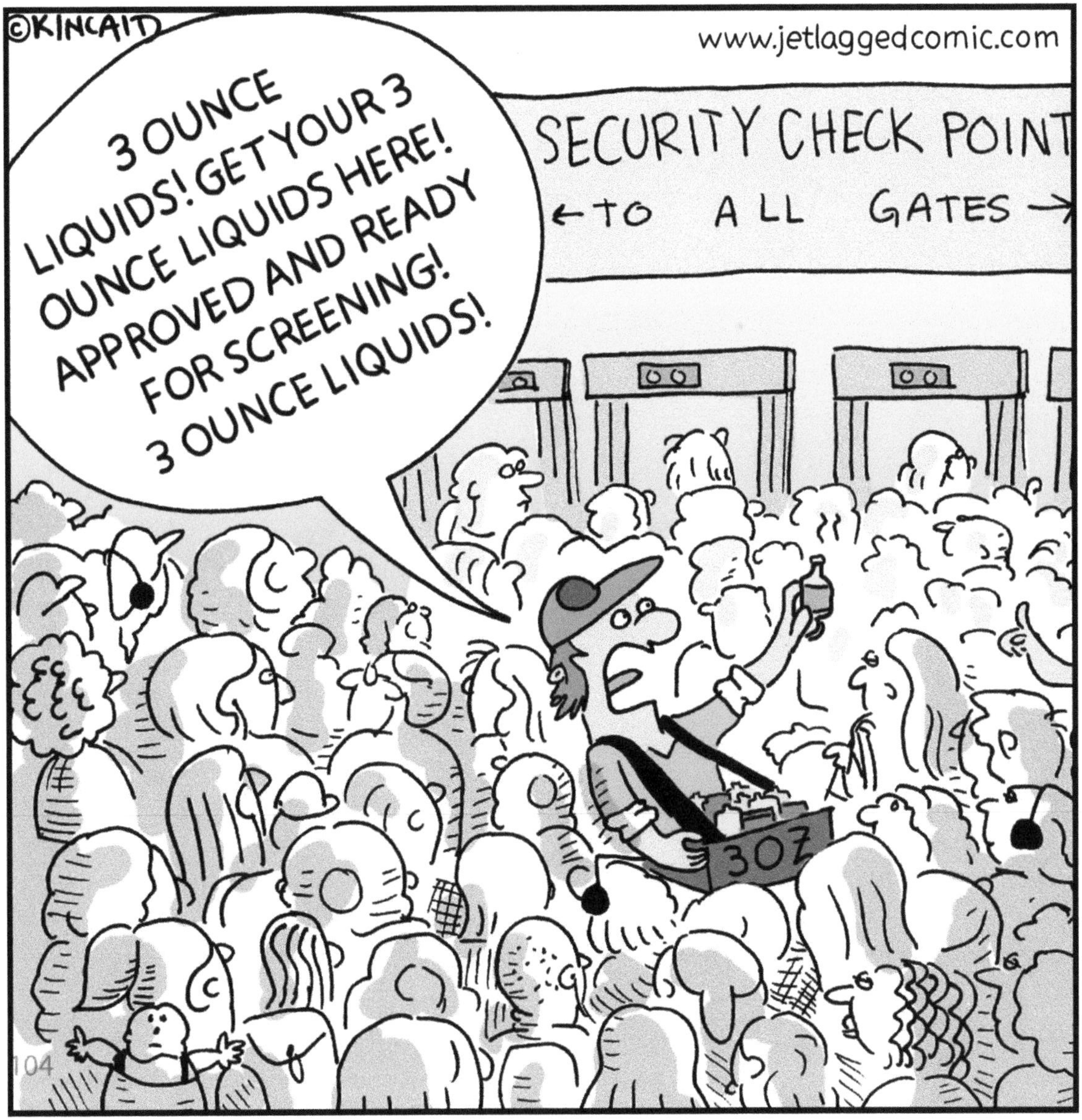
©KINCAID
www.jetlaggedcomic.com
3 OUNCE LIQUIDS! GET YOUR 3 OUNCE LIQUIDS HERE! APPROVED AND READY FOR SCREENING! 3 OUNCE LIQUIDS!
SECURITY CHECK POINT
← TO ALL GATES →
3OZ
104

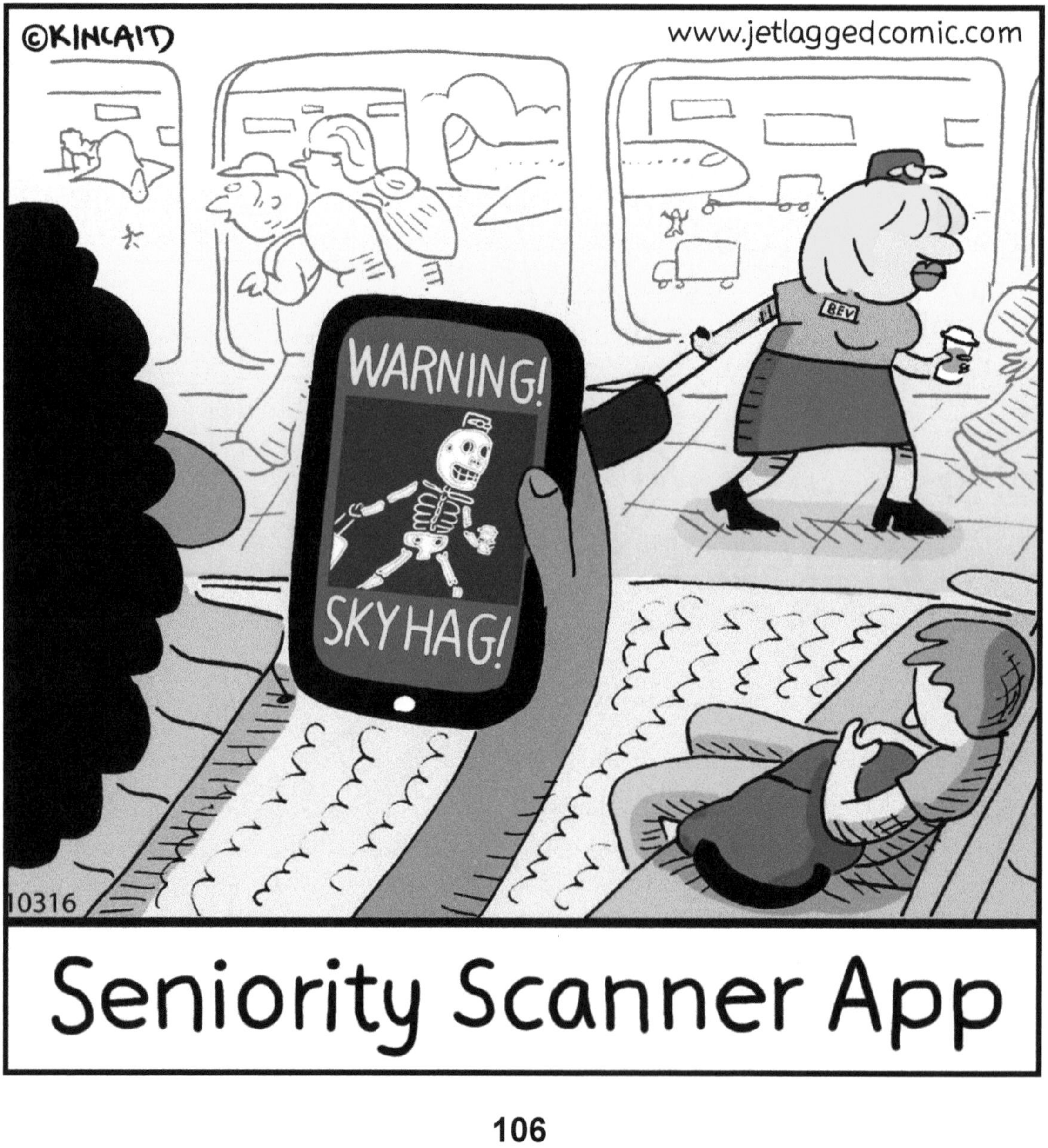
©KINCAID
www.jetlaggedcomic.com
WARNING!
SKYHAG!
BEV
10316

Seniority Scanner App

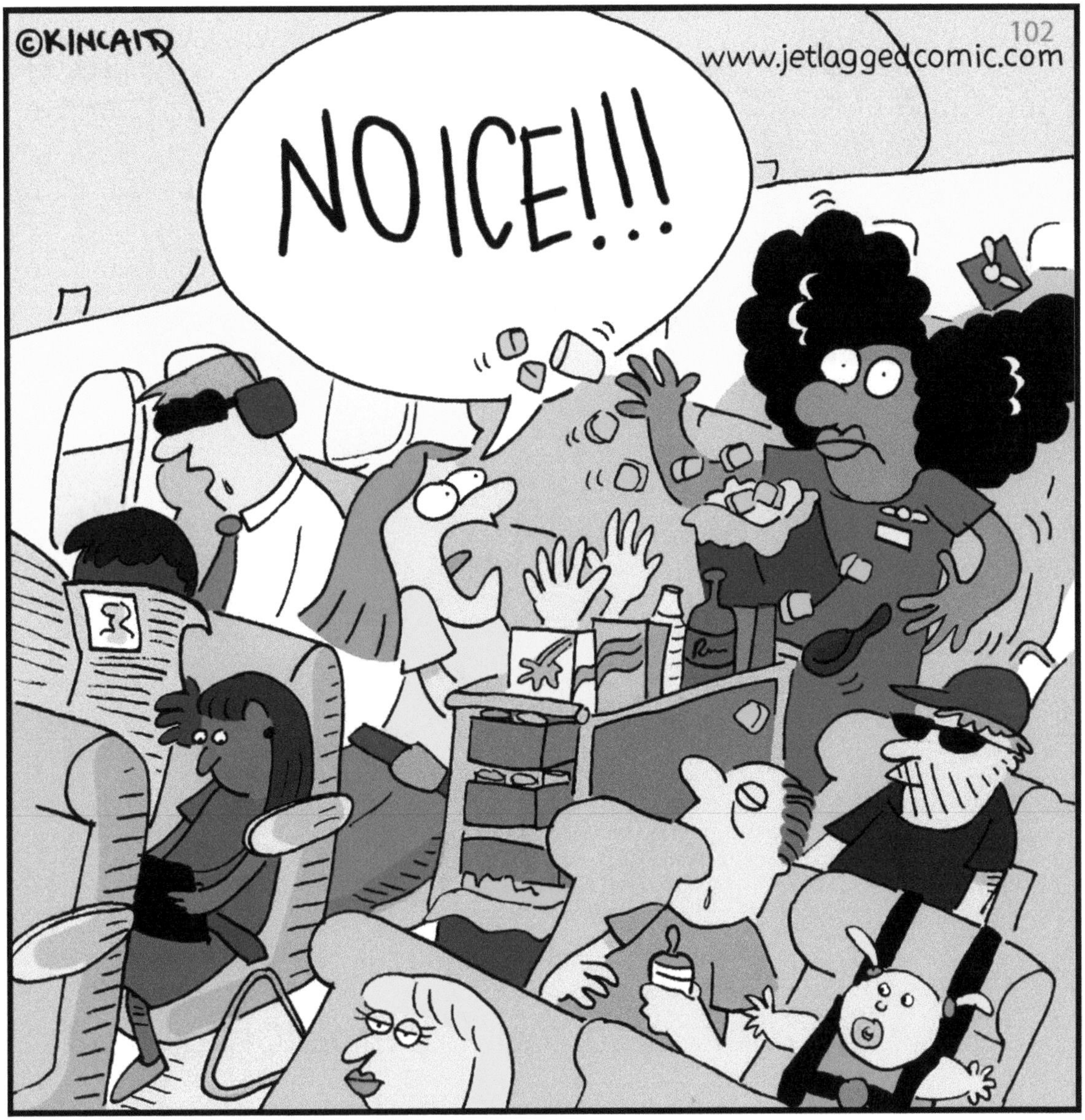
©KINCAID
102
www.jetlaggedcomic.com
NO ICE!!!

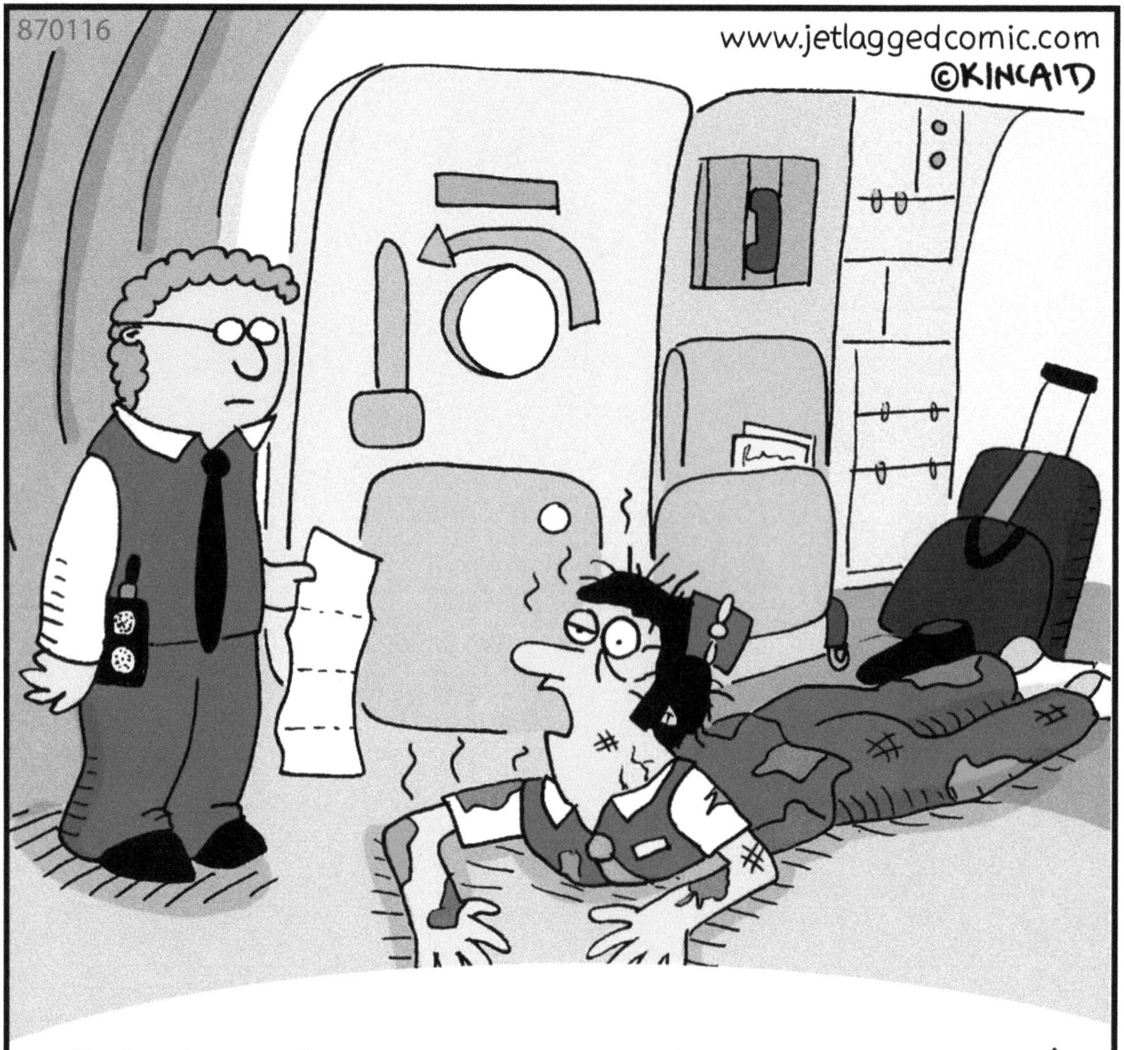
870116
www.jetlaggedcomic.com
©KINCAID

"That trip looked so much better on paper."

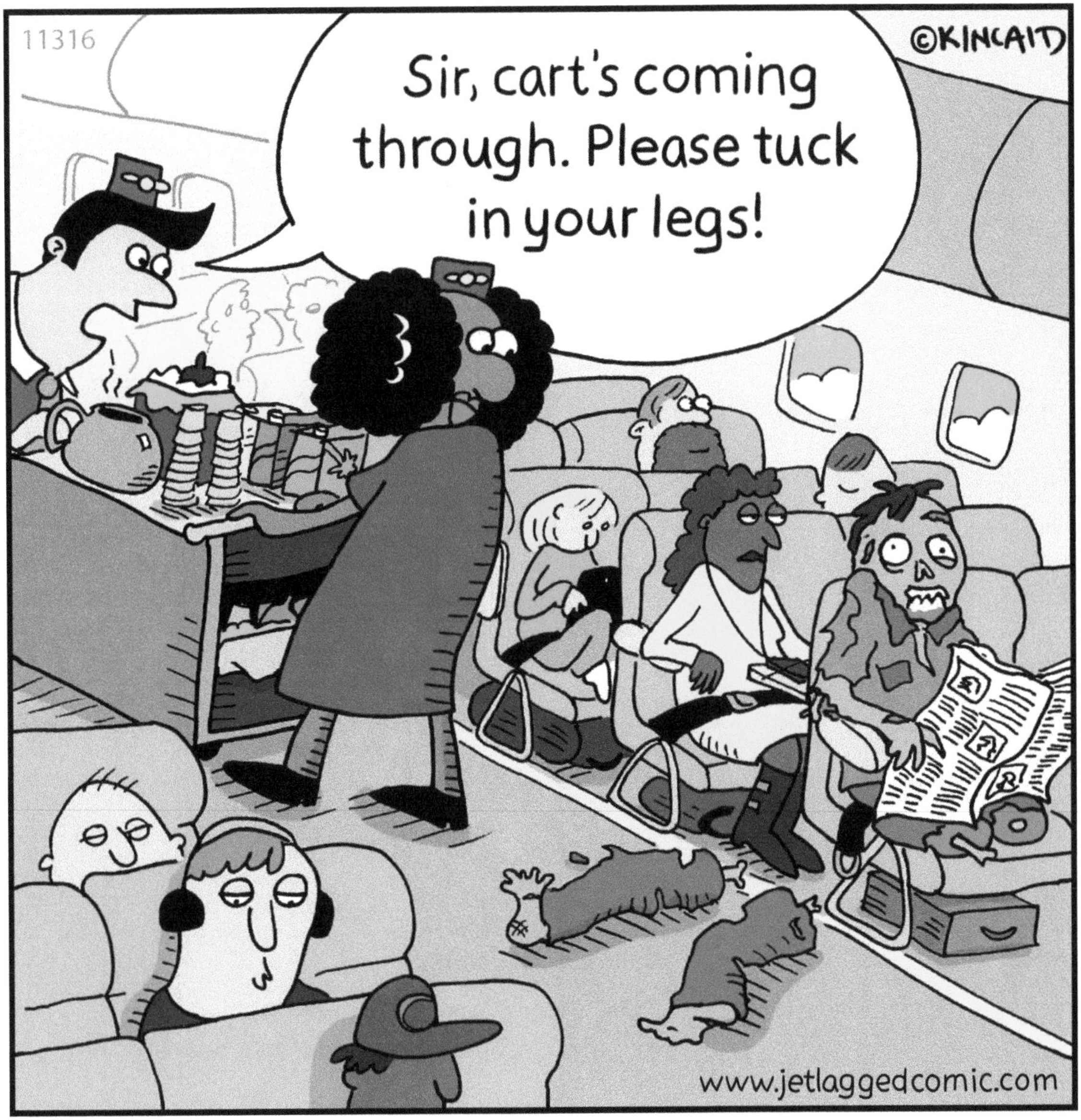
11316
©KINCAID
Sir, cart's coming through. Please tuck in your legs!
www.jetlaggedcomic.com

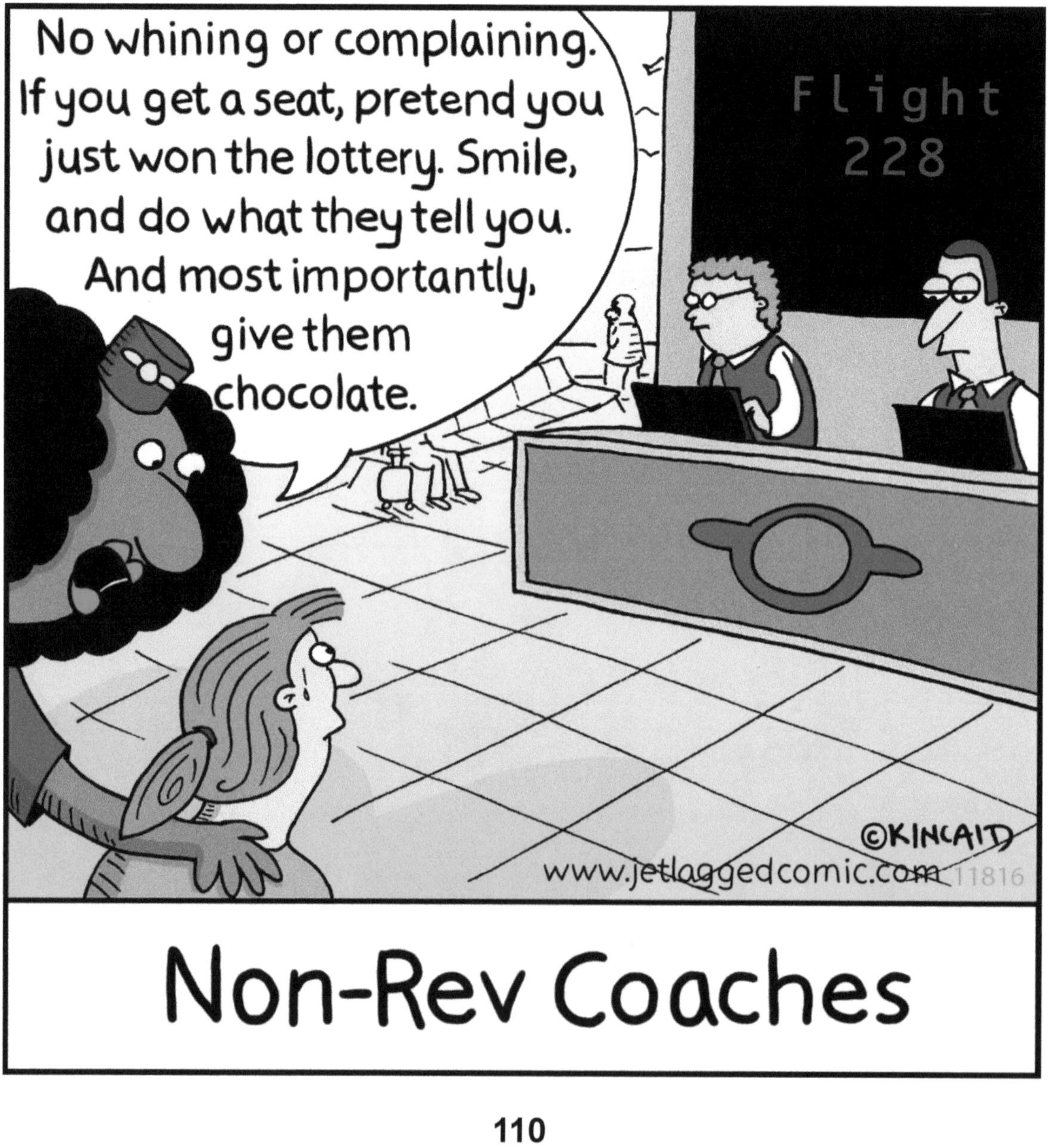
No whining or complaining. If you get a seat, pretend you just won the lottery. Smile, and do what they tell you. And most importantly, give them chocolate.
Flight 228
©KINCAID
www.jetlaggedcomic.com 11816

Non-Rev Coaches

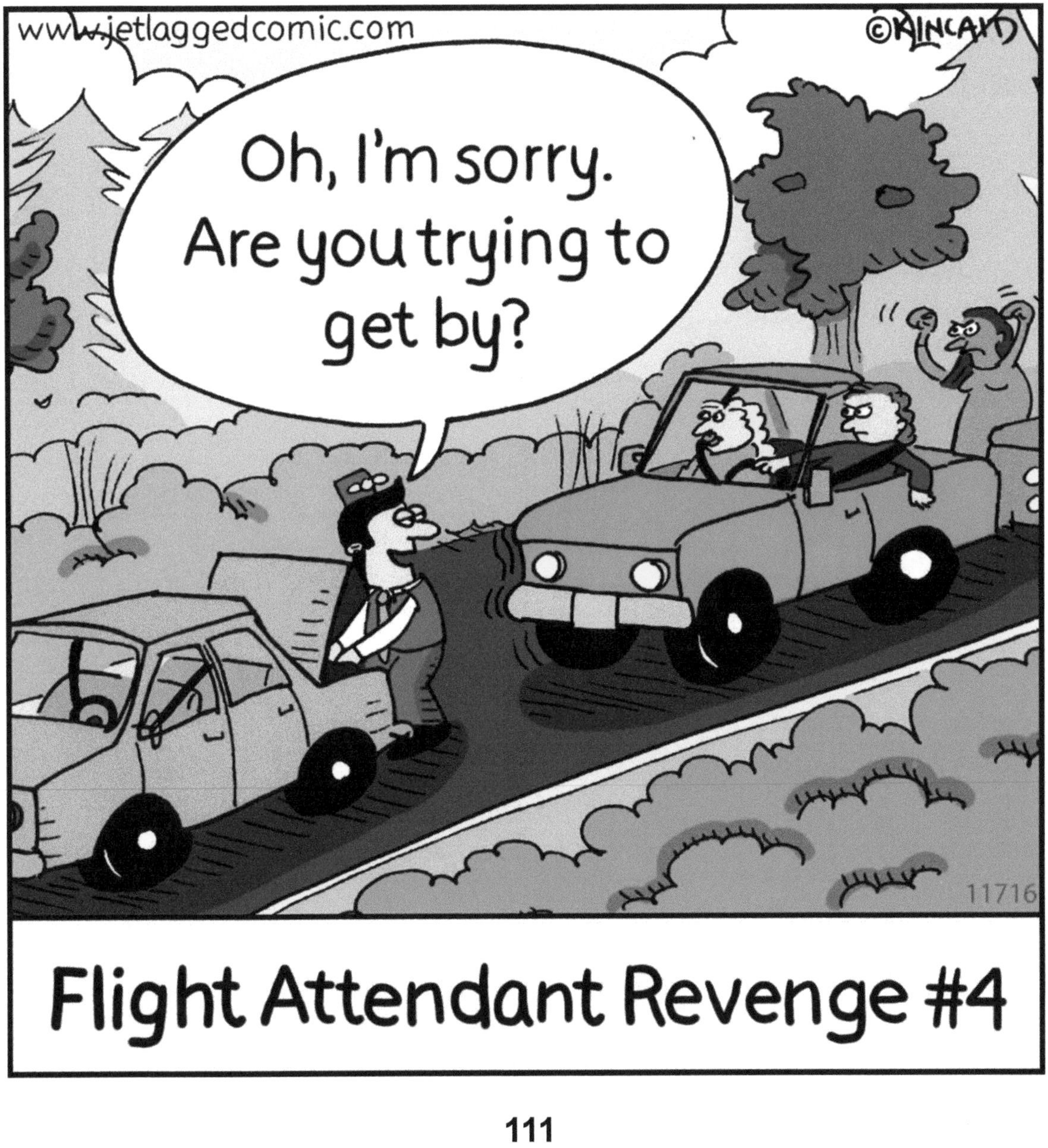
www.jetlaggedcomic.com
©KINCAID
Oh, I'm sorry. Are you trying to get by?
11716

Flight Attendant Revenge #4

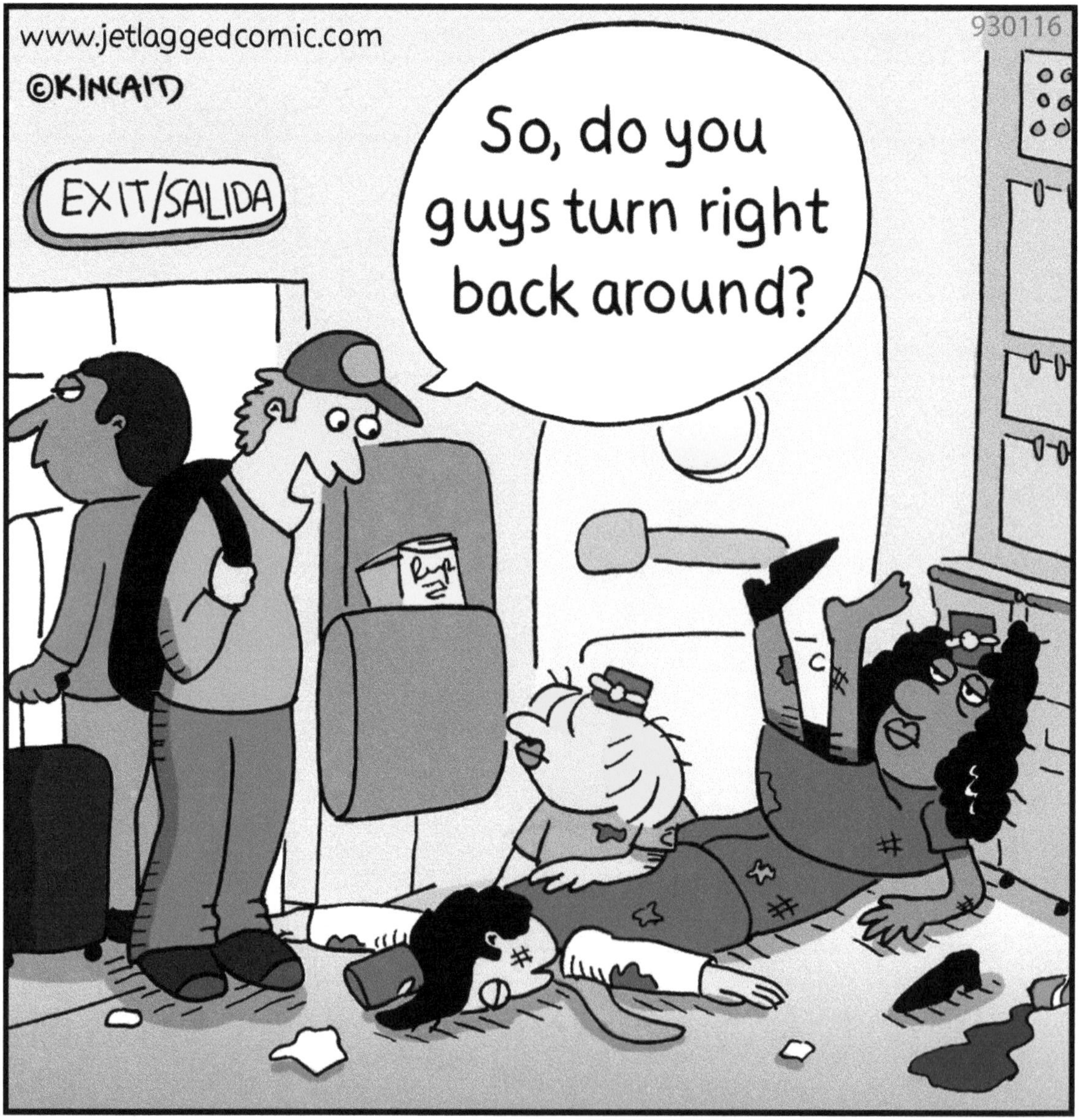
www.jetlaggedcomic.com
©KINCAID
930116
EXIT/SALIDA
So, do you guys turn right back around?

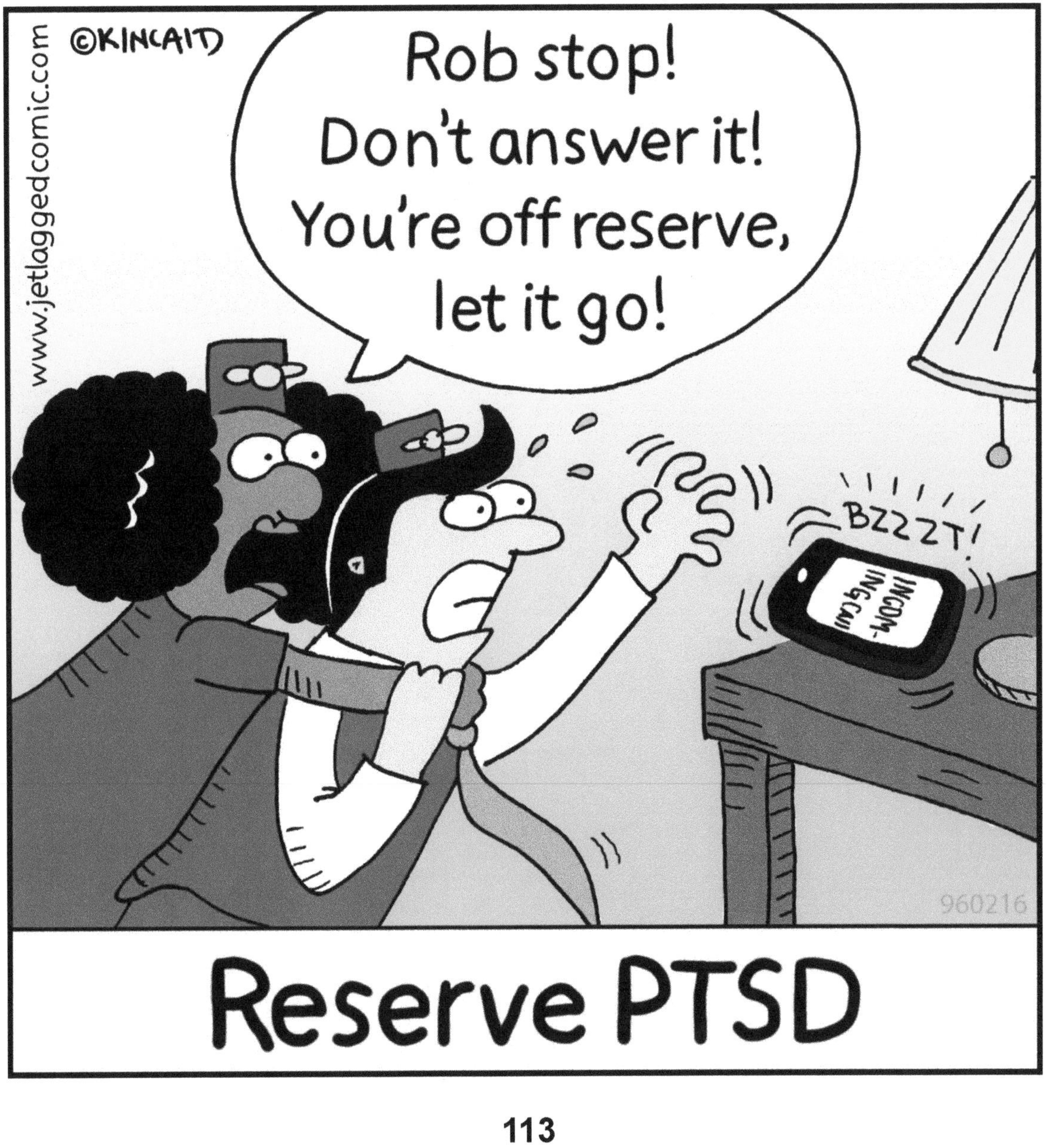
©KINCAID
www.jetlaggedcomic.com
Rob stop! Don't answer it! You're off reserve, let it go!
BZZZT!
INCOM-ING CAll
960216

Reserve PTSD

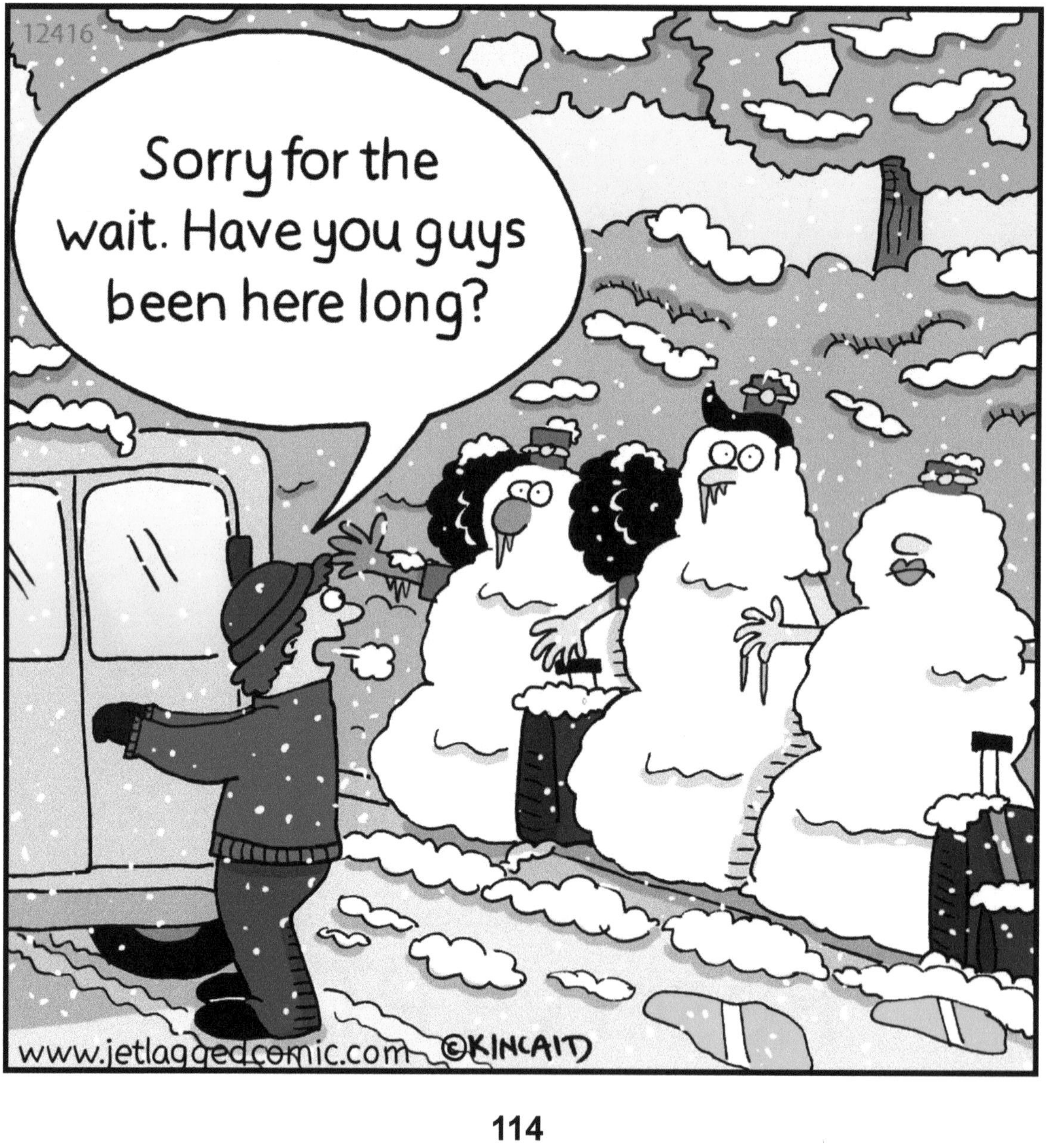
12416
Sorry for the wait. Have you guys been here long?
www.jetlaggedcomic.com
©KINCAID

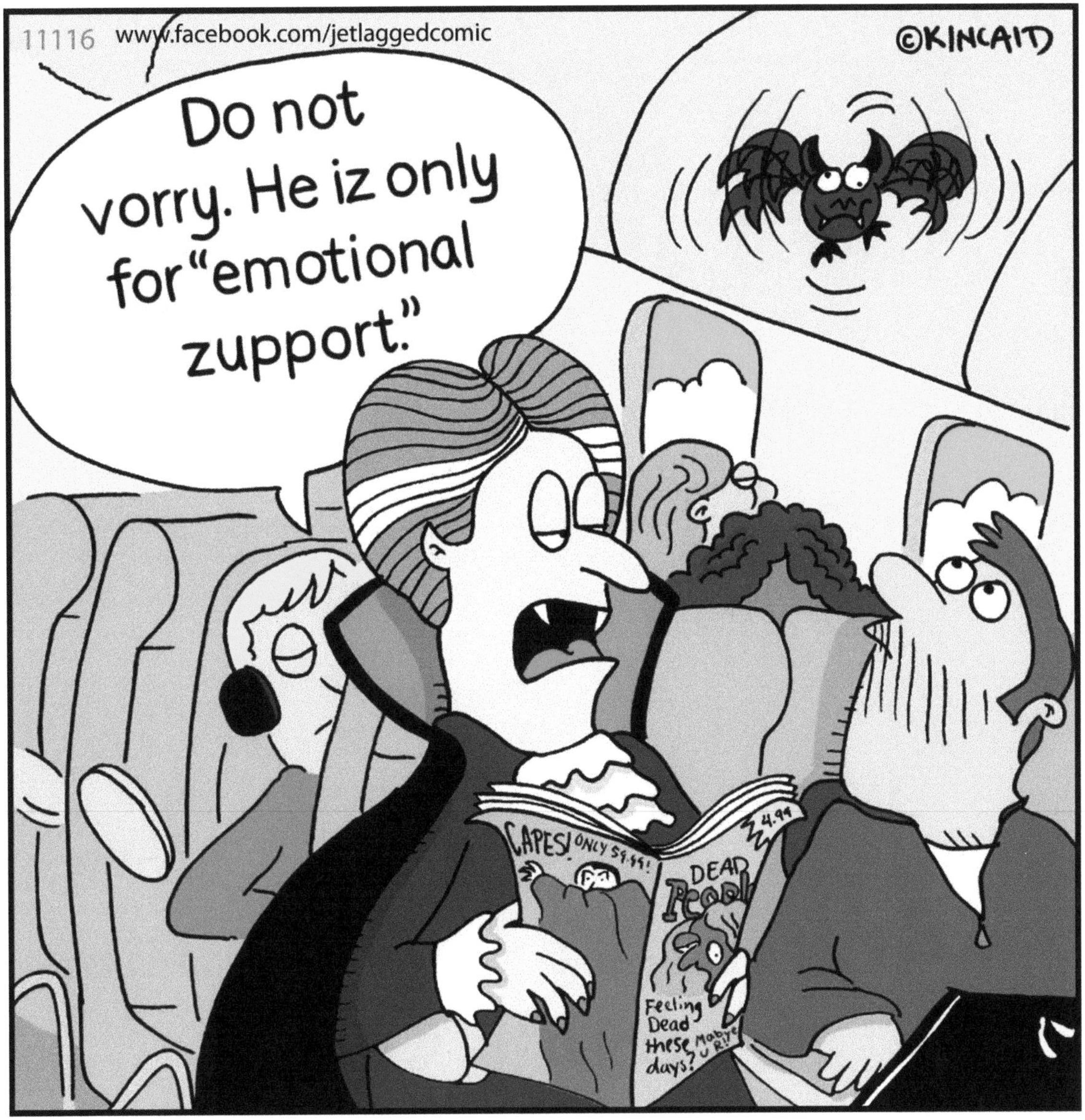
11116 www.facebook.com/jetlaggedcomic
©KINCAID
Do not vorry. He iz only for "emotional zupport."
CAPES! ONLY $9.99!
4.99
DEAD
Feeling Dead these days?

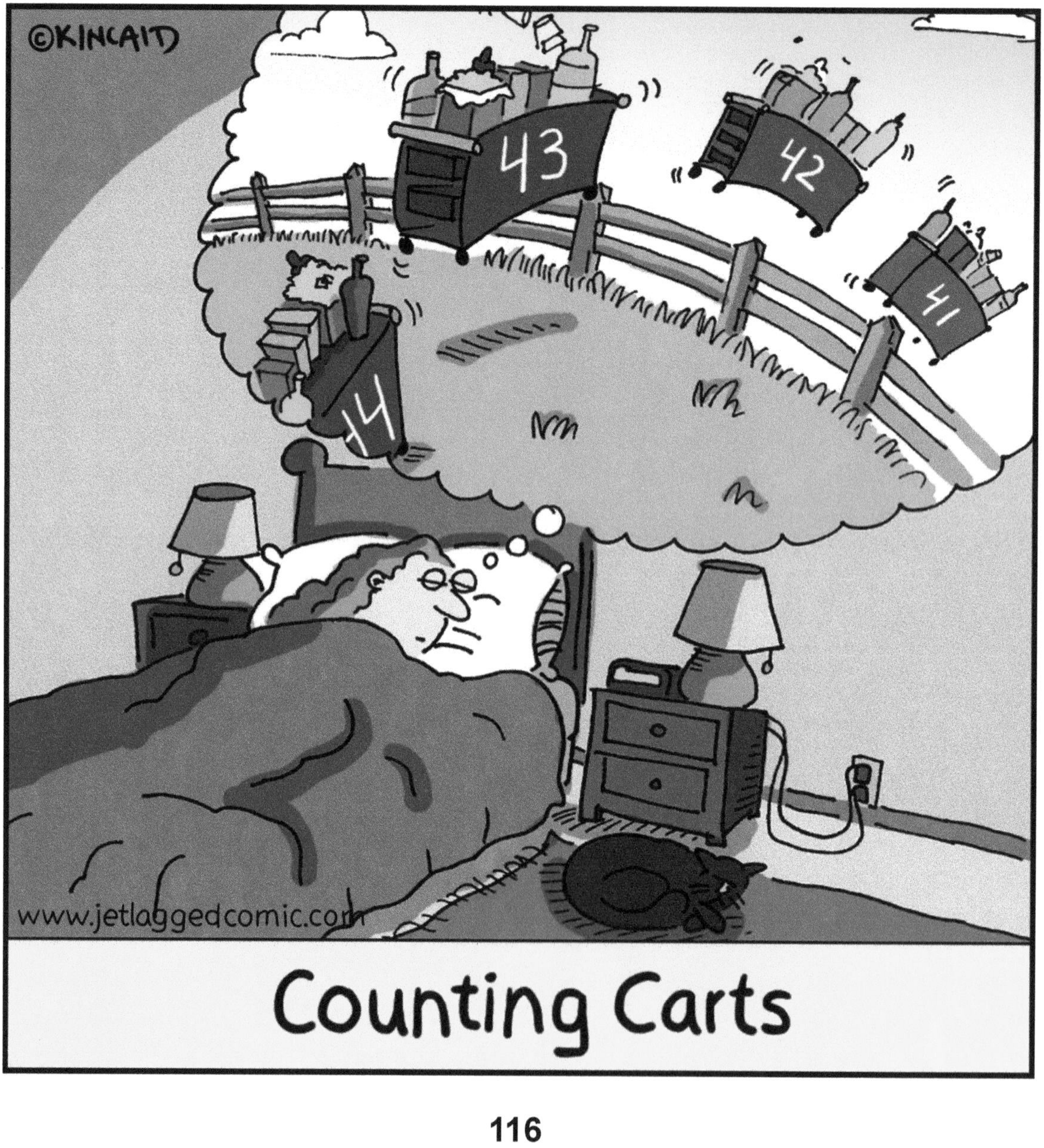
©KINCAID
43
42
41
44
www.jetlaggedcomic.com

Counting Carts

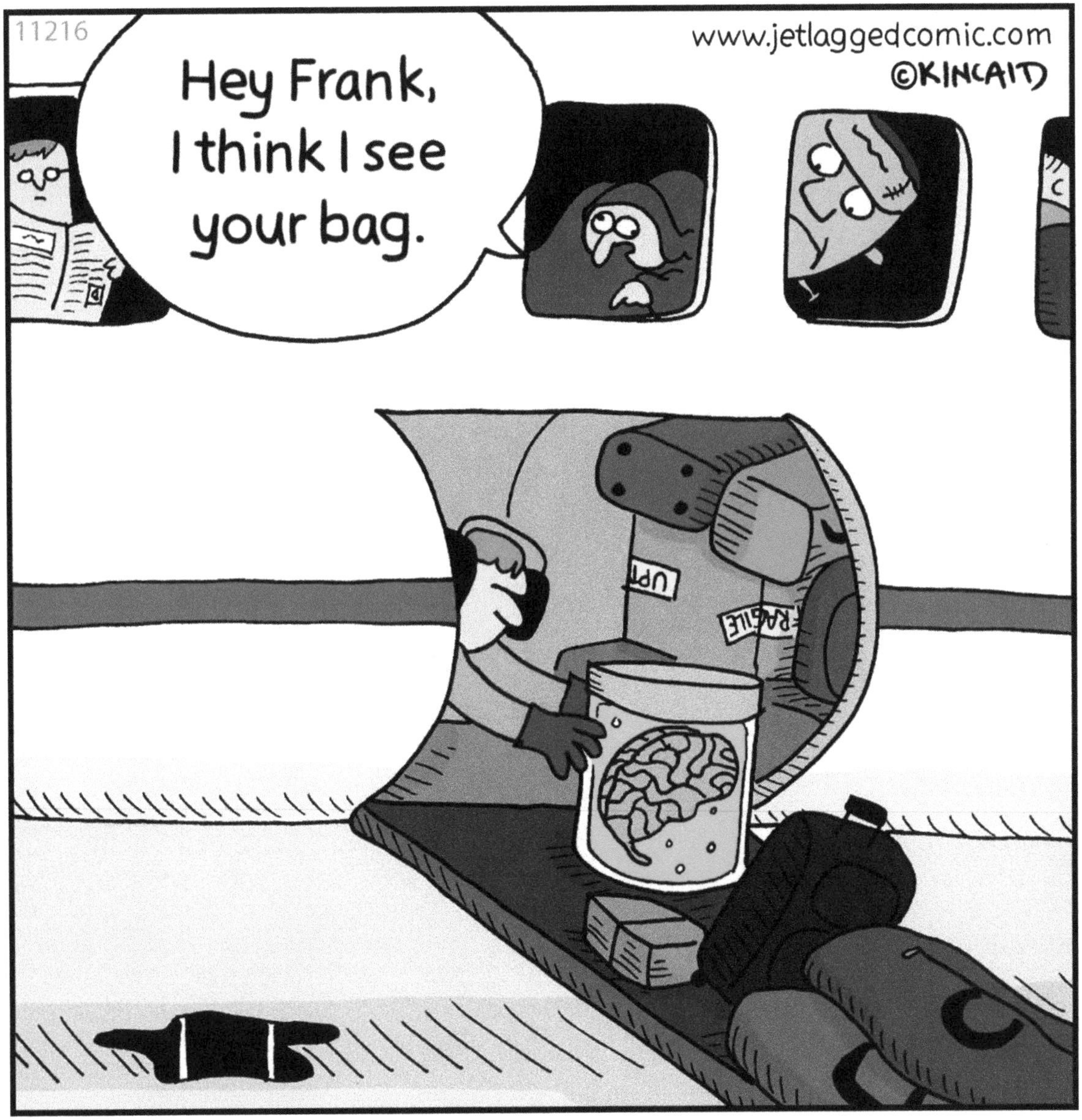
11216
www.jetlaggedcomic.com
©KINCAID
Hey Frank, I think I see your bag.
UP
FRAGILE

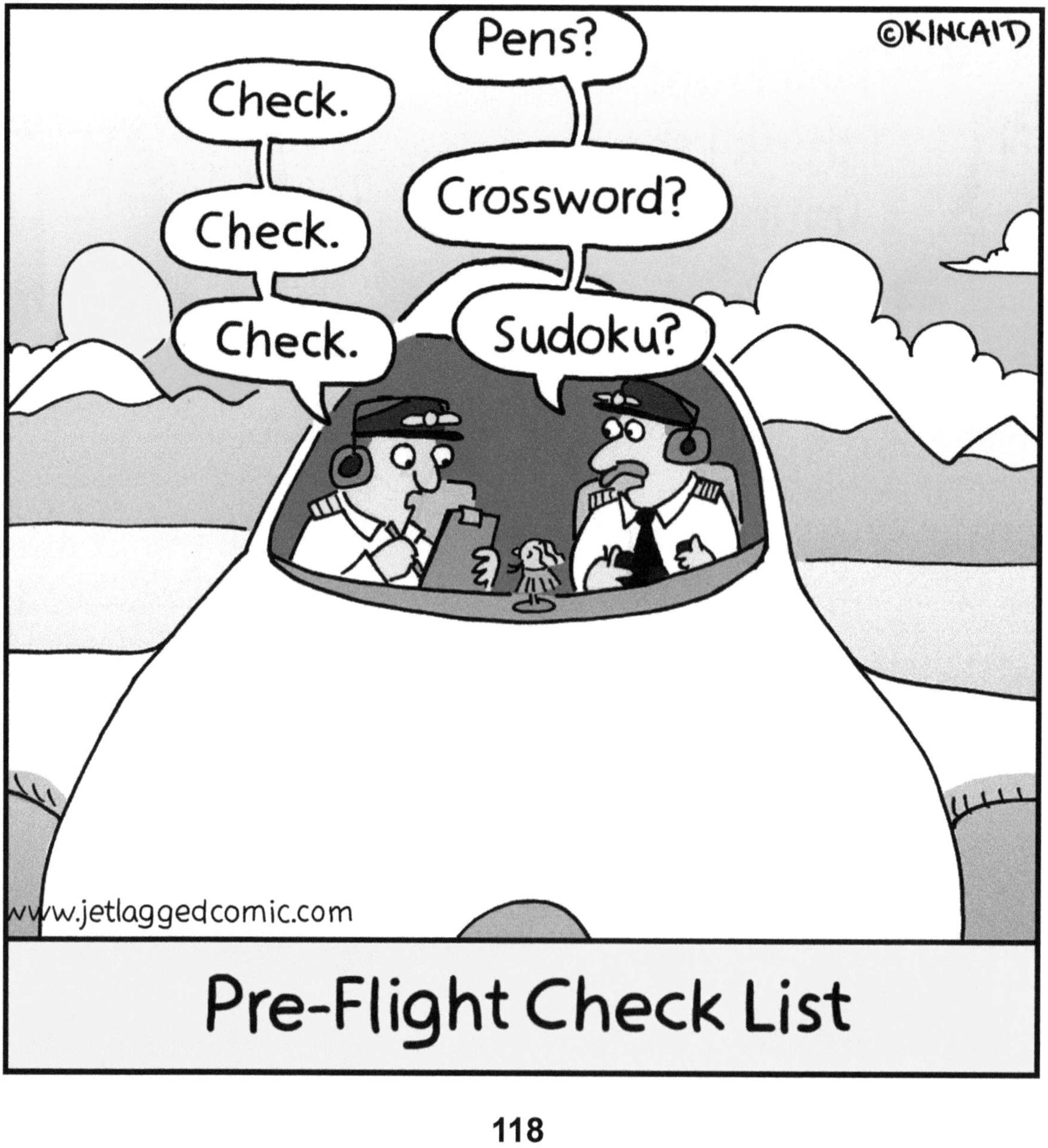
©KINCAID
Pens?
Check.
Crossword?
Check.
Sudoku?
Check.
www.jetlaggedcomic.com

Pre-Flight Check List

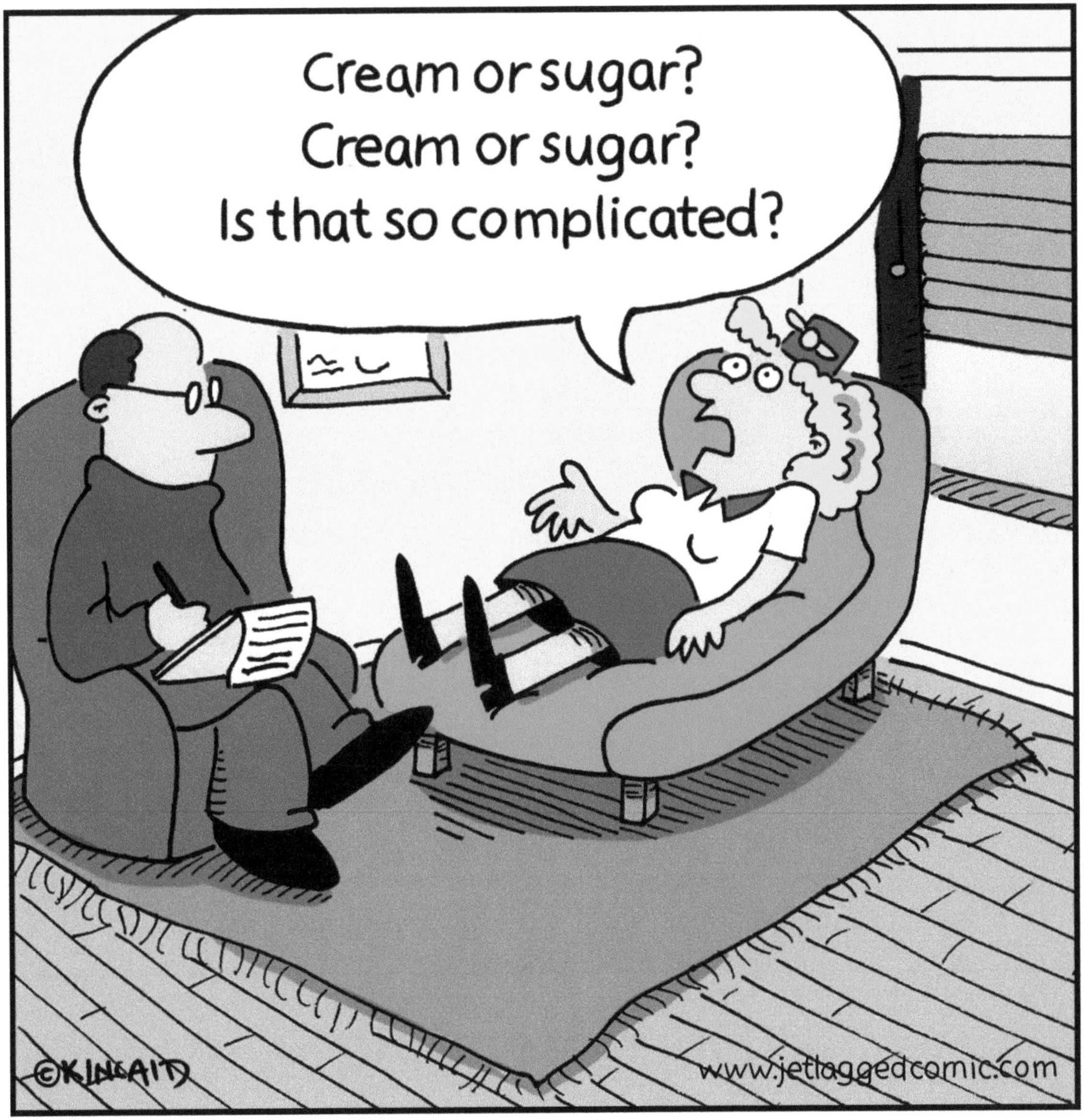
Cream or sugar?
Cream or sugar?
Is that so complicated?
©KINCAID
www.jetlaggedcomic.com

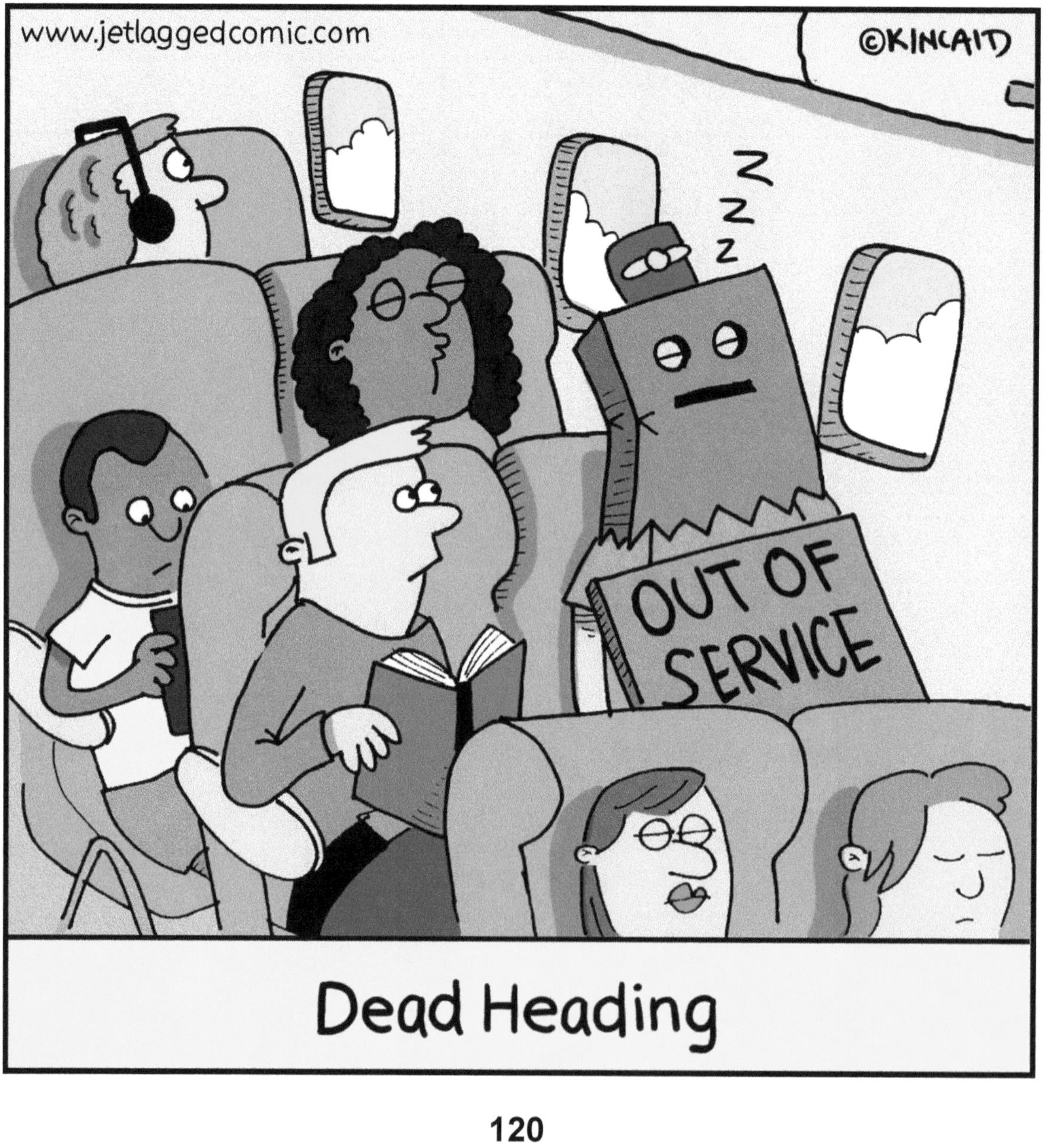
www.jetlaggedcomic.com
©KINCAID
Z Z Z
OUT OF SERVICE

Dead Heading

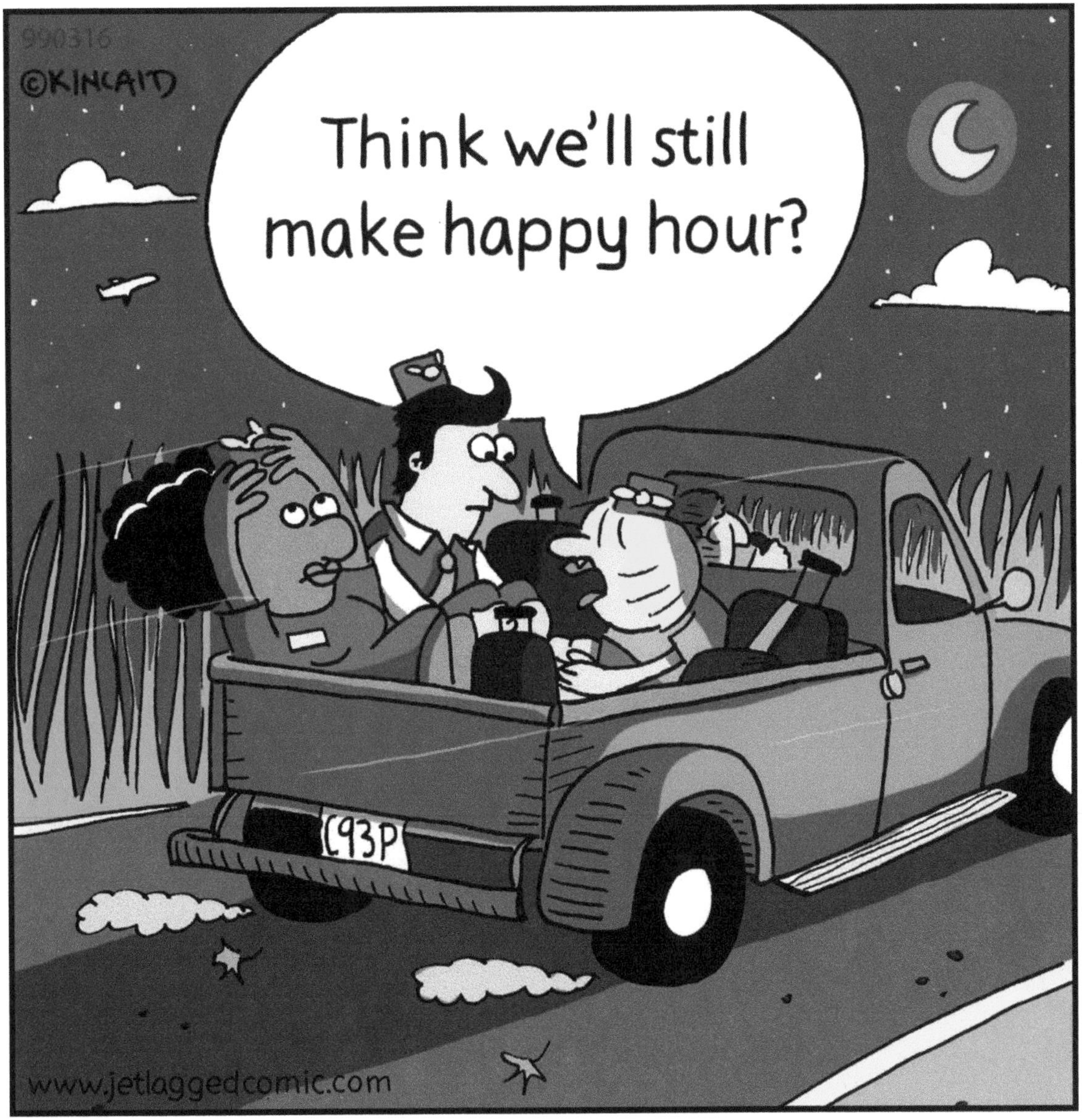
990316
©KINCAID
Think we'll still make happy hour?
C93P
www.jetlaggedcomic.com

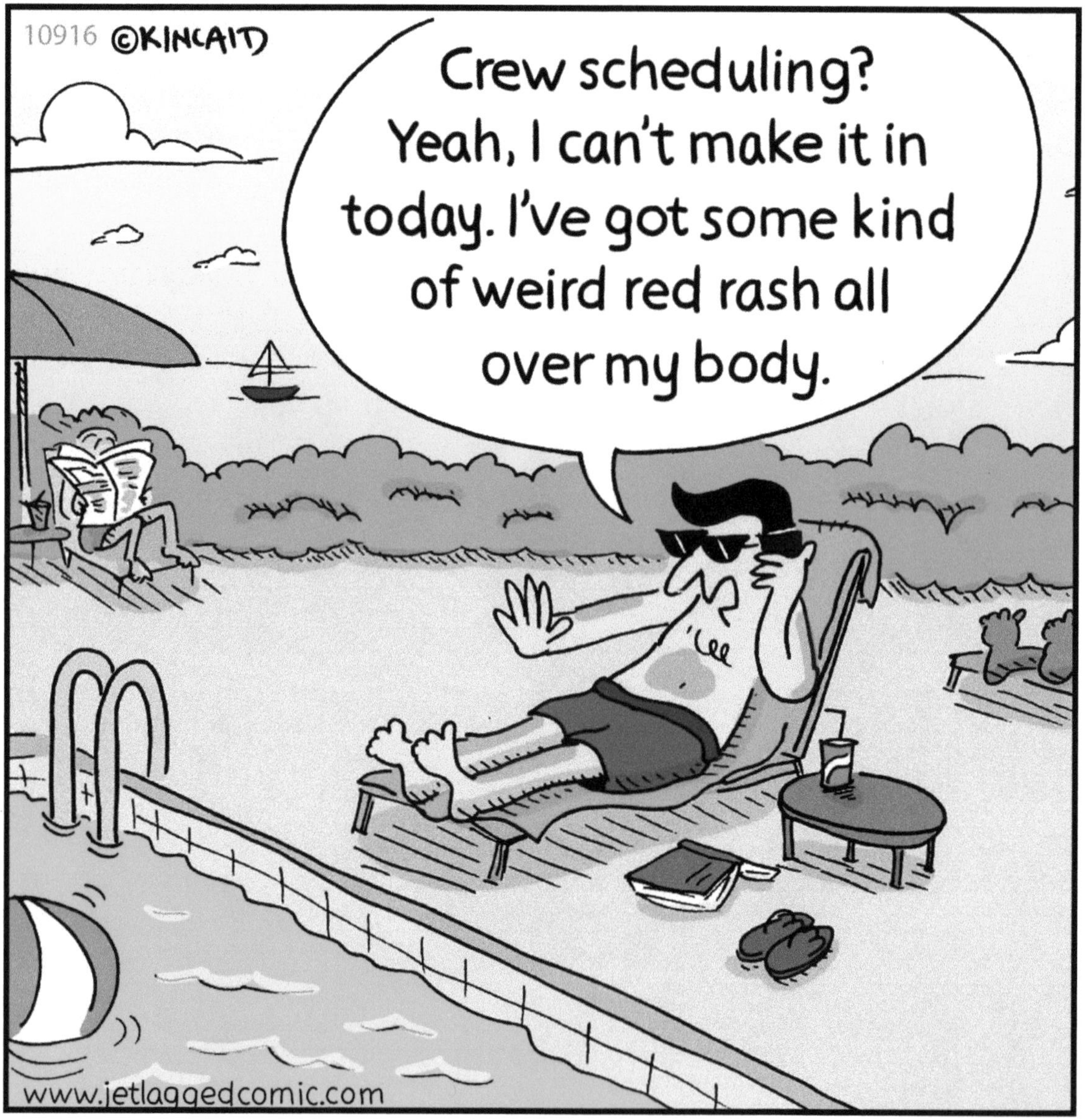
10916 ©KINCAID
Crew scheduling? Yeah, I can't make it in today. I've got some kind of weird red rash all over my body.
www.jetlaggedcomic.com

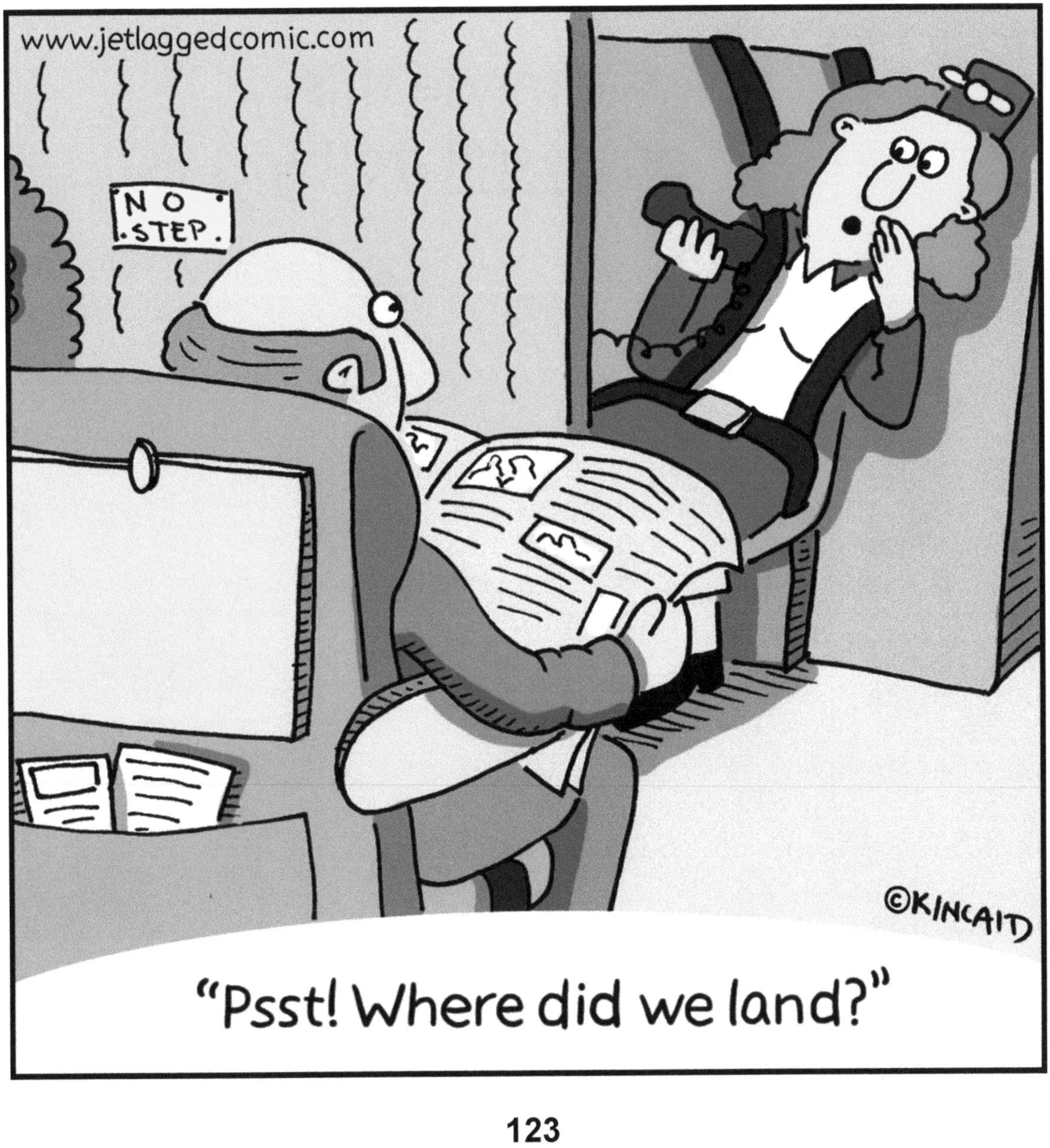
www.jetlaggedcomic.com
NO STEP.
©KINCAID

"Psst! Where did we land?"

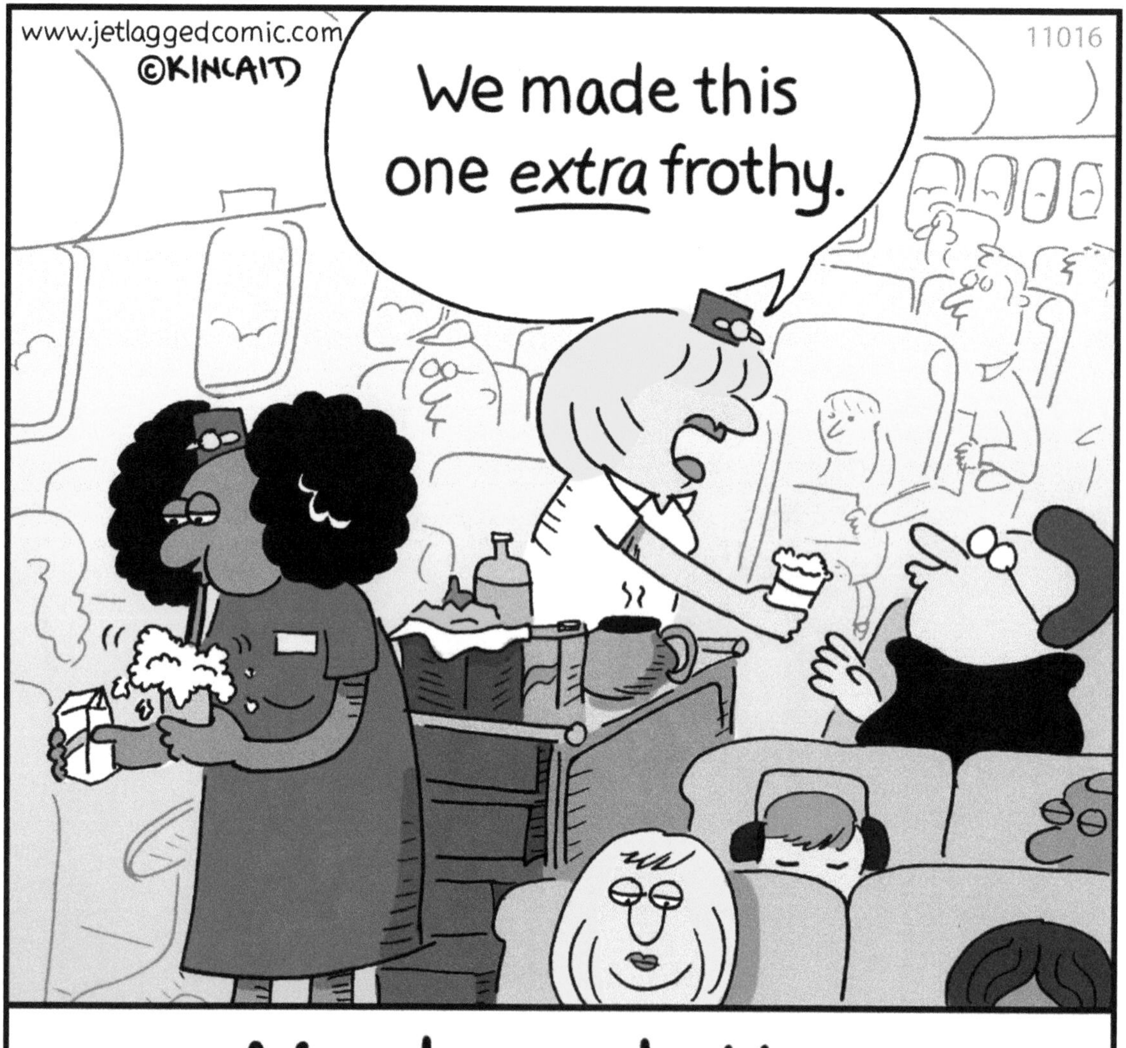
www.jetlaggedcomic.com
©KINCAID
11016
We made this one *extra* frothy.

Airplane lattes

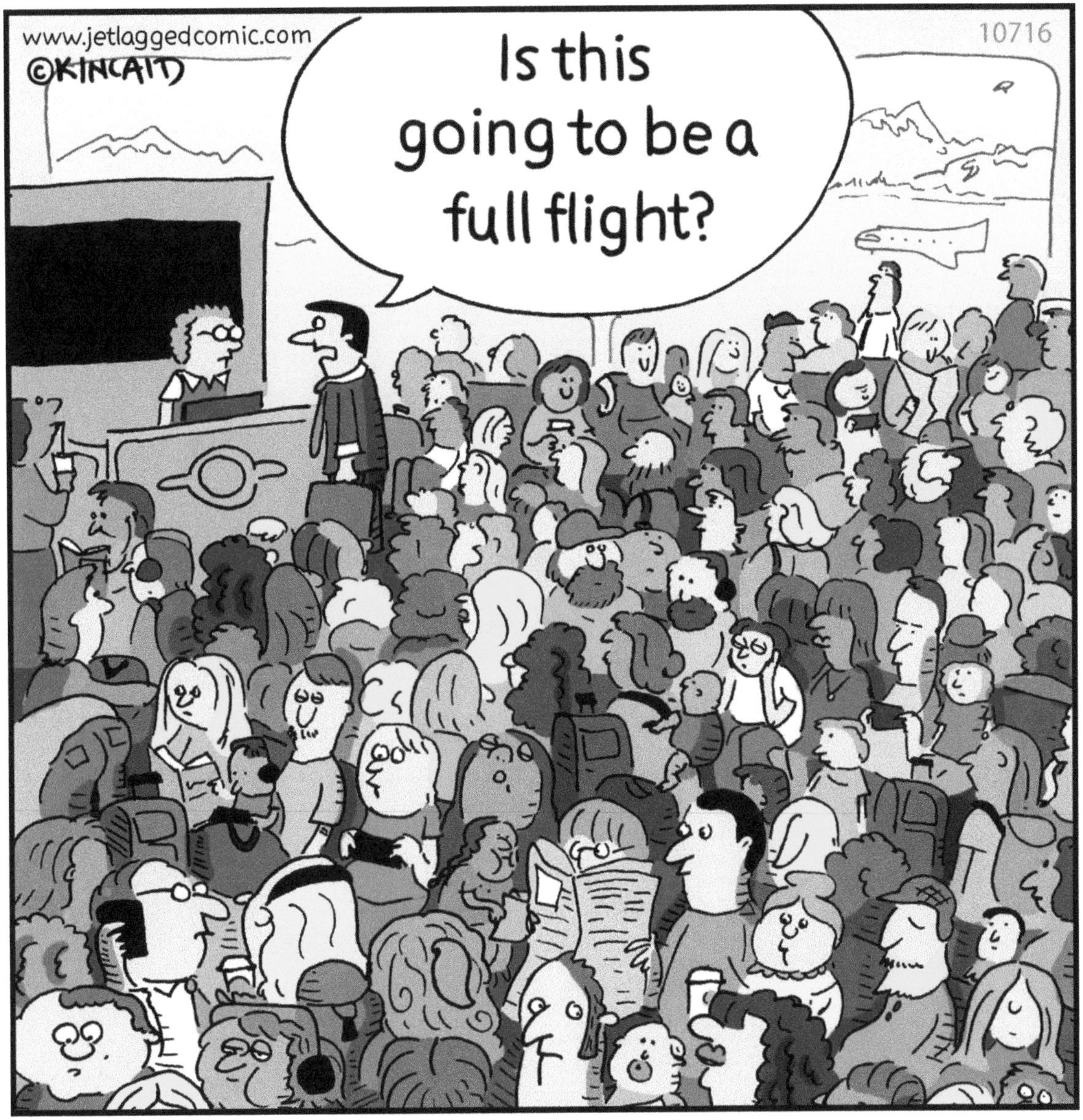
www.jetlaggedcomic.com
©KINCAID
10716
Is this going to be a full flight?

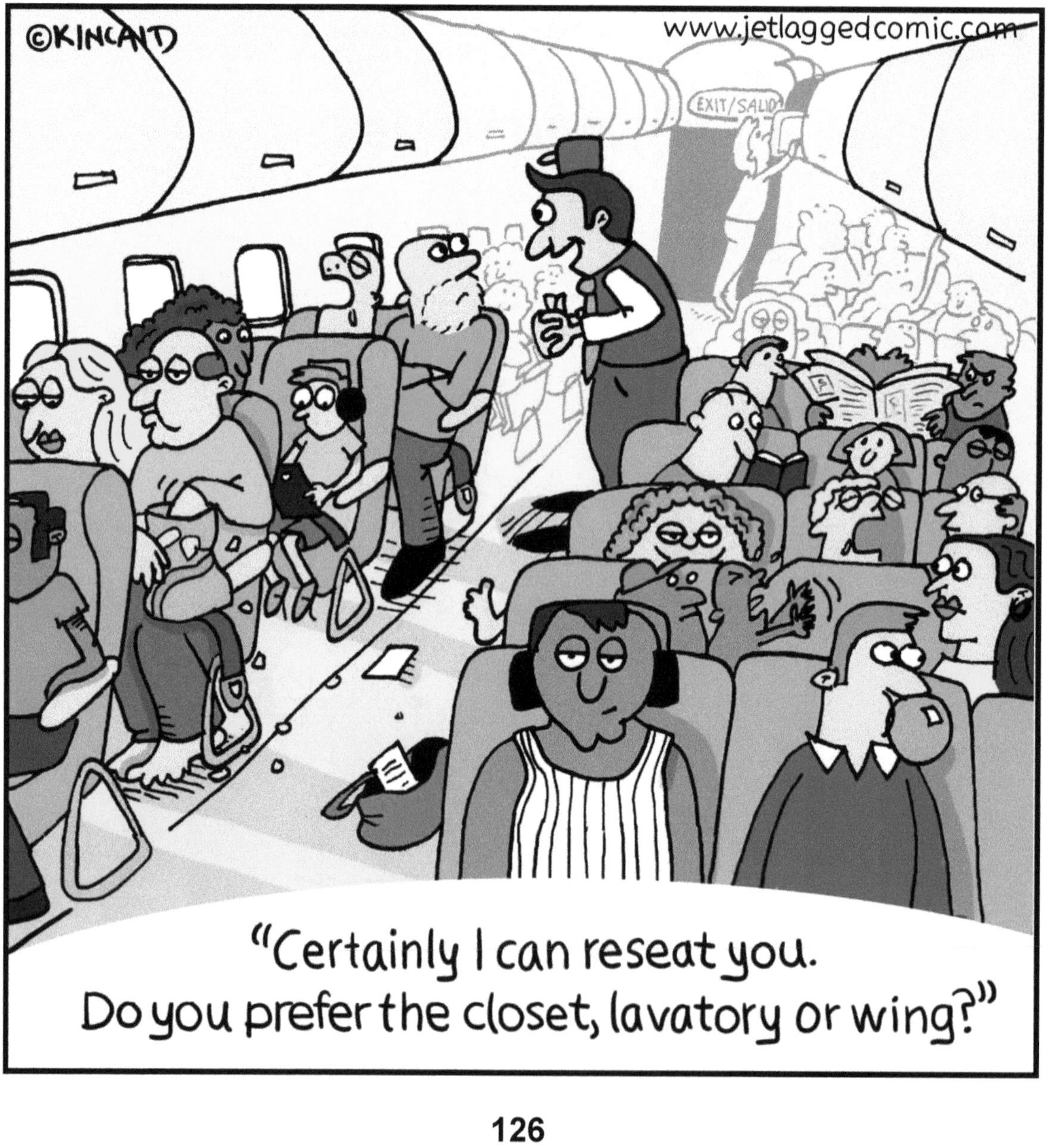
©KINCAID
www.jetlaggedcomic.com
EXIT/SALID

"Certainly I can reseat you.
Do you prefer the closet, lavatory or wing?"

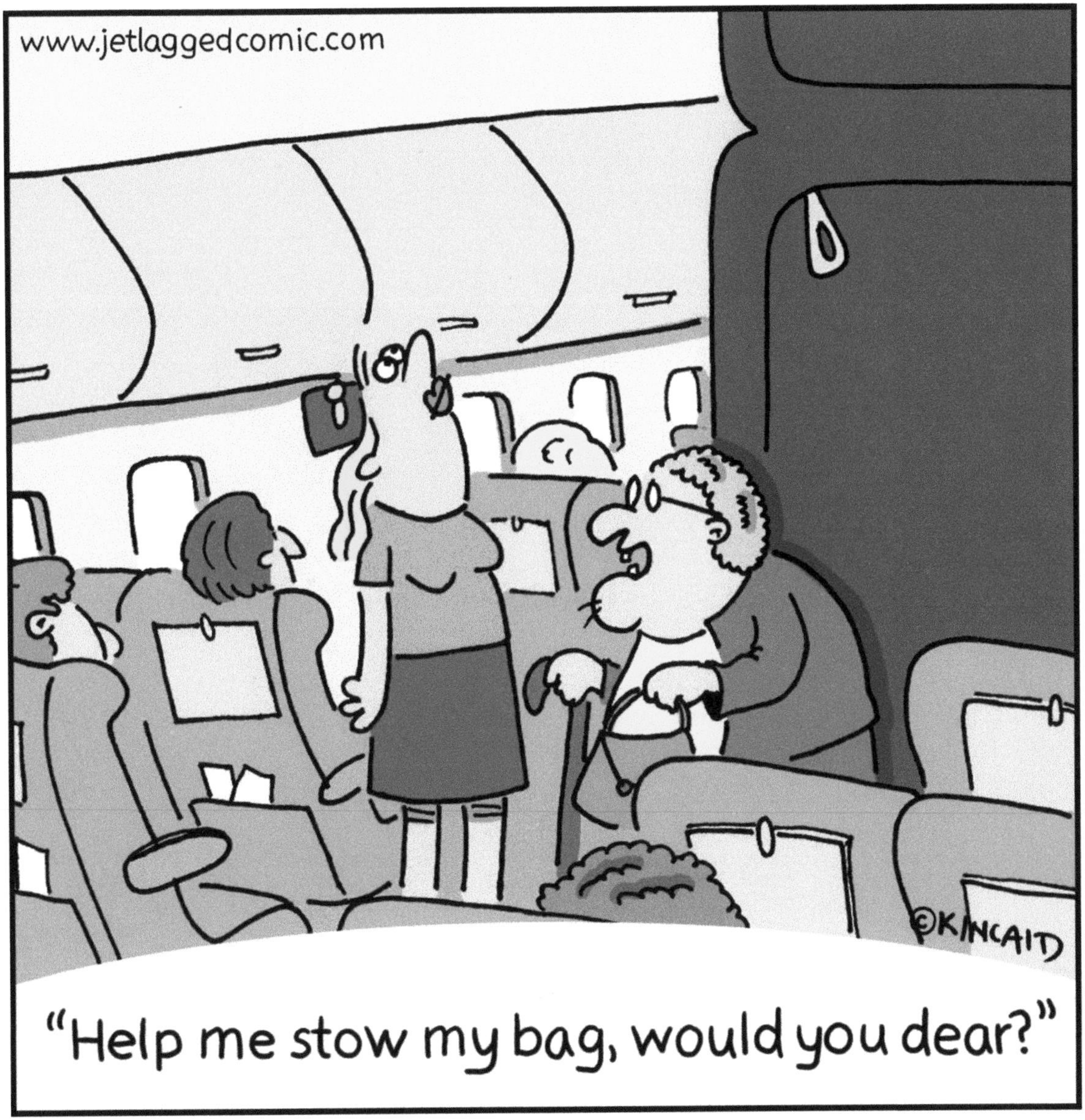
www.jetlaggedcomic.com
©KINCAID

"Help me stow my bag, would you dear?"

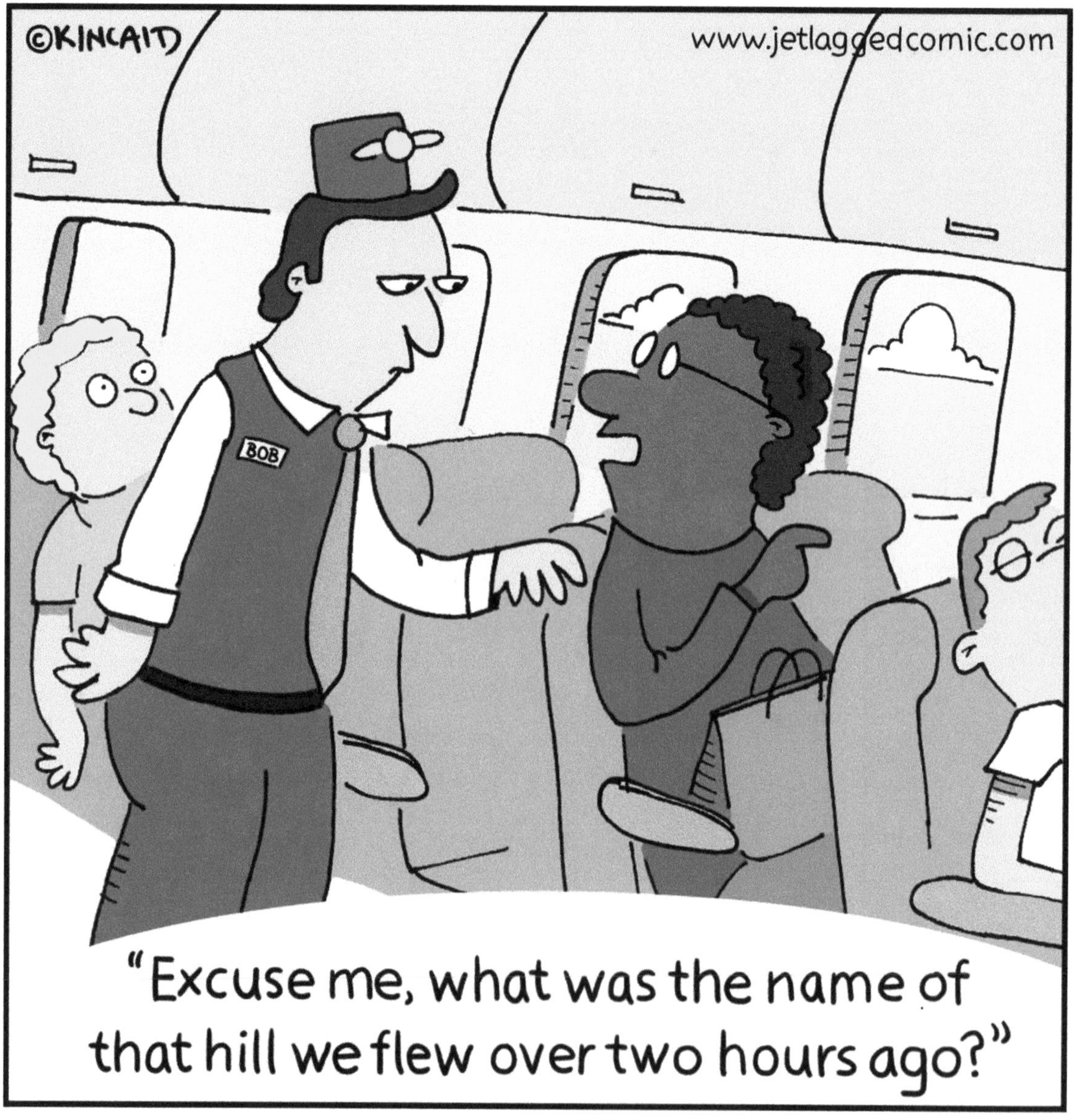
©KINCAID
www.jetlaggedcomic.com
BOB
"Excuse me, what was the name of that hill we flew over two hours ago?"

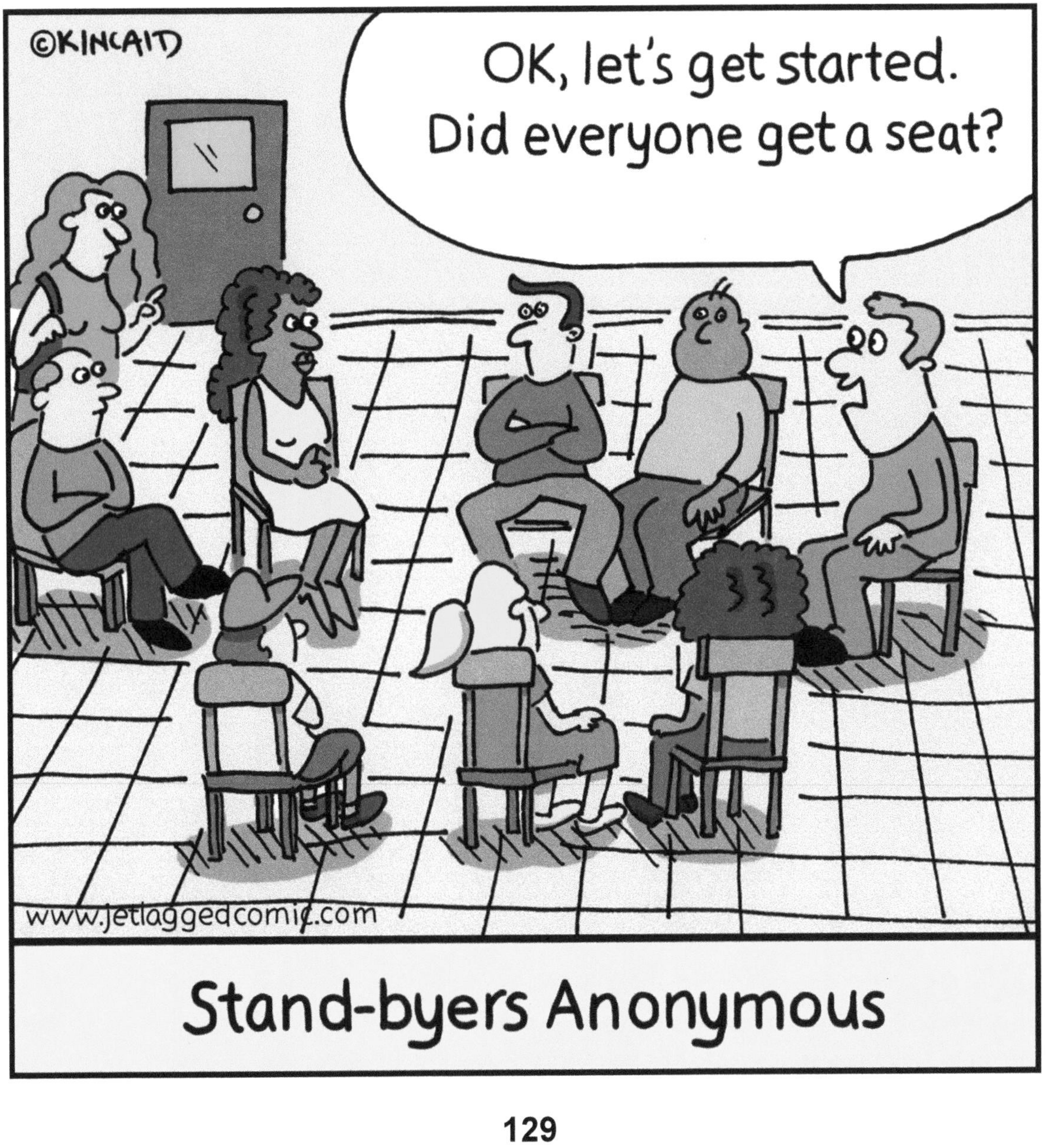
©KINCAID
OK, let's get started. Did everyone get a seat?
www.jetlaggedcomic.com

Stand-byers Anonymous

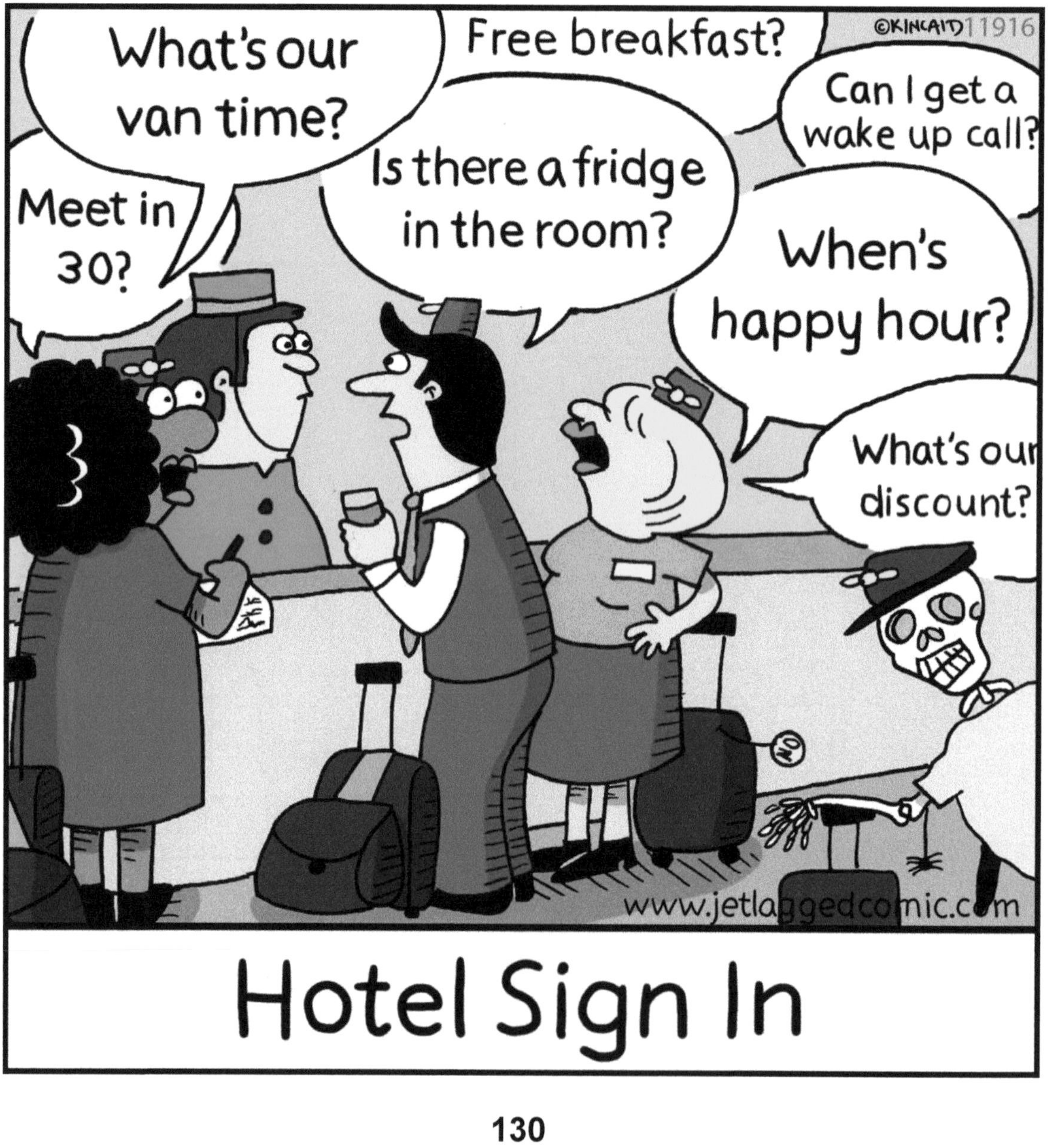

©KINCAID 11916
What's our van time?
Free breakfast?
Can I get a wake up call?
Meet in 30?
Is there a fridge in the room?
When's happy hour?
What's our discount?
www.jetlaggedcomic.com

Hotel Sign In

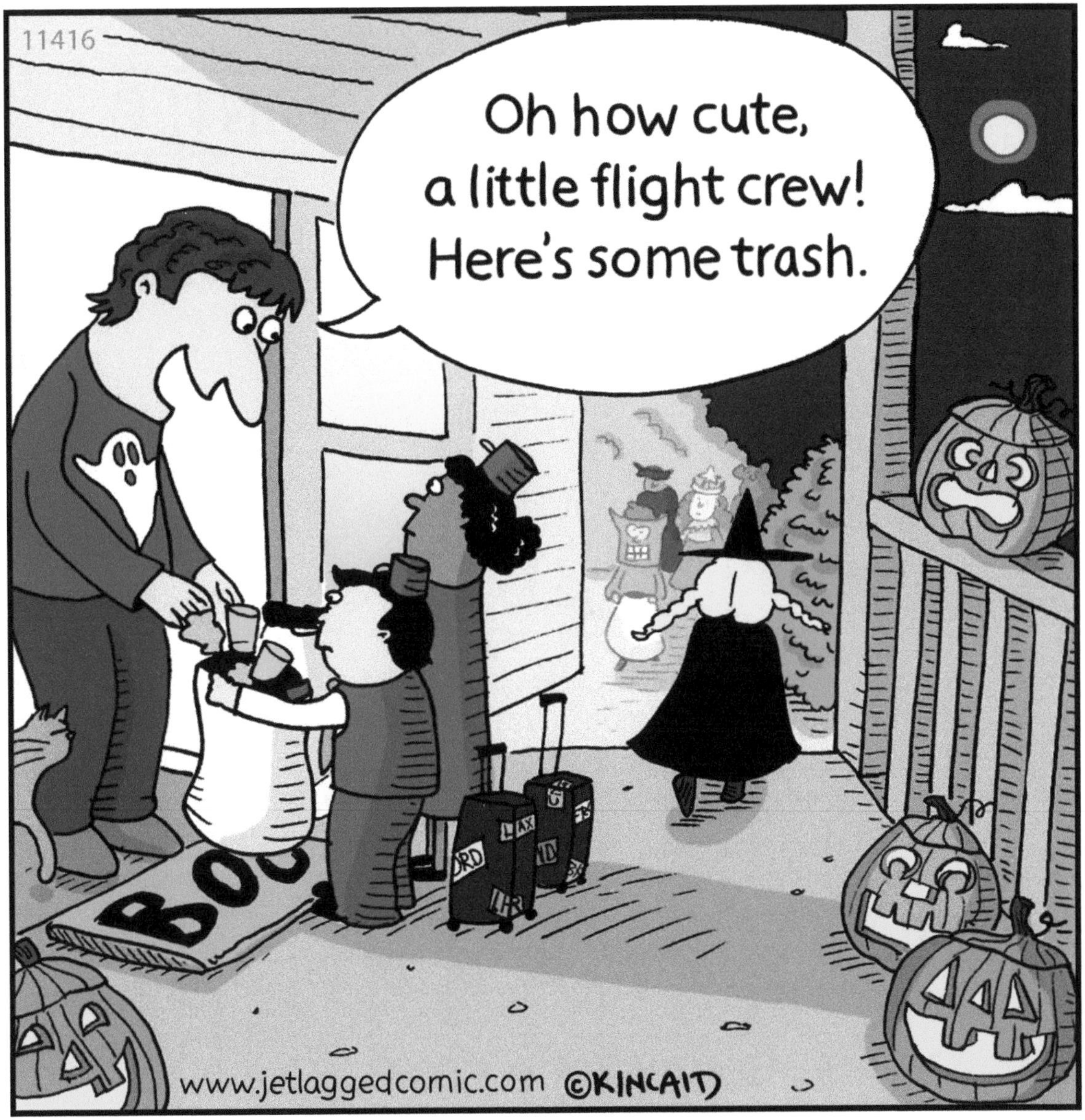
11416
Oh how cute, a little flight crew! Here's some trash.
BOO
LAX
ORD
www.jetlaggedcomic.com ©KINCAID

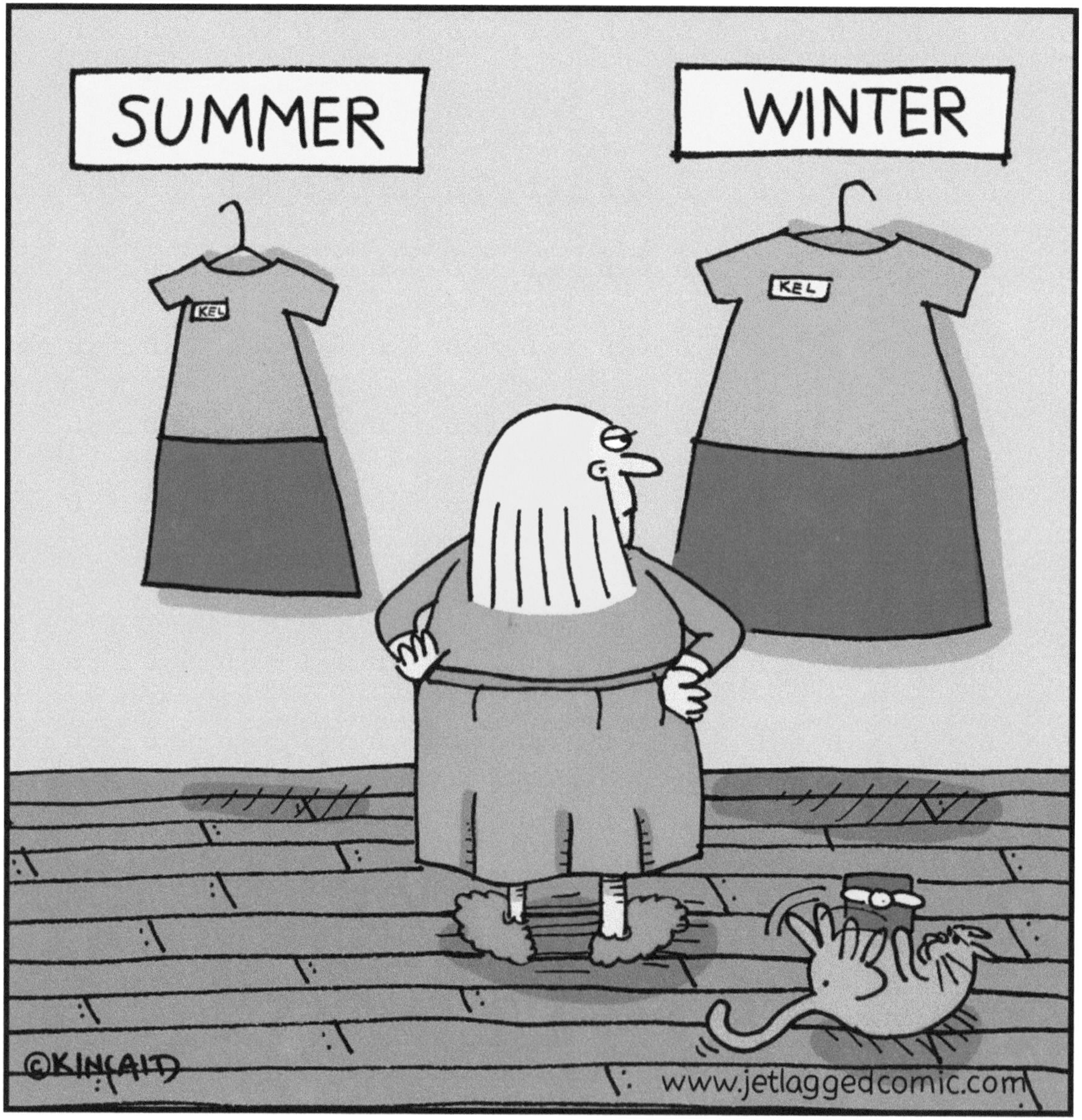
SUMMER
WINTER
KEL
KEL
©KINCAID
www.jetlaggedcomic.com

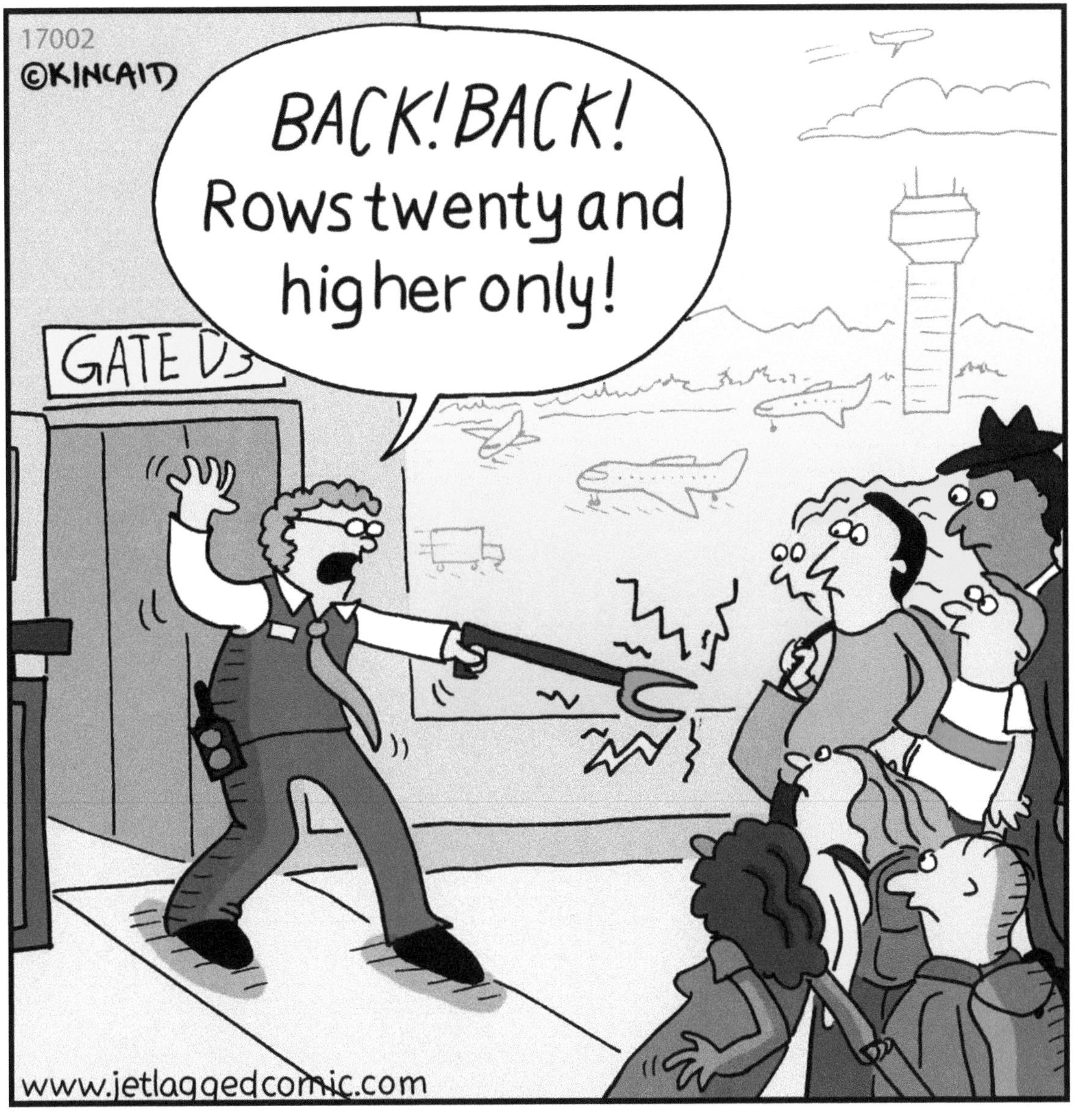
17002
©KINCAID
BACK! BACK! Rows twenty and higher only!
GATE D3
www.jetlaggedcomic.com

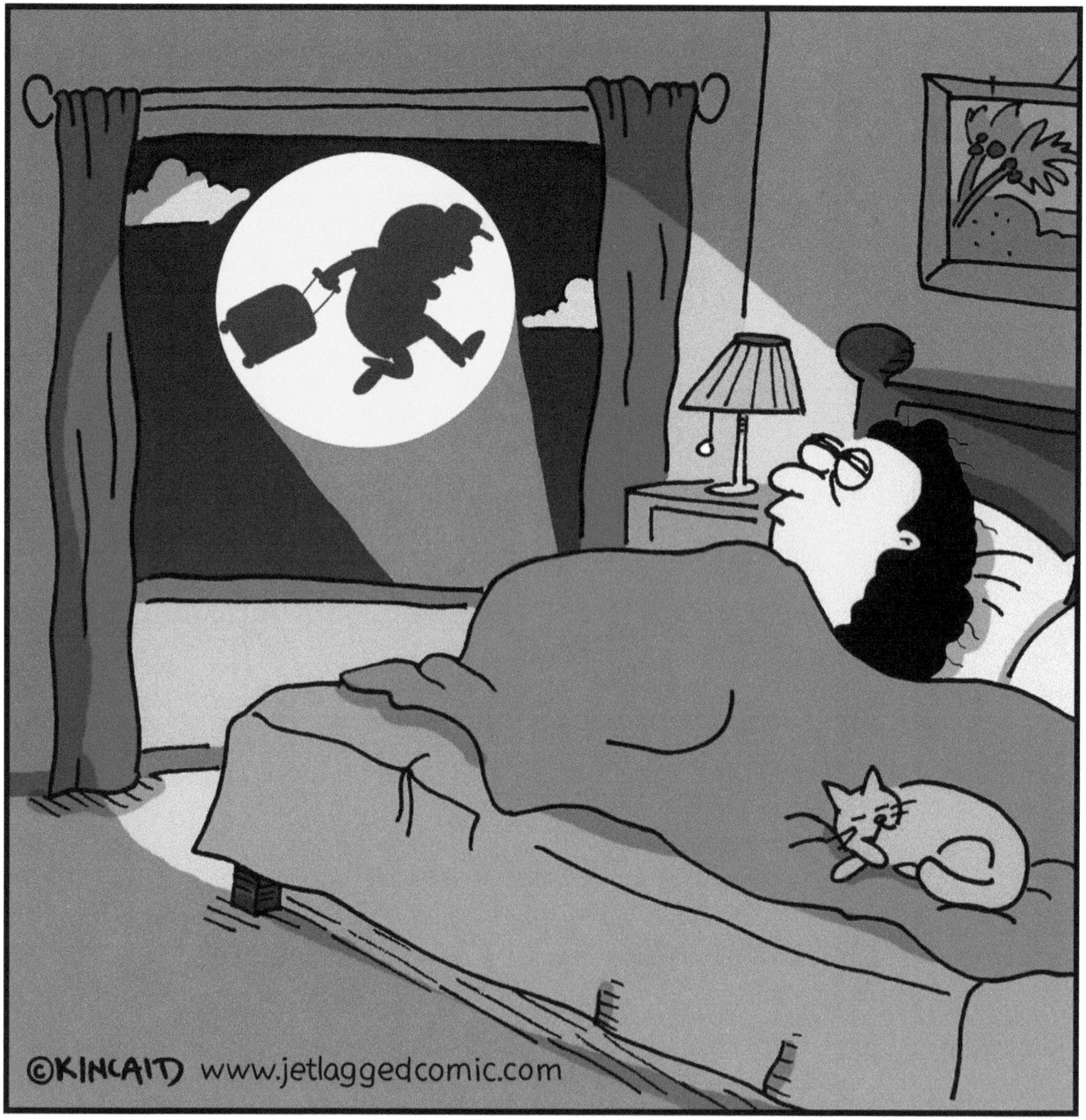
©KINCAID www.jetlaggedcomic.com

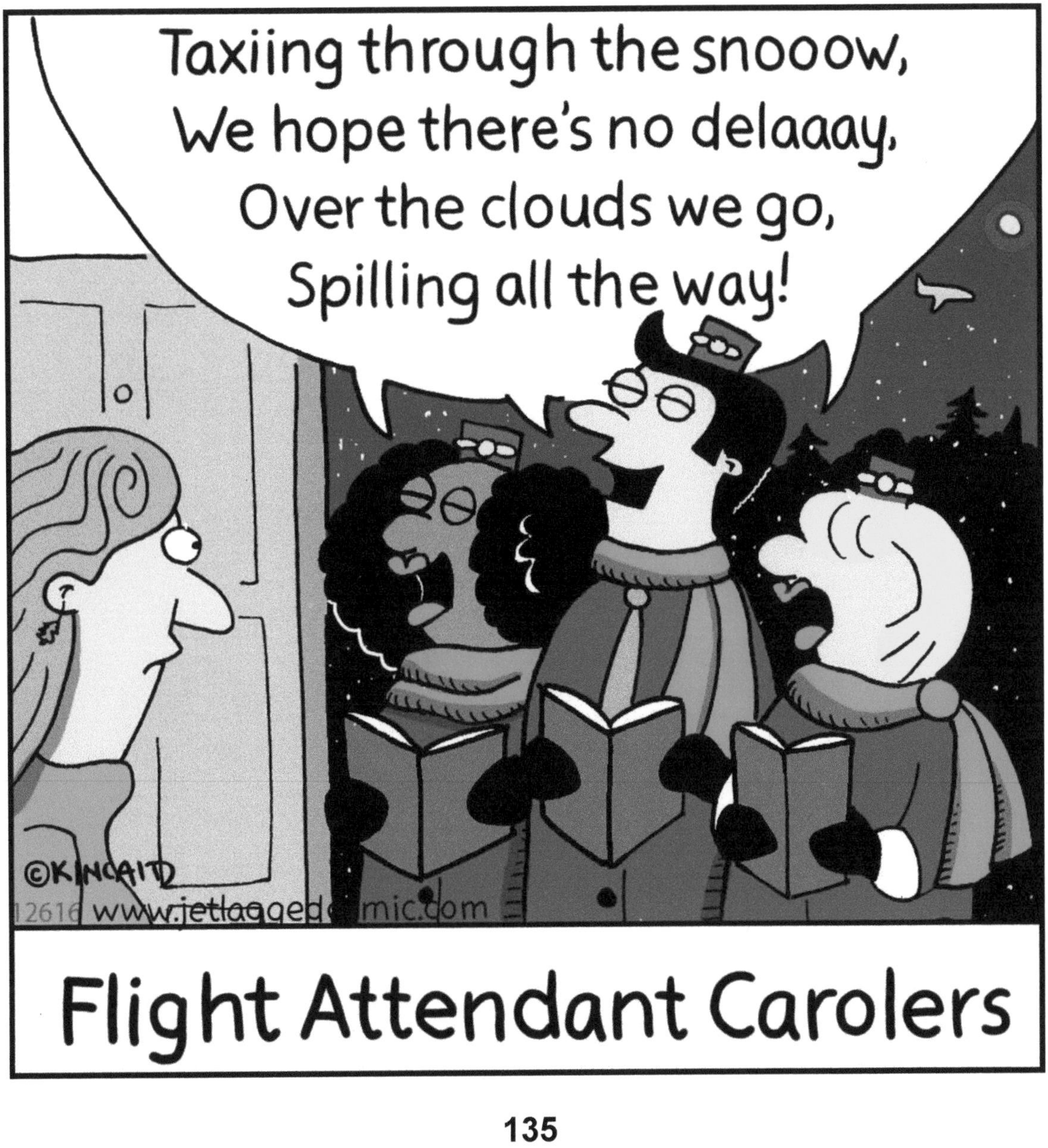
Taxiing through the snooow,
We hope there's no delaaay,
Over the clouds we go,
Spilling all the way!
©KINCAID

Flight Attendant Carolers

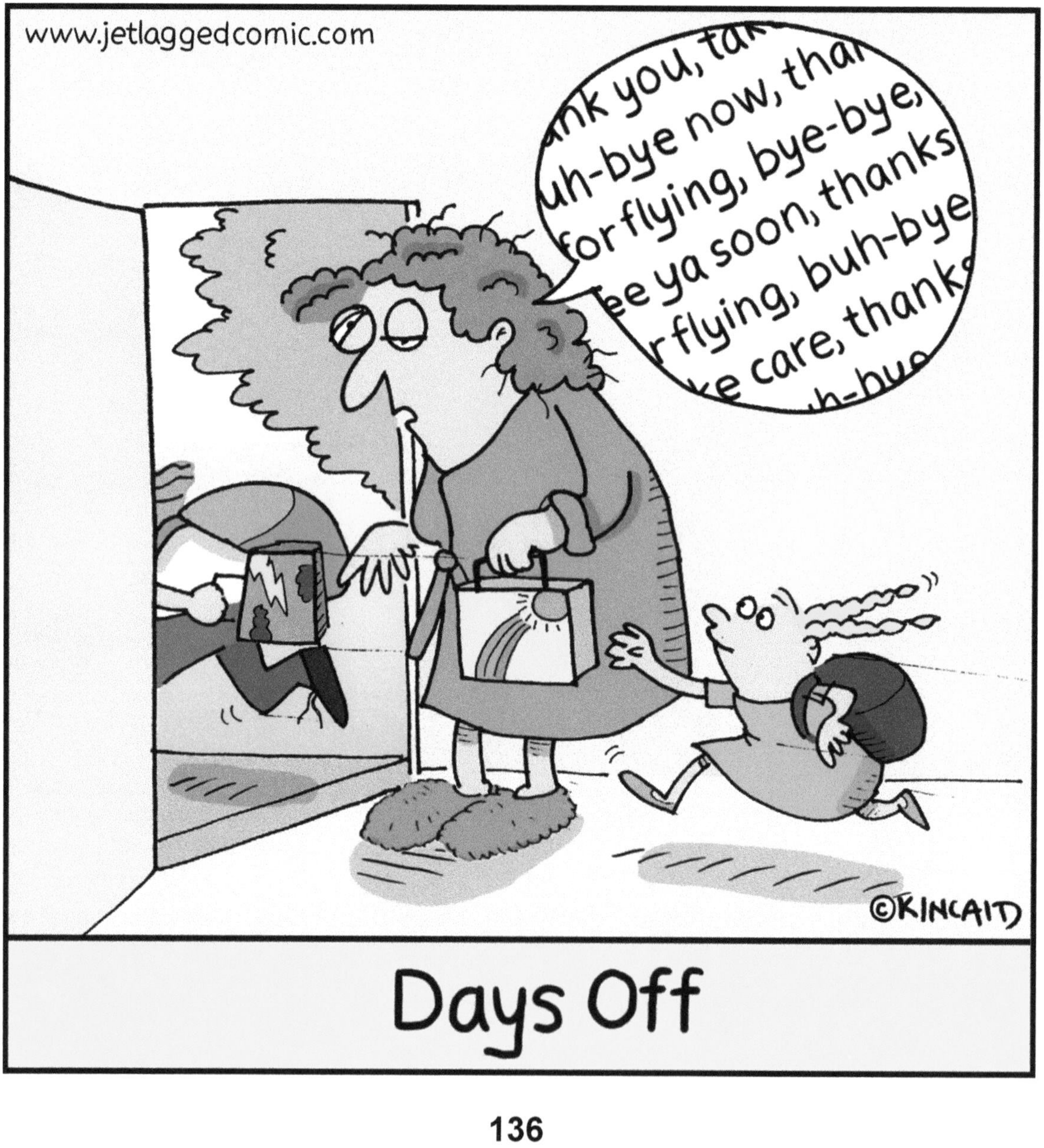
www.jetlaggedcomic.com
nk you, ta
uh-bye now, tha
for flying, bye-bye,
for flying, bye-bye, thanks
ee ya soon, thanks
r flying, buh-bye
ke care, thank
©KINCAID

Days Off

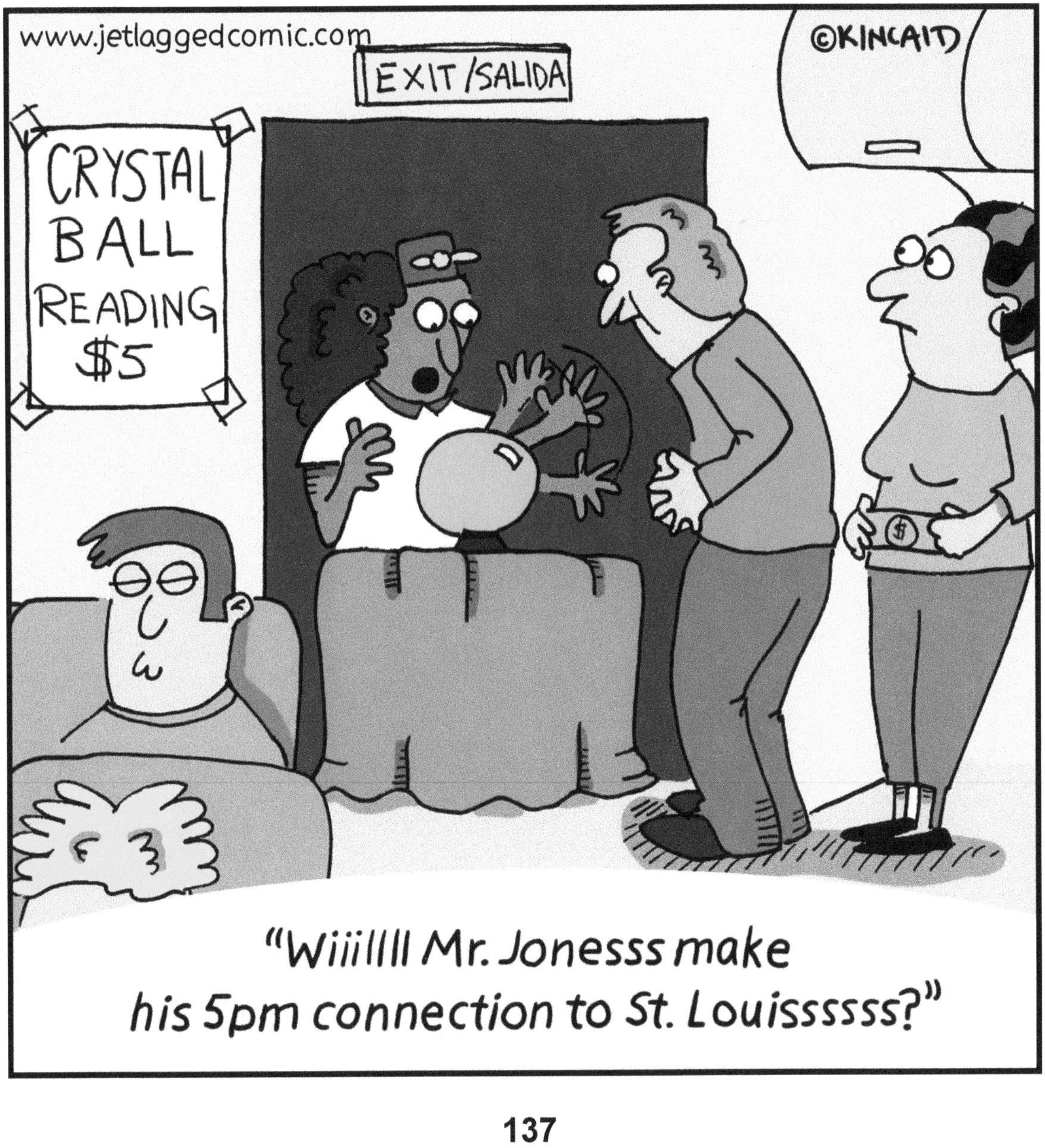
www.jetlaggedcomic.com
©KINCAID
EXIT/SALIDA
CRYSTAL BALL READING $5

"Wiiillll Mr. Jonesss make his 5pm connection to St. Louisssss?"

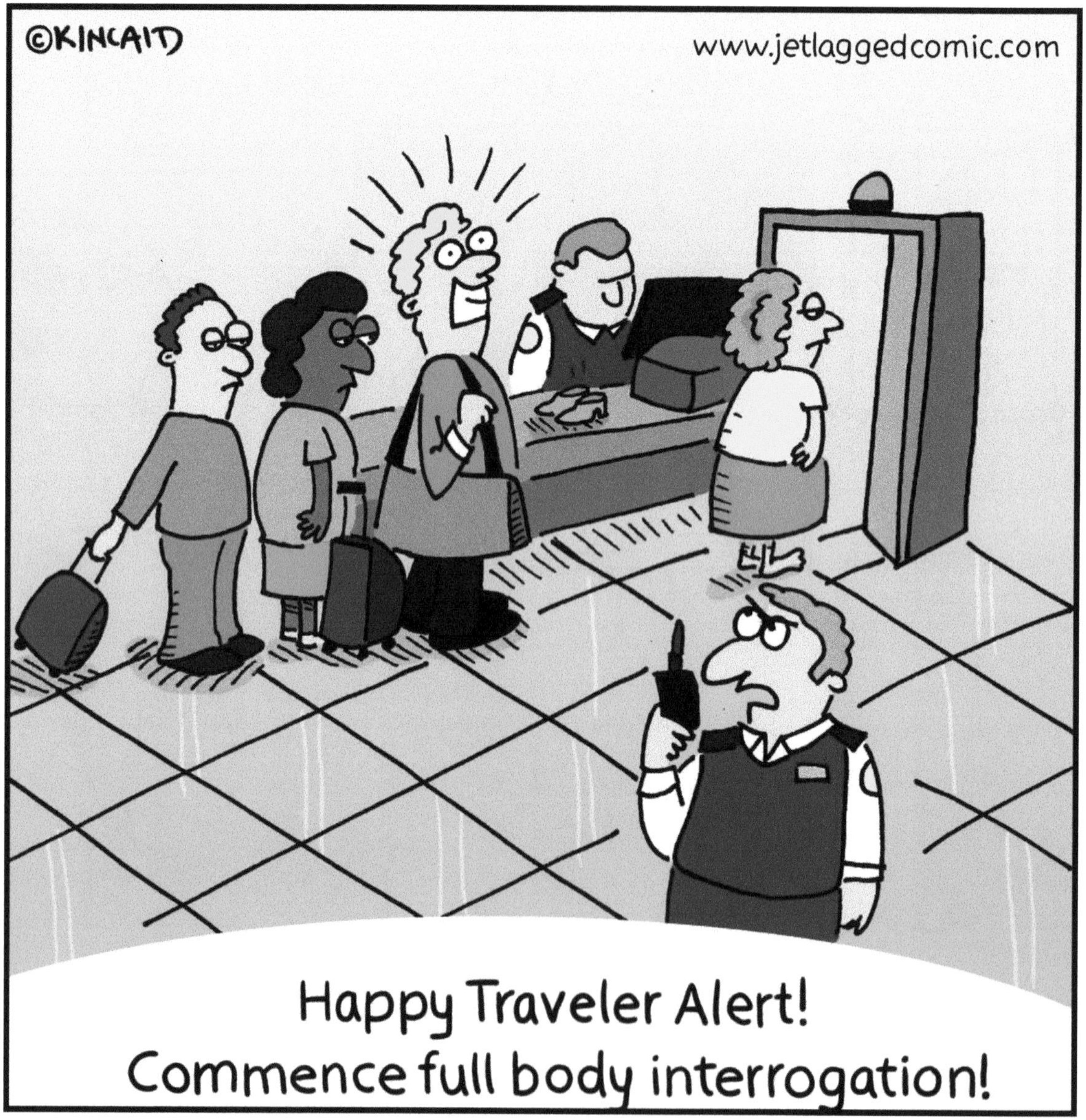
©KINCAID
www.jetlaggedcomic.com
Happy Traveler Alert!
Commence full body interrogation!

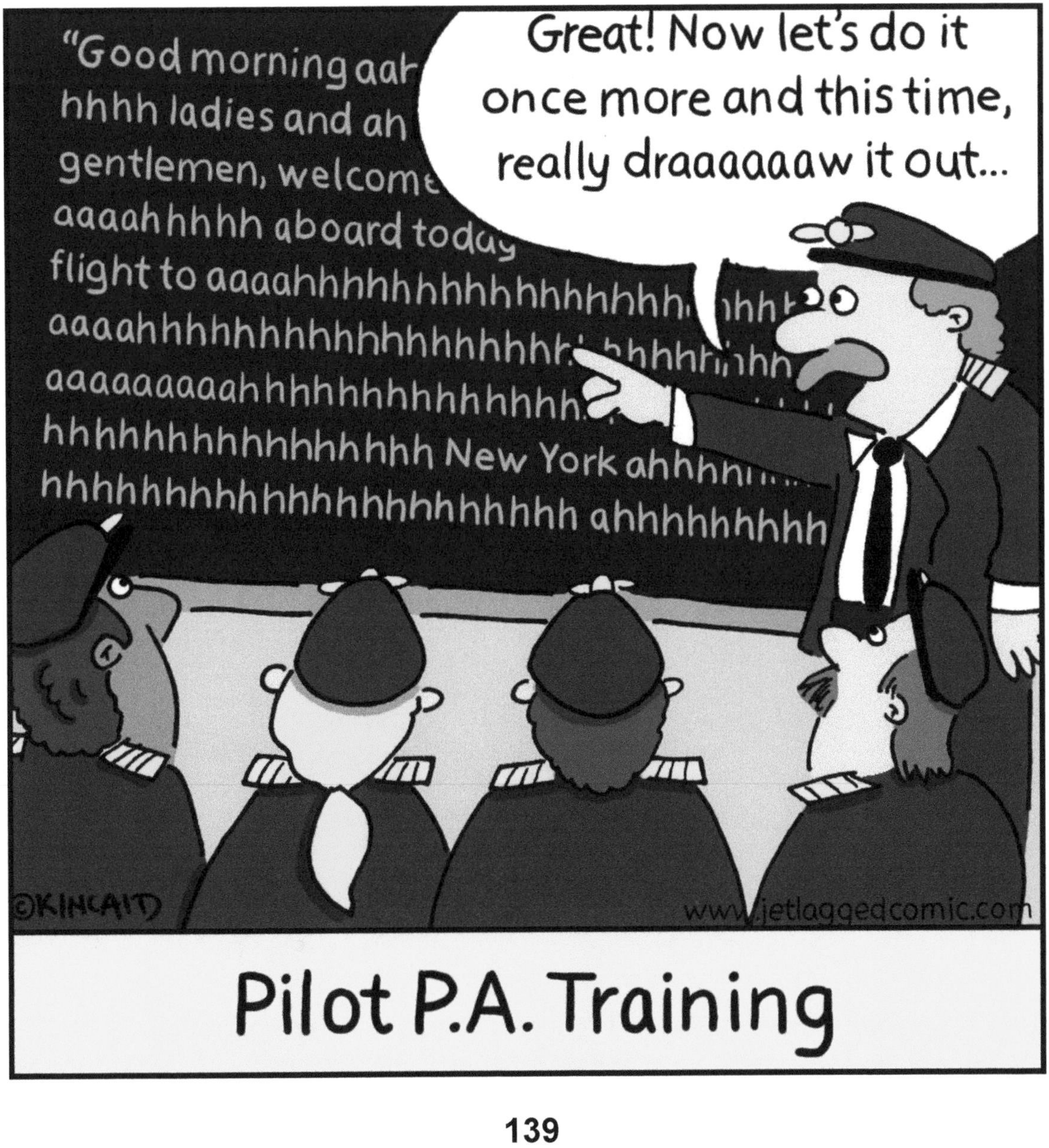
"Good morning aah
hhhh ladies and ah
gentlemen, welcome
aaaah hhhh aboard today
flight to aaaahhhhhhhhhhhhhhhh
aaaahhhhhhhhhhhhhhhhh
aaaaaaaaah hhhhhhhhhhhhhh
hhhhhhhhhhhhhhh New York ahhhh
hhhhhhhhhhhhhhhhhhhhhh ahhhhhhhhh
Great! Now let's do it once more and this time, really draaaaaaw it out...
©KINCAID
www.jetlaggedcomic.com

Pilot P.A. Training

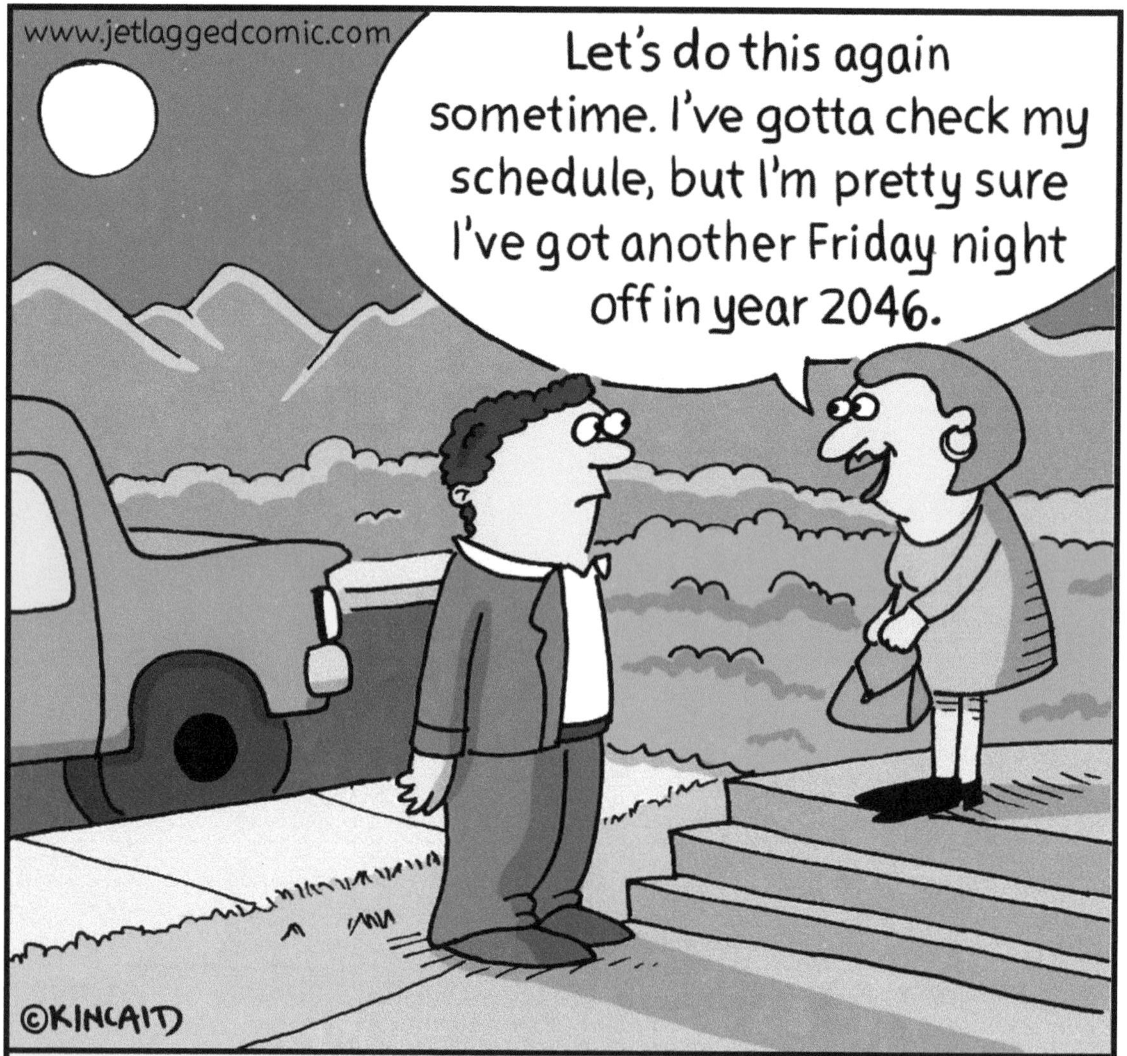
www.jetlaggedcomic.com
Let's do this again sometime. I've gotta check my schedule, but I'm pretty sure I've got another Friday night off in year 2046.
©KINCAID

When Reserves Date

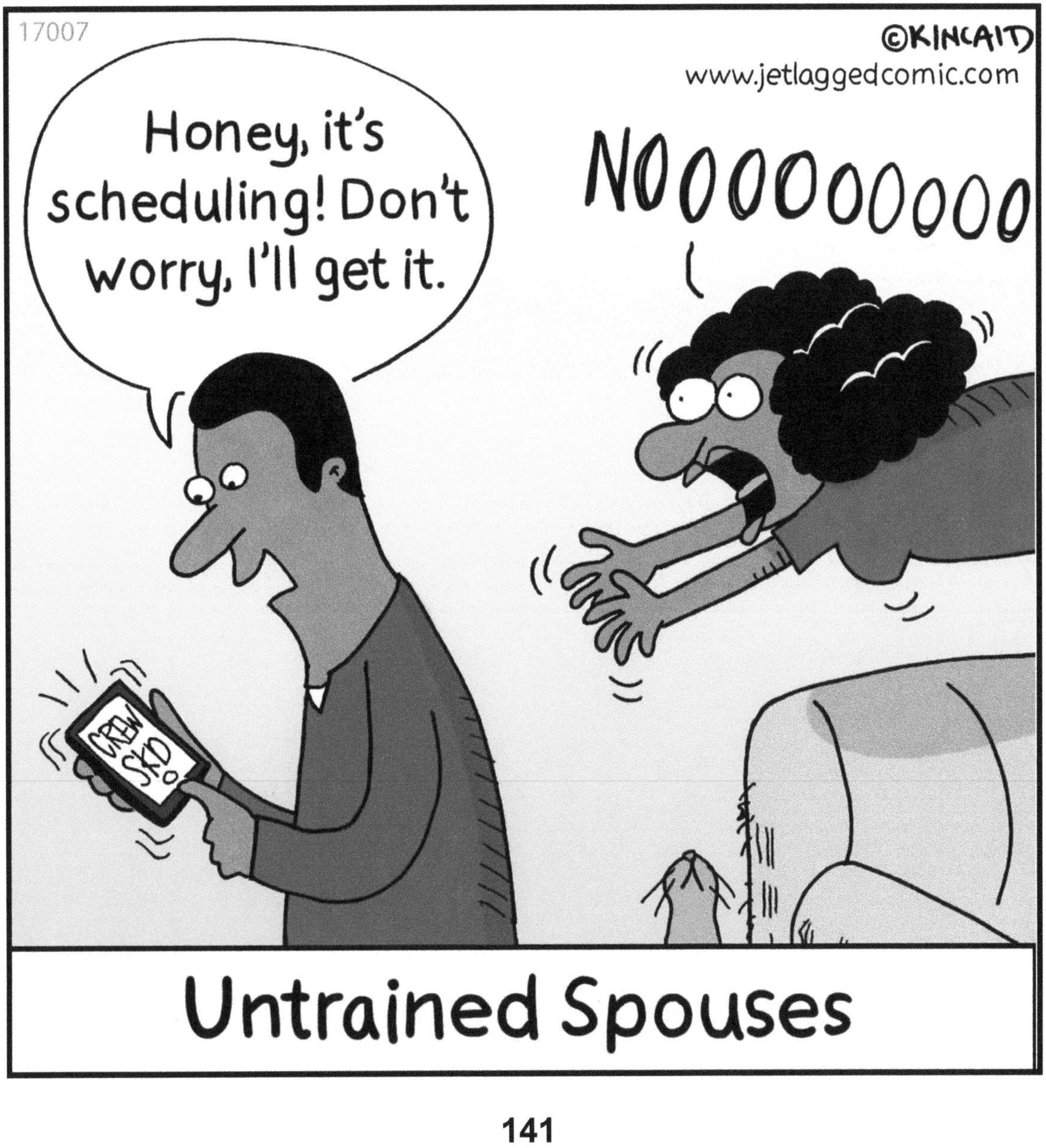
17007
©KINCAID
www.jetlaggedcomic.com
Honey, it's scheduling! Don't worry, I'll get it.
NOOOOOOOOOO
CREW SKD

Untrained Spouses

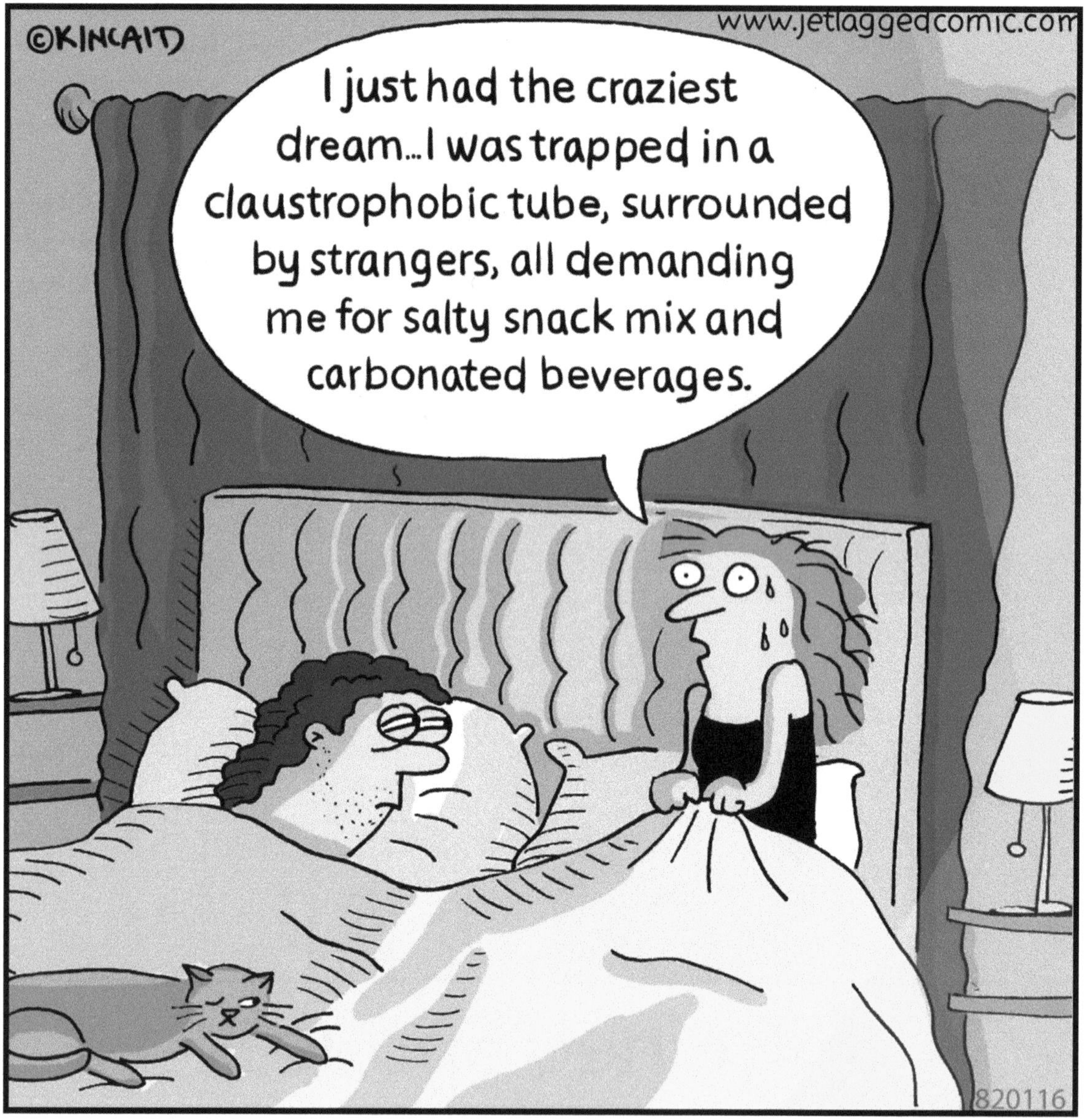
©KINCAID
www.jetlaggedcomic.com
I just had the craziest dream...I was trapped in a claustrophobic tube, surrounded by strangers, all demanding me for salty snack mix and carbonated beverages.
820116

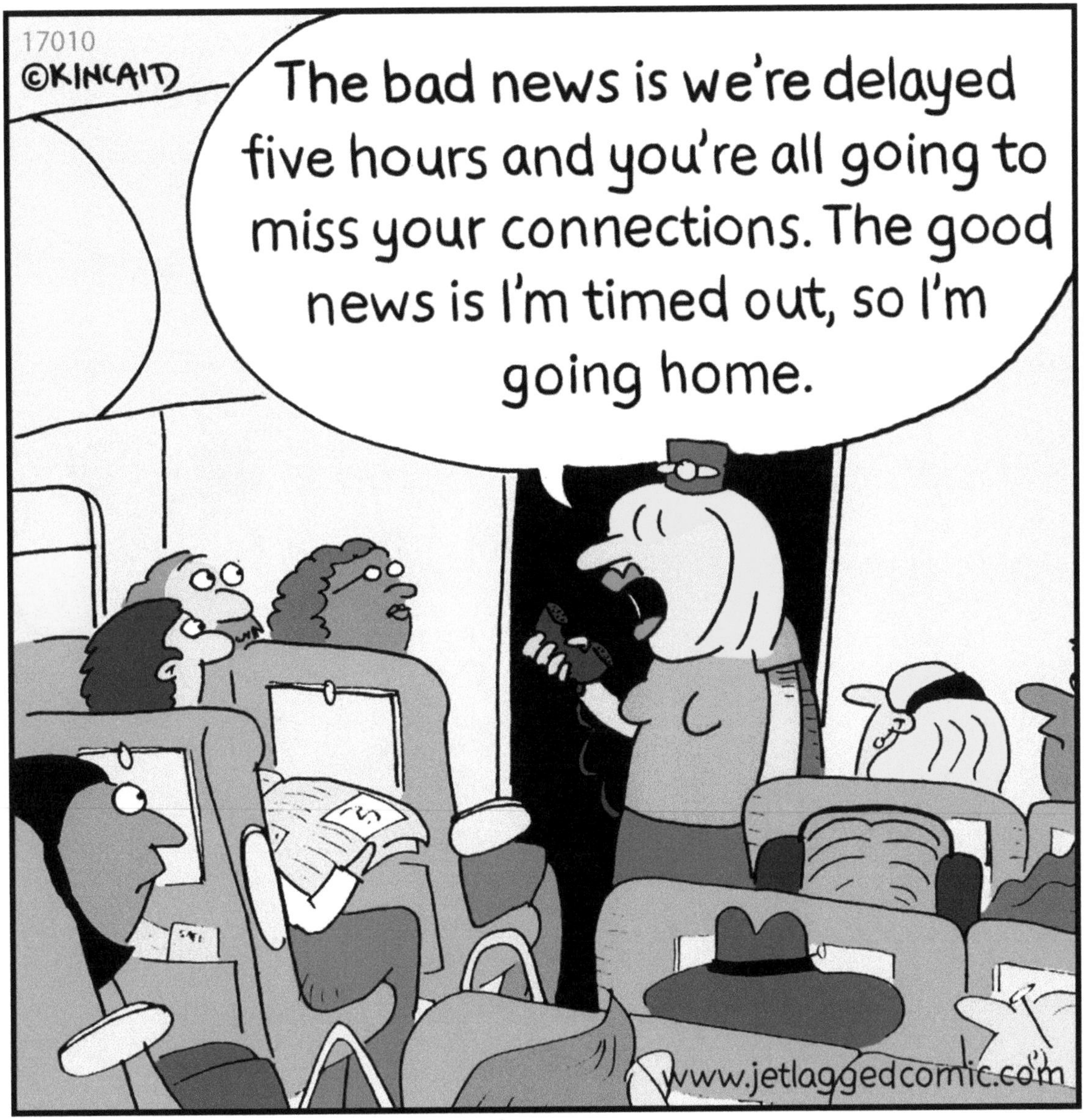
17010
©KINCAID
The bad news is we're delayed five hours and you're all going to miss your connections. The good news is I'm timed out, so I'm going home.
www.jetlaggedcomic.com

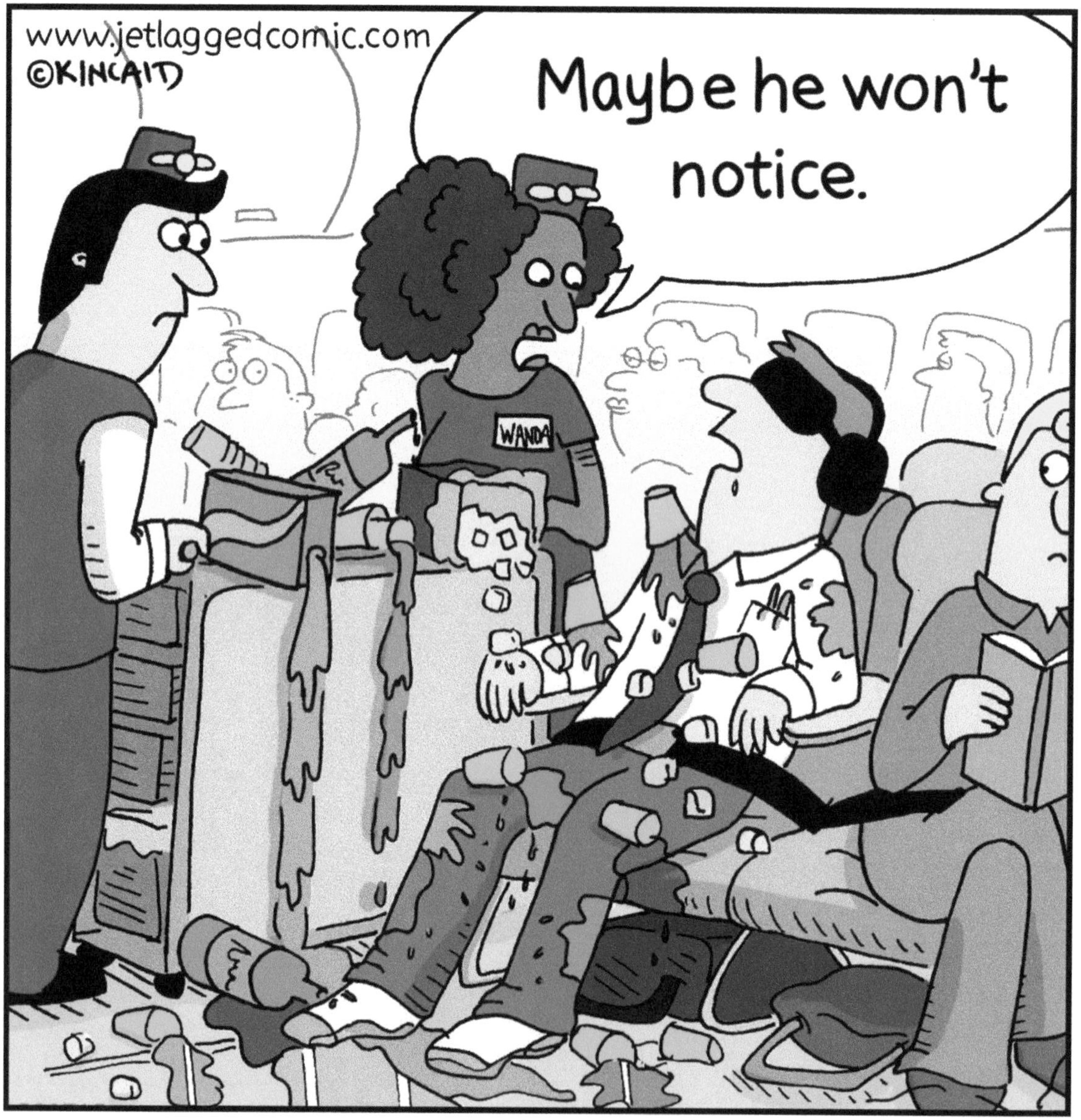
www.jetlaggedcomic.com
©KINCAID
Maybe he won't notice.
WANDA

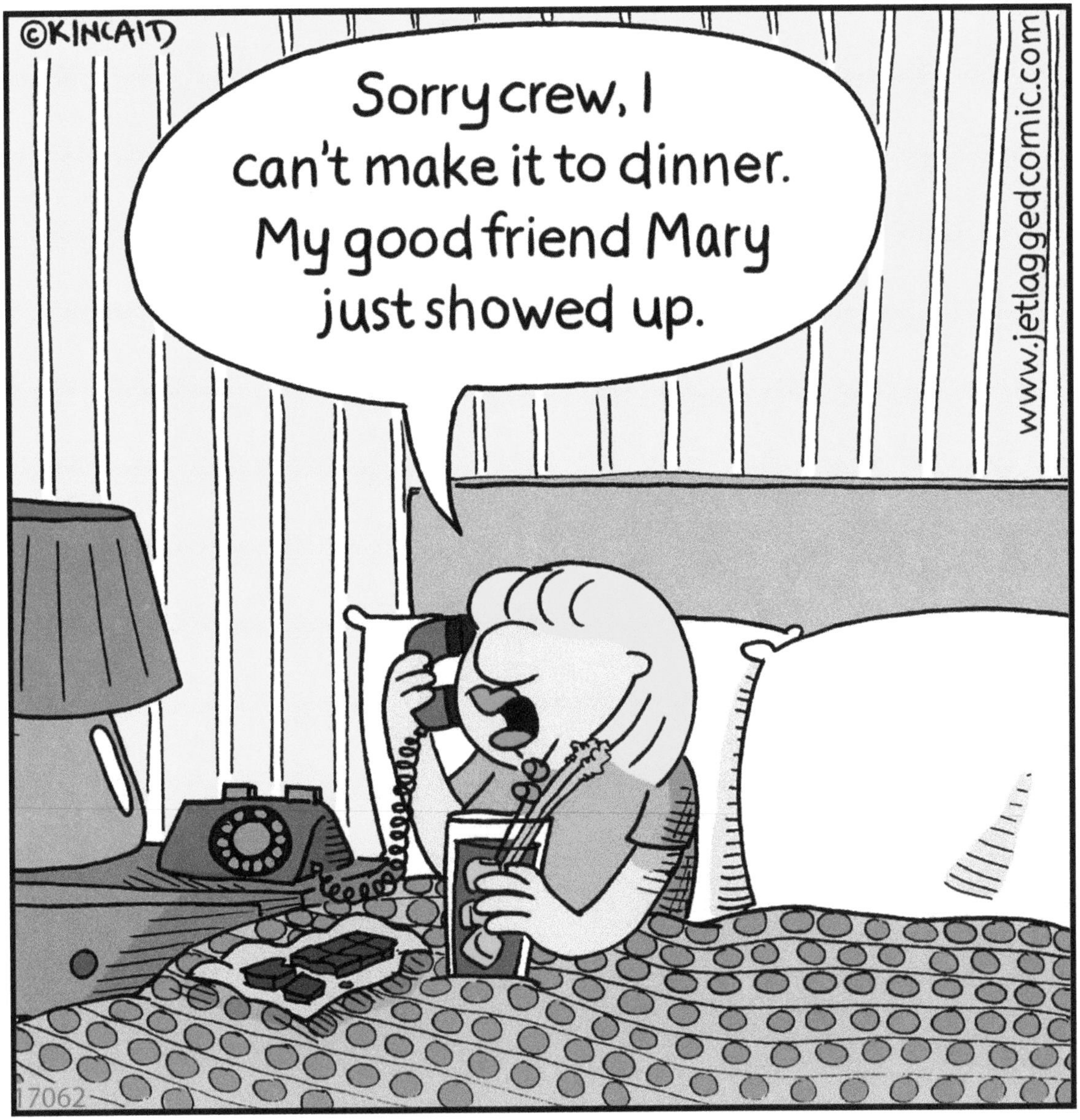
©KINCAID
Sorry crew, I can't make it to dinner. My good friend Mary just showed up.
www.jetlaggedcomic.com
17062

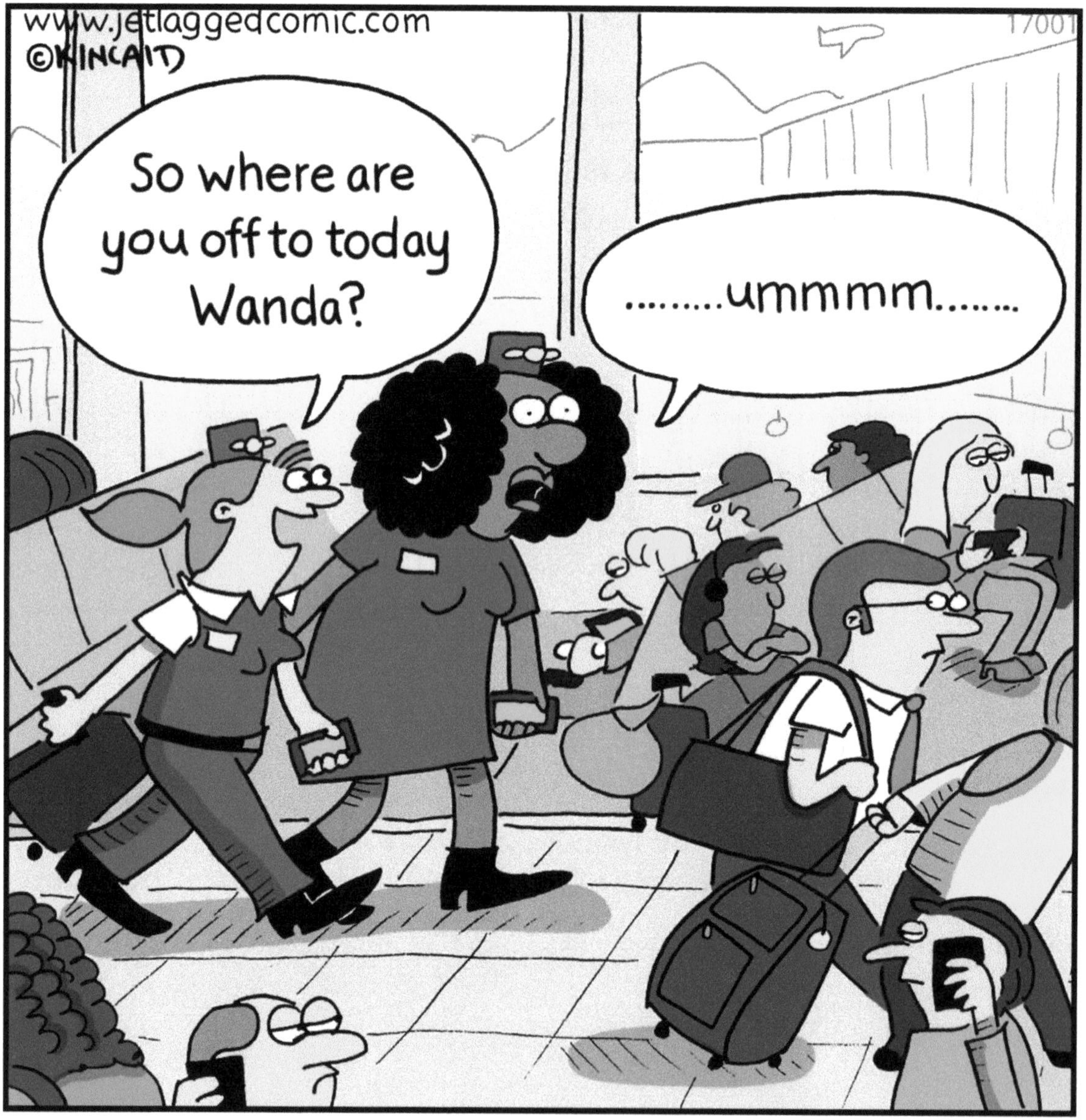
www.jetlaggedcomic.com
©KINCAID
So where are you off to today Wanda?
.........ummmm........

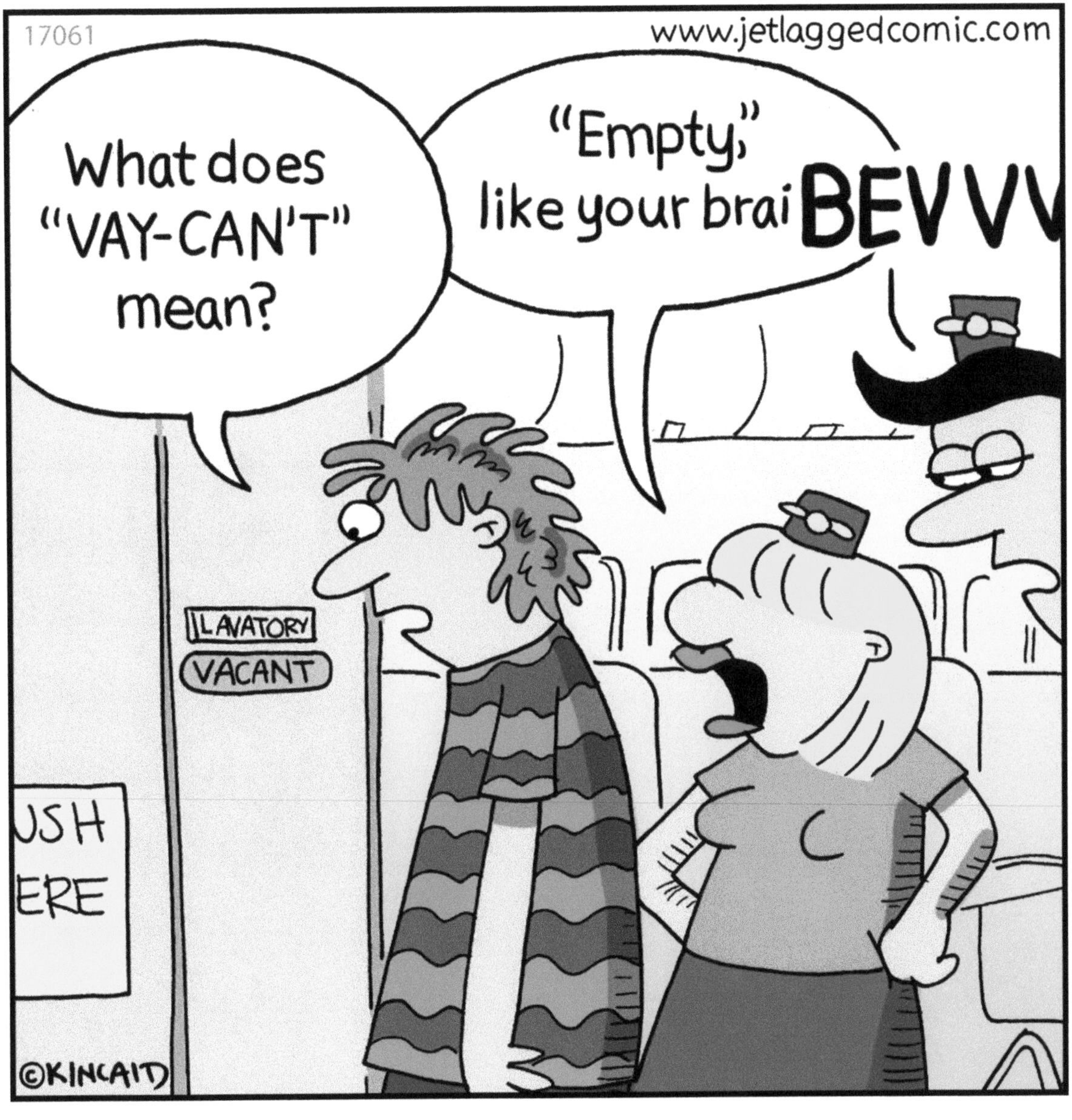
17061
www.jetlaggedcomic.com
What does "VAY-CAN'T" mean?
"Empty," like your brai
BEVVV
LAVATORY
VACANT
USH
ERE
©KINCAID

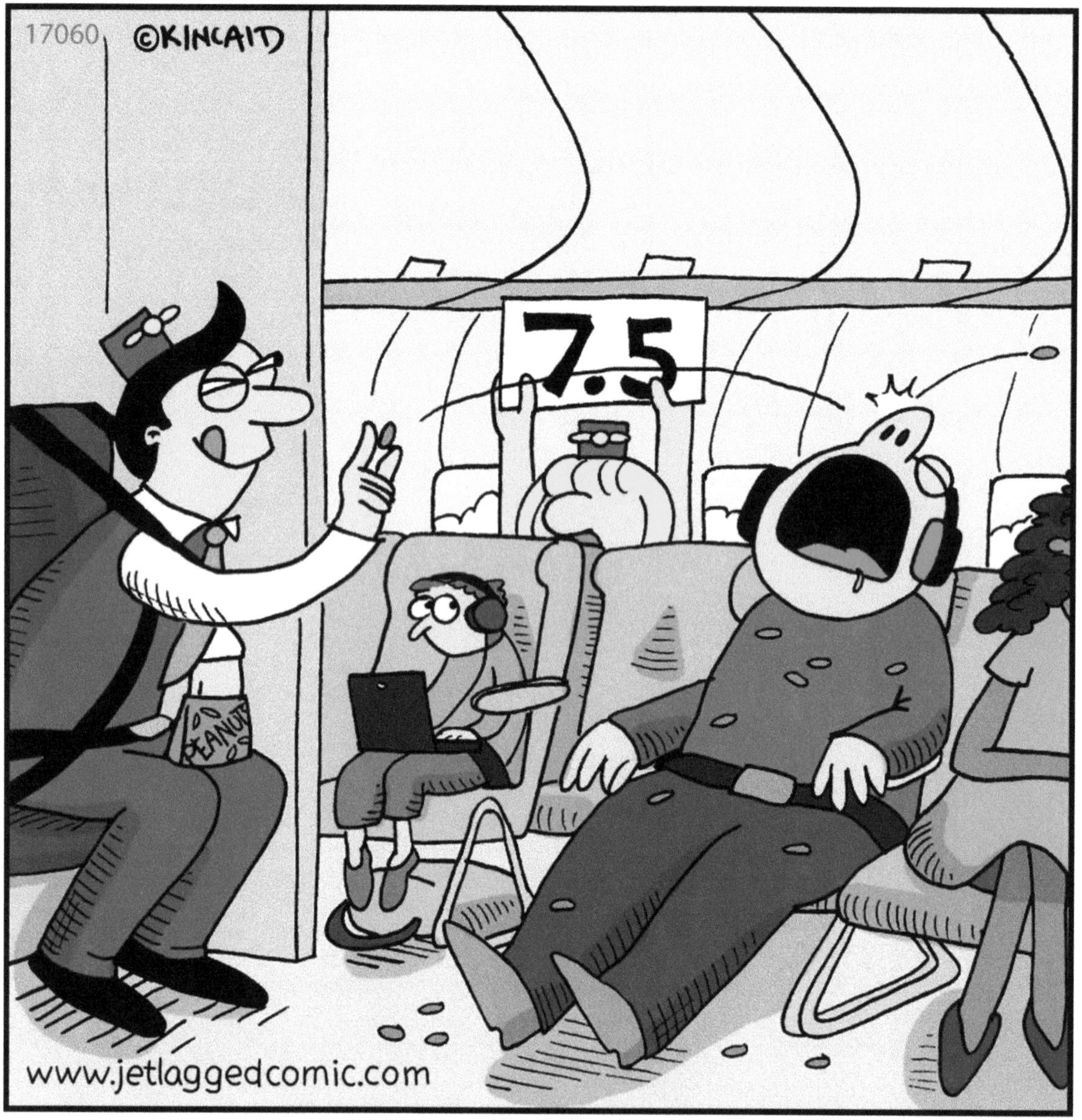
17060
©KINCAID
7.5
PEANUTS
www.jetlaggedcomic.com

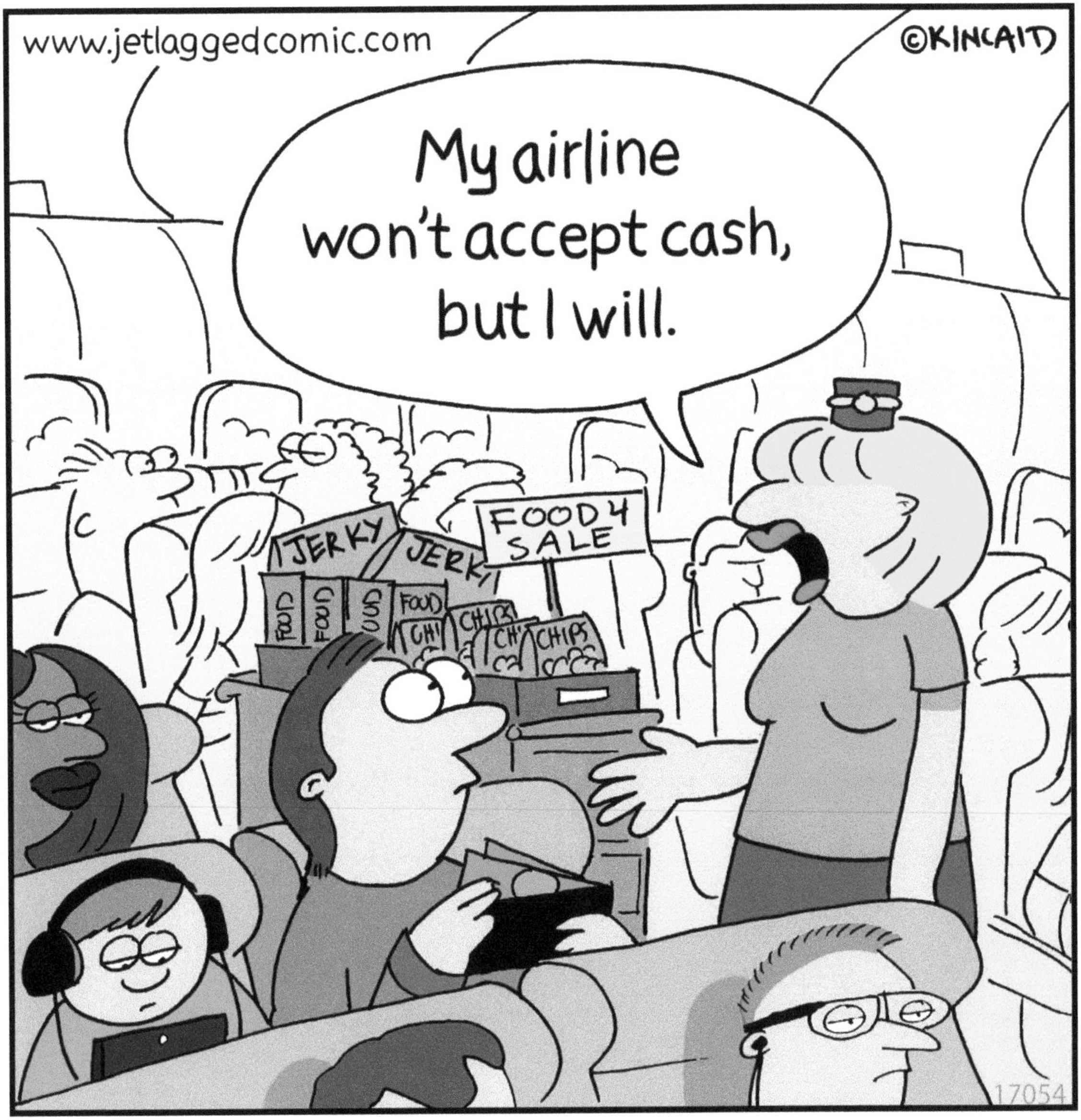
www.jetlaggedcomic.com
©KINCAID
My airline won't accept cash, but I will.
JERKY
JERKY
FOOD 4 SALE
FOOD
FOOD
FOOD
CHIPS
CHIPS
17054

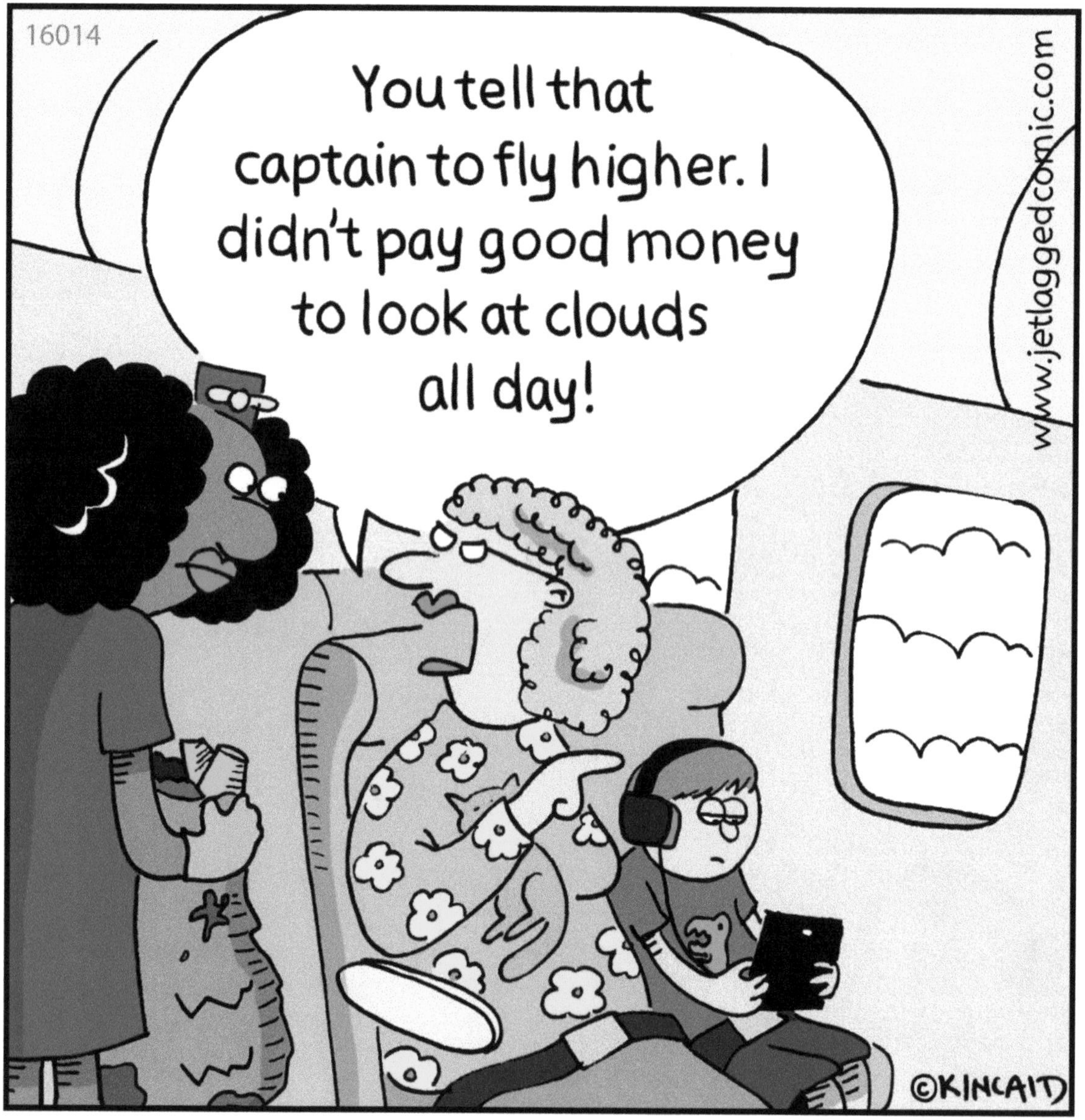
16014
You tell that captain to fly higher. I didn't pay good money to look at clouds all day!
www.jetlaggedcomic.com
©KINCAID

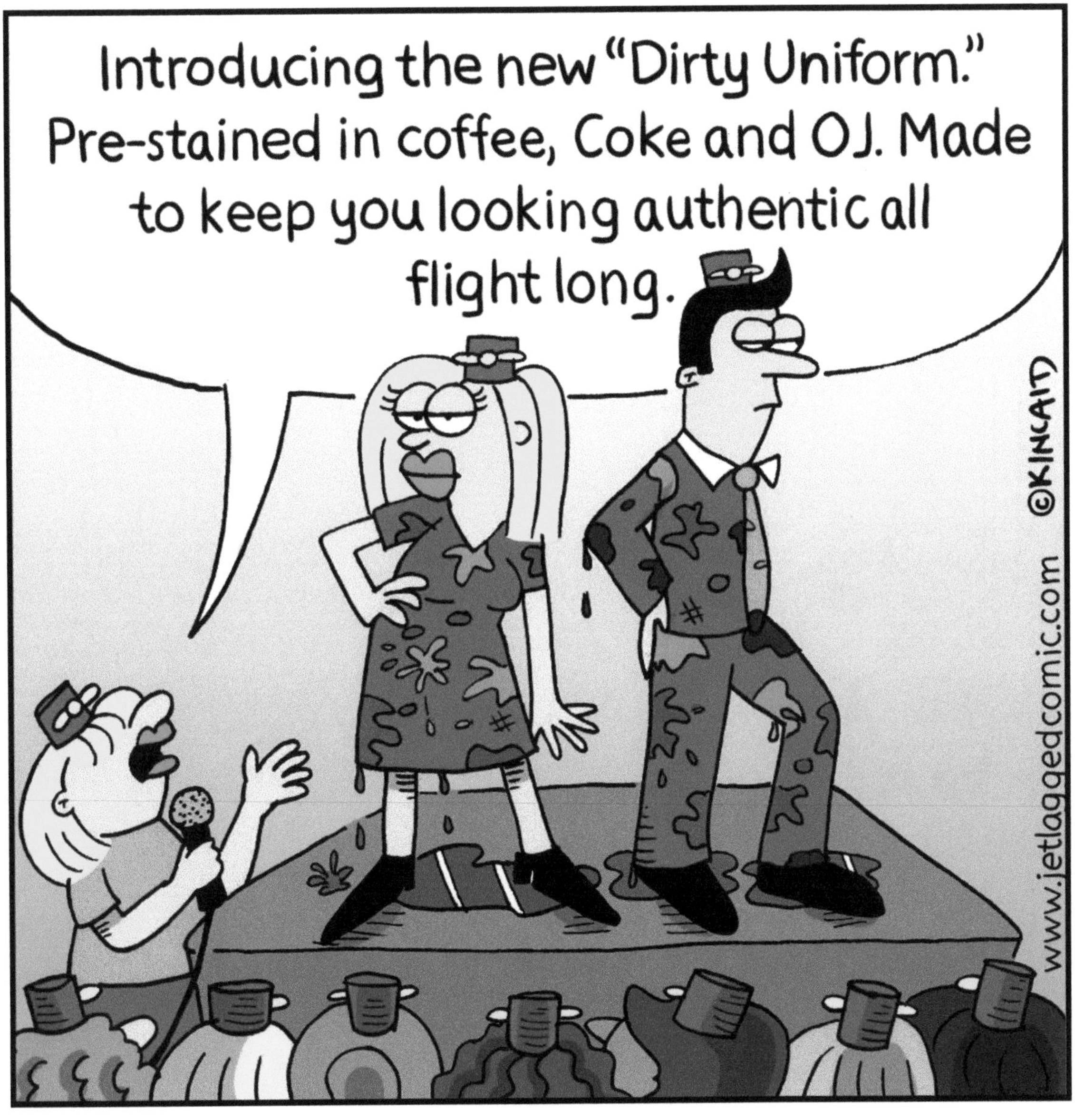
Introducing the new "Dirty Uniform." Pre-stained in coffee, Coke and OJ. Made to keep you looking authentic all flight long.
©KINCAID
www.jetlaggedcomic.com

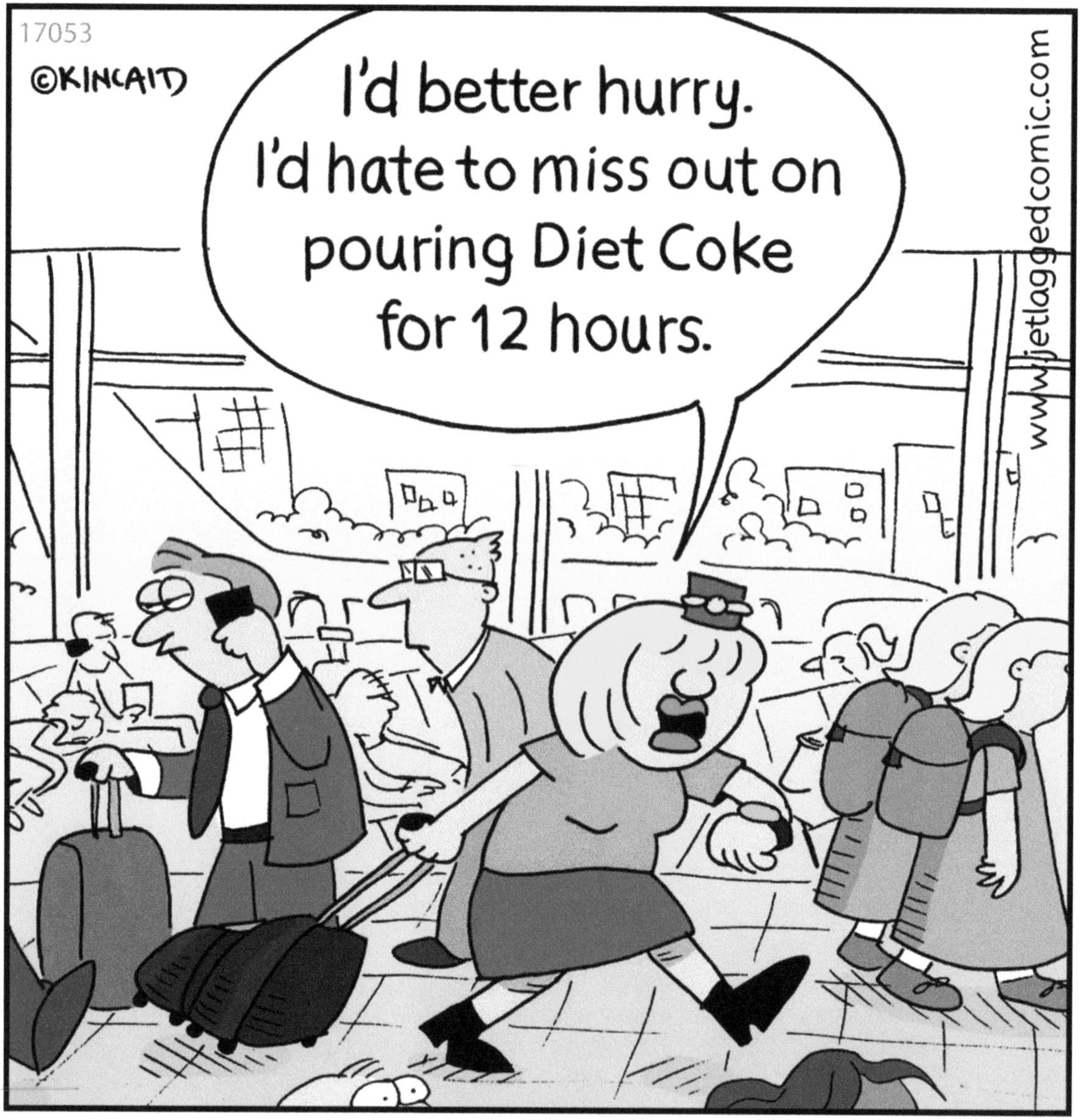
17053
©KINCAID
I'd better hurry.
I'd hate to miss out on
pouring Diet Coke
for 12 hours.
www.jetlaggedcomic.com

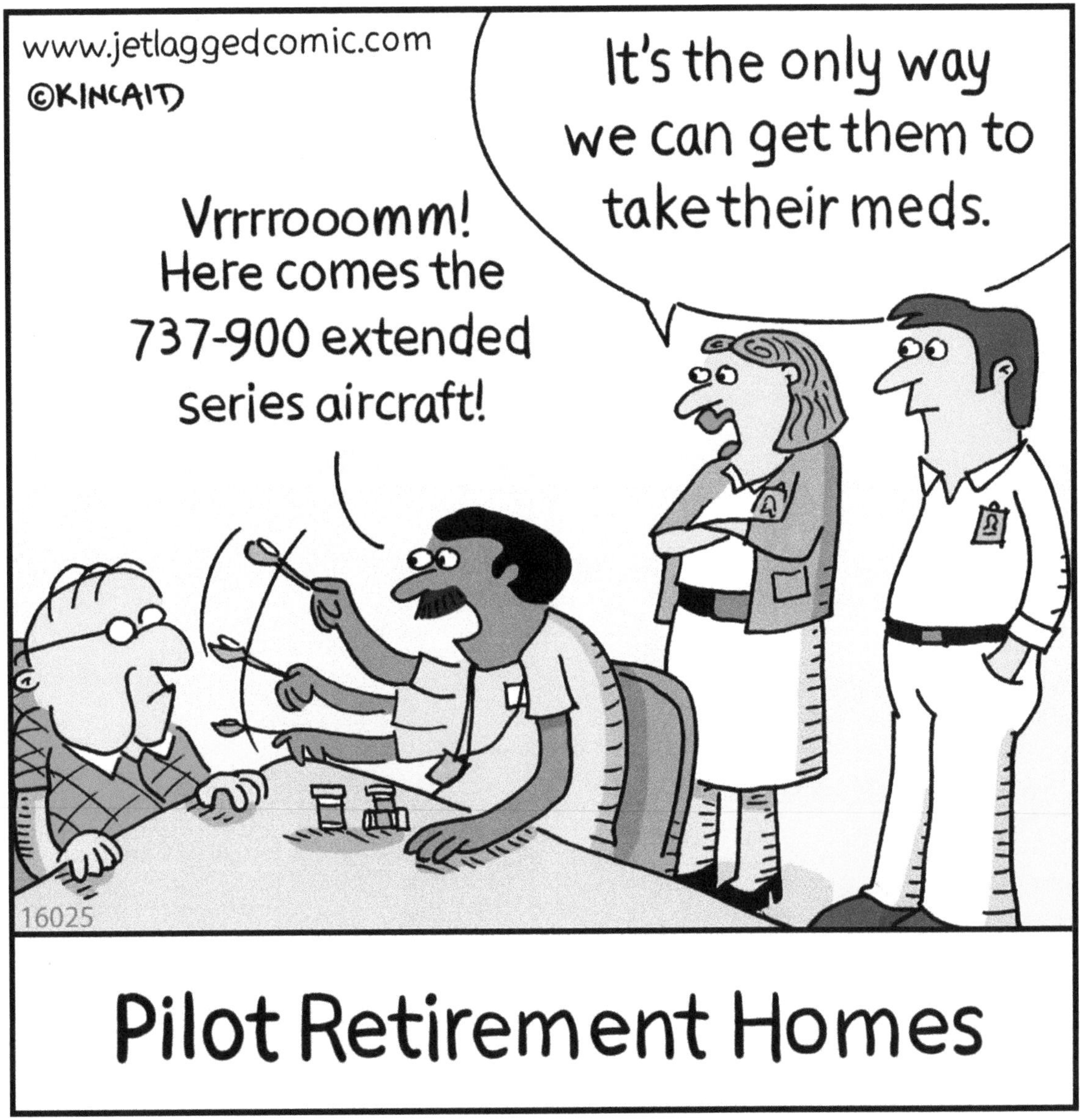
www.jetlaggedcomic.com
©KINCAID
Vrrrrooomm! Here comes the 737-900 extended series aircraft!
It's the only way we can get them to take their meds.
16025
Pilot Retirement Homes

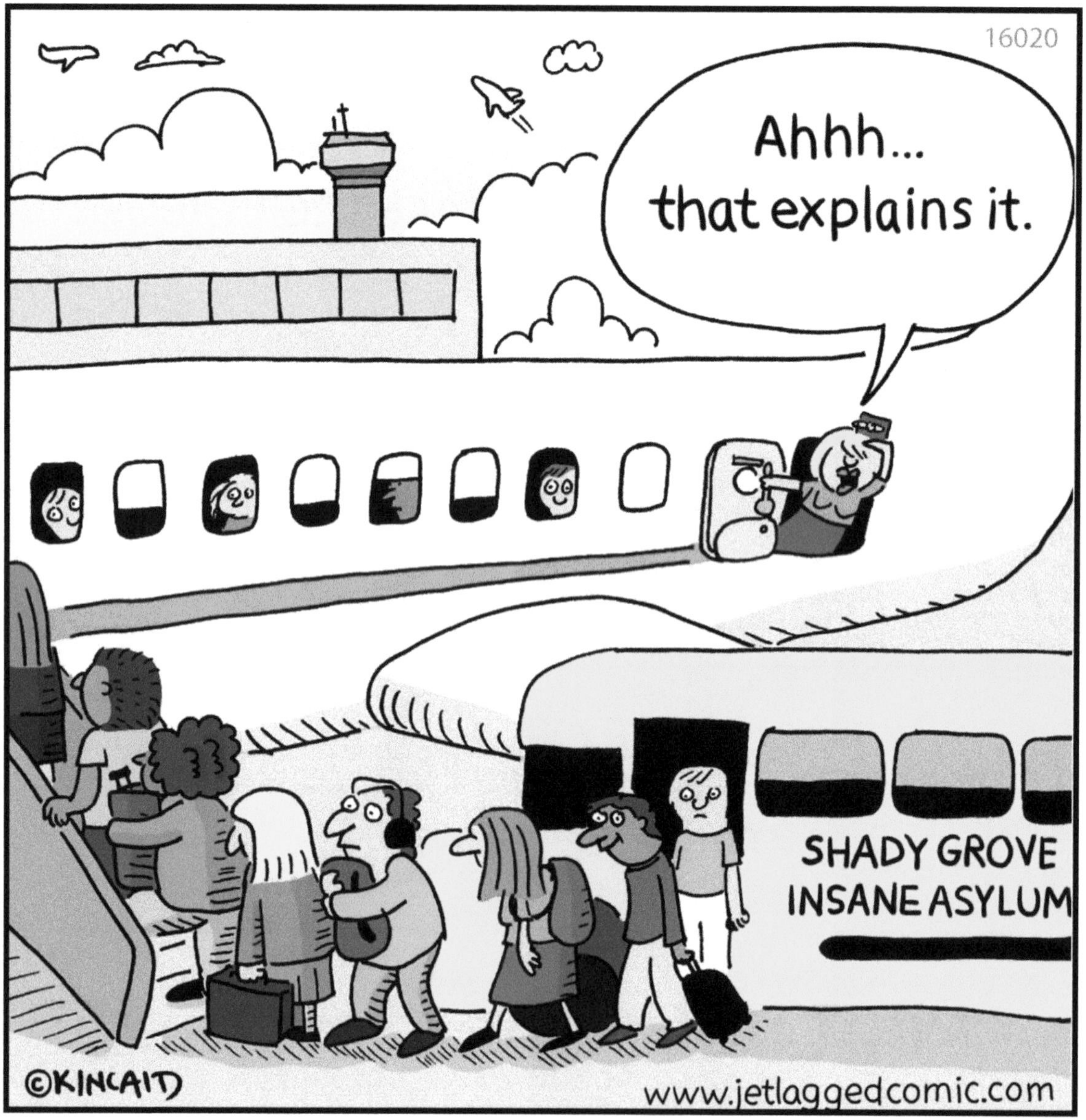
16020
Ahhh...
that explains it.
SHADY GROVE
INSANE ASYLUM
©KINCAID
www.jetlaggedcomic.com

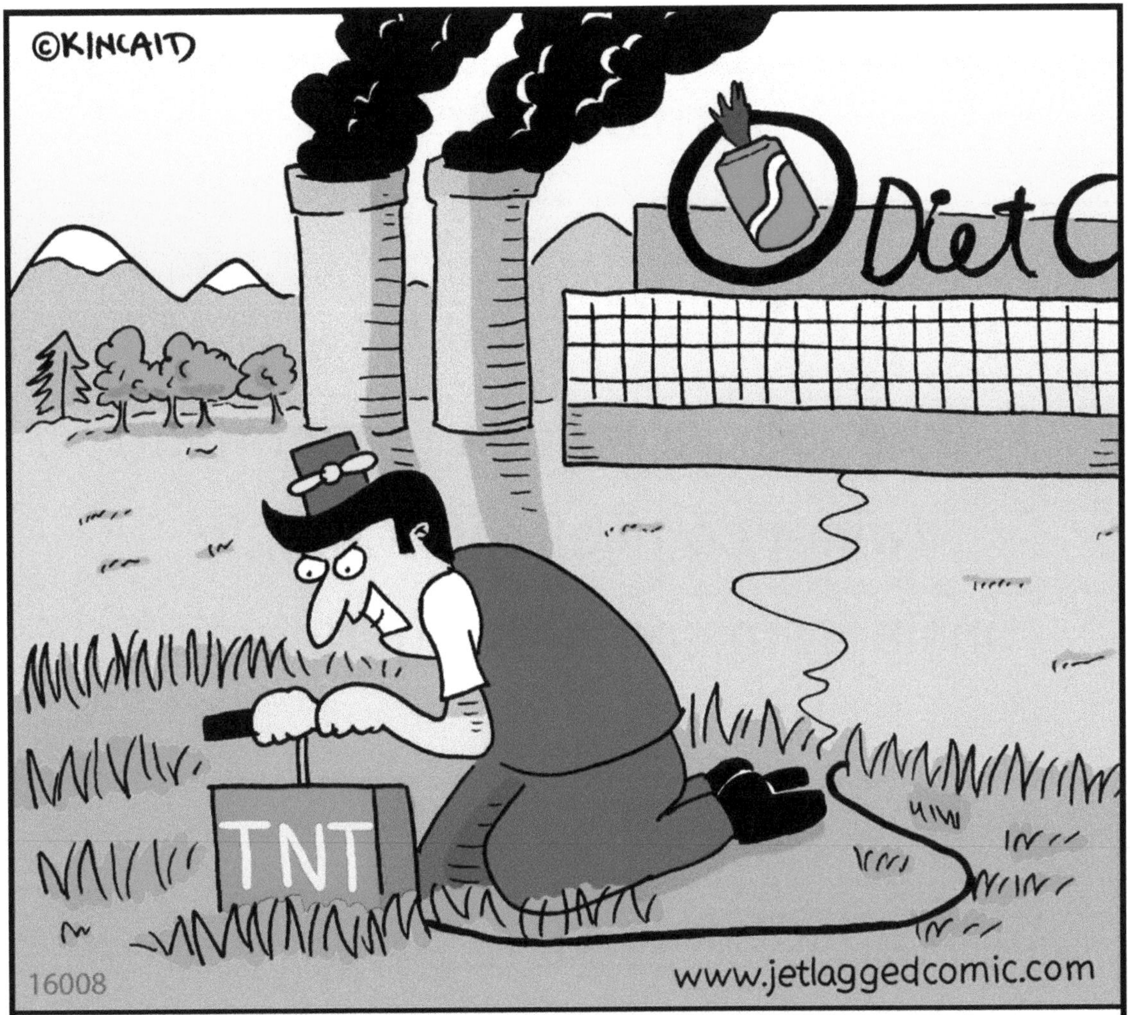
©KINCAID
Diet C
TNT
16008
www.jetlaggedcomic.com

Flight Attendant Revenge #5

Also in the Jetlagged Comic Series

Airplane Mode

Be a Fan of Jetlagged Comic!

facebook.com/jetlaggedcomic

twitter.com/jetlaggedcomic

instagram.com/jetlaggedcomics

Sign up for Jetlagged's Fan Club at
www.jetlaggedcomic.com

and get FREE weekly cartoons to your inbox!

CPSIA information can be obtained
at www.ICGtesting.com
Printed in the USA
BVHW020432170919
558624BV00001B/3/P